Philosophy of Digital Currencies

Current systems are failing the poor because these systems are unable to provide the financial inclusion needed for basic subsistence and commerce, which in turn would drive micro- and macro-economic growth. This book introduces the reader to a new way of thinking about how value can be created, captured, measured, and understood, economically and financially, and within the context of social contracts. It underscores the need to revisit such models through technological advancements, namely, Industrial Revolution 4.0, in order to solve pressing global issues such as economic inclusion and poverty eradication.

The book proposes that for humanity to make the leap forward and for any real sustainable development to occur, the world needs a disruptive approach to value creation using currency systems, considering that currencies underpin value exchange. This disruption will result in a level of decentralization that facilitates peer-to-peer value exchange and drives financial inclusion, all of which should be underscored by a new, digital social contract. The author asserts that a time-based digital currency could address these issues by creating a new and truly inclusive currency model that allows economies to gain more value than previously possible. In addition, by leveraging 4IR technologies, a currency system can be designed where each unit of money accurately reflects the context and range of socio-economic factors that influence each human interaction.

This book is aimed at futurists, technologists, researchers, policymakers, and anyone that is curious about how technology could make a difference in our collective futures. It cuts across a range of subject areas from economics, finance, philosophy, innovation to social development and takes an interdisciplinary approach to present a logical framework and theoretical foundation for the monetization of time as a digital currency.

Ugochukwu Chigoziem Ikpeazu is Lecturer at the EU Business School, Switzerland. His research, as well as professional and entrepreneurial experiences, focuses on technology, strategy, and social development.
Ahtiso.com

Routledge Studies in the Economics of Innovation

The *Routledge Studies in the Economics of Innovation* series is our home for comprehensive yet accessible texts on the current thinking in the field. These cutting-edge, upper-level scholarly studies and edited collections bring together robust theories from a wide range of individual disciplines and provide in-depth studies of existing and emerging approaches to innovation, and the implications of such for the global economy.

China's Innovation Economy
Artificial Intelligence and the New Silk Road
Jon-Arild Johannessen

The Dynamics of the Innovation Divide between China and Europe
National and Regional Dimensions
Edited by Arkadiusz Michal Kowalski

A Systemic Approach to Continuous Change in the Innovation Economy
Jon-Arild Johannessen

Industrial Revolution 4.0
Economic Foundations and Practical Implications
Edited by Stanisław Mazur

Global Innovation, Finance, and International Commerce
F. John Mathis and Raja M. Almarzoqi

Philosophy of Digital Currencies
A Theory of Monetizing Time
Ugochukwu Chigoziem Ikpeazu

The New Silk Road and the Innovation Economy in China
Jon-Arild Johannessen

For more information about this series, please visit: www.routledge.com/Routledge-Studies-in-the-Economics-of-Innovation/book-series/ECONINN

Philosophy of Digital Currencies

A Theory of Monetizing Time

Ugochukwu Chigoziem Ikpeazu

Routledge
Taylor & Francis Group
LONDON AND NEW YORK

First published 2023
by Routledge
4 Park Square, Milton Park, Abingdon, Oxon OX14 4RN

and by Routledge
605 Third Avenue, New York, NY 10158

Routledge is an imprint of the Taylor & Francis Group, an informa business

British Library Cataloguing-in-Publication Data
A catalogue record for this book is available from the British Library

ISBN: 978-1-032-36139-0 (hbk)
ISBN: 978-1-032-36141-3 (pbk)
ISBN: 978-1-003-33041-7 (ebk)

DOI: 10.4324/9781003330417

Typeset in Bembo
by SPi Technologies India Pvt Ltd (Straive)

The Pillars of Creation. NASA, ESA, and the Hubble Heritage Team (STScI/AURA).

"A Lifetime Trading" by Ugochukwu Chigoziem Ikpeazu, Benin Republic, 2016.

Contents

Figures

Tables

Preface

In the opening pages of this book, you were presented with two images; take a moment to think about what those images represented to you.

The first was a picture from space (an image from NASA of the flame nebula), with all its beauty, reminiscent of the magnitude of the universe. The second image was that of a resilient female trader in a remote West African village. These two images were chosen because in principle, humans can, and will, thrive in both contexts. Our needs may change slightly, but they will largely stay the same. As a species, we are likely to still be driven by our physiological needs to eat, sleep, and procreate, among other things (Abraham Maslow describes these needs well in the "hierarchy of needs"). But once these needs are met, history has shown that we quickly start to reach for more (Yuval Noah Harari makes a compelling argument for this in the opening chapters of his book titled *Homo Deus* (2015)). This is where the concept of "value" comes in. Whether economic, social, moral, or other, humanity is always going to grapple with the concept of what we value, and how we value resources. This is especially true of economic value. Once our species becomes the multiplanetary species that it is most likely going to become, we will need to trade and exchange value in new ways and across new horizons. You might ask, why consider value exchange on another planet when we have not overcome the social and economic challenges on this planet? This is exactly the challenge; the fact that we have not yet overcome the social and economic challenges here on earth, despite largely having the tools to do so. Technology is facilitating exponential advancements in the human experience, and yet millions of people are living in realities that are characterized by abject poverty and socio-economic exclusion. Current economic systems and financial models are failing the poor because these systems are unable to provide the financial inclusion needed for basic subsistence and commerce, which in turn would drive micro and macro-economic growth. This inability to ensure financial inclusion is linked to currency models, which may have become limited in their ability to effectively capture, store, and transfer economic value. These currency models of course do not function in a vacuum; instead, currencies are part of a larger network of services, infrastructure, policies, and ideologies that make up contemporary societies.

The impact of limited financial inclusion is an inadequate situation because it means that economies are stagnant and cannot benefit from the full productivity potential within their reach. This also means that billions of people stay marginalized since they are often relegated to the informal economy, and to economic/social activities that are not protected or regulated by government (ILO, 1993). The limitations of current approaches to value also mean delays in reaching the targets set out in the Sustainable Development Goals. Considering this situation, this book set out to present an alternative approach to capturing and transferring economic value in the form of a digital currency pegged to units of time (just as currencies where once pegged to gold or other commodities).

In addition to exploring the evolving nature of social interactions and economic value, using a mixed methodology, the research behind the book sought to understand whether consumers in low-resource settings are open to using alternative stores of value as a means of payment. This research was complemented by a series of analyses that expound on the role that the private sector plays in a new social contract, private sector–driven innovation, as well as the evolution of value theory through the periods of industrial revolutions. Furthermore, the book presents an analysis and justification on why digitally monetized time should be considered as a store of economic value as well as why it should be converted into a financial instrument in the form of a digital currency.

This series of discussions shows, among other things, that through history, money/currency has evolved to reflect social realities. The limitations to money/currency as a store of value and means of exchange mean that citizens in marginalized settings cannot access markets; neither can they participate in the economic productivity that contributes to micro and macro-economic growth. Based on this, the book posits that money/currency must evolve again to reflect current social realities. There are already calls for this all around the world.

To effectively present this alternative store of value, the book starts by laying the foundation for human interaction which through history has been defined by the social contract in the context of the state. It is within this context of the state that resource management takes place, because one of the reasons why individuals enter into the social contract is to facilitate collective resource management. The book goes into further detail on the subject of economic value to highlight how this has historically been defined and measured, as well as to define the concept of utility as one of primary economic importance. Once the relationship between social interaction (in the context of the state) and resource management (value and utility) is clearly established, the book addresses the subject of the digital economy, to highlight how value is created and captured in/through the digital economy. Current perspectives on value in the digital economy focus on the monetization of digital assets such as user data, and less on leveraging the digital economy and digital technologies to unlock social and economic value, which is a key pillar of this book. The book then looks at the literature on the concept of "time" before building on assumptions of the passing of time from linear and dynamic perspectives. An important development to note is that on 31 July 2021, scientists were able to identify light coming from behind a black hole, confirming Einstein's theory of general relativity (ESA, 2021). This may have potential long-term implications on how time is perceived; however, this does not affect the assumptions and conclusions presented in this book.

All of these subjects come together to form the core thesis of the book. The findings and analysis show that for any real sustainable development to occur, the world needs a disruptive approach to creating and capturing value using currency systems. This disruption should force a rethink of how financial systems interact with individuals and how we measure "economic value". A rethink of how value is measured would allow humanity to effectively restructure financial models and leverage technologies in a manner that ultimately improves the life of the individual by facilitating their access to a new type of social and financial system. This would in turn increase the contribution of marginalized communities to macroeconomic output. The justifications for time as a store of economic value and valuable digital currency are hinged on four key factors. First, time is the common denominator to all productivity capable individuals (a **common denominator**). Second, a digital currency based on time would allow each unit of currency to be calculated factoring in as much information as possible (the **calculability/computation implication**). Third, this currency would allow units of currency and the value that they hold, to build on each other (the **building block factor**). Finally, a time-based digital currency would be easily generated at the point of value creation (point of use), using software that is easily deployable through mobile applications (the **deployability factor**).

This book seeks to monetarize time, as an alternative approach to capturing economic value for social development. To achieve this, the book lays the theoretical foundation for a time-based digital that effectively leverages fourth industrial revolution technologies in the context of an evolving social contract. Furthermore, the book attempts to situate the concept of a time-based digital currency within the evolution of social and economic structures, and sustainable/inclusive development. The book also highlights the role that specific technologies can play in mainstreaming a global time-based digital currency, with the objective of facilitating a new wave of financial inclusion and value creation for the fourth industrial revolution. Through each historical stage of industrial revolution, we have leveraged technology to propel the human experience forward. The fourth industrial revolution presents another opportunity to redesign this experience in a socially and economically inclusive manner. Beyond this, it also presents an opportunity to advance the concept of **vivos experientia**.

Bibliography

ESA, 2021. *Light Echo From Behind a Black Hole Confirms Einstein's Theory of General Relativity.* [Online] Available at: https://scitechdaily.com/light-echo-from-behind-a-black-hole-confirms-einsteins-theory-of-general-relativity/ [Accessed 4 August 2021].

Harris, R., 2021. *Progress in Poverty Reduction Over the Last Decade.* [Online] Available at: https://www.borgenmagazine.com/poverty-reduction-over-the-last-decade/ [Accessed 25 July 2021].

ILO, 1993. *Informal economy.* [Online] Available at: https://www.ilo.org/ilostat-files/Documents/description_IFL_EN.pdf [Accessed 26 July 2021].

Jones, E. & Knaack, P., 2019. *Global Financial Regulation: Shortcomings and Reform Options.* [Online] Available at: https://onlinelibrary.wiley.com/doi/full/10.1111/1758-5899.12656 [Accessed 25 July 2021].

Lis, S. F. d & Urbiola, P., 2020. *Retail Central Bank Digital Currencies: Means of Payment vs Store of Value*. [Online] Available at: https://www.suerf.org/policynotes/15609/retail-central-bank-digital-currencies-means-of-payment-vs-store-of-value [Accessed 3 May 2021].

PDXCoin, n.d. *Are Cryptocurrencies Still Far Away from a Reliable Store of Value?*. [Online] Available at: https://pdxcoin.io/news/reliable-store-of-value.html [Accessed 3 May 2021].

Roser, M. & Ortiz-Ospina, E., 2019. *Global Extreme Poverty*. [Online] Available at: https://ourworldindata.org/extreme-poverty [Accessed 5 August 2021].

Sugisaki, S., 1997. *The Global Financial System: Status Report--Address by Shigemitsu Sugisaki*. [Online] Available at: https://www.imf.org/en/News/Articles/2015/09/28/04/53/sp111897 [Accessed 25 July 2021].

World Bank, 2018a. *Decline of Global Extreme Poverty Continues but Has Slowed: World Bank*. [Online] Available at: https://www.worldbank.org/en/news/press-release/2018/09/19/decline-of-global-extreme-poverty-continues-but-has-slowed-world-bank [Accessed 25 July 2021].

World Bank, 2018b. *Financial Inclusion*. [Online] Available at: https://www.worldbank.org/en/topic/financialinclusion/overview [Accessed 25 July 2021].

World Data Lab, 2021. *World Poverty Clock*. [Online] Available at: https://worldpoverty.io/headline [Accessed 25 July 2021].

Acknowledgements

If this goes down in history as anything worth reading, anything worth considering, then I dedicate this to you, my family, and to you, humanity. If it doesn't, I still dedicate my intentions to you. Let every idea be another step forward in the right direction.

Ugochukwu Chigoziem Ikpeazu

1 Conquering the Next Millennium

> *Imagine a life where you could engage in a value-creating activity, anywhere, anyhow. Imagine that it was possible to automatically record that value that you had created, as currency on a virtual wallet, without you having to take any specific additional steps. Imagine in that world, you could go anywhere in your immediate community, or even travel across continents, and spend that value (those digital currencies) without having to open a new account, or convert currencies, with transaction settling and universal wallet updates happening in real-time.*
>
> – Ugochukwu Chigoziem Ikpeazu

If you think (or read) back to early reflections on human interaction, you will find that the state or community are central concepts that humanity has used to define interaction. When we speak of human interaction here, we are not focusing on the mundane, yet creative, ways that humans have chosen to fill gaps of silence. No, instead, we are focusing on the more primal reasons that push a survival-oriented animal to exchange, share, and trade among other things. Throughout history, value has been measured in the context of human-to-human and human-to-resource interactions (whether as individuals or groups). It is these interactions that historically evolved into communities and ultimately into states as we know them today.

"Interaction" is a recurring and core theme in this book. The subject of the "state" is a lengthy discussion that begins on how states are formed and continues into how they evolve, considering contemporary states and societies. To highlight the evolution of this subject, we will examine of the thought processes of philosophers from around the world, including looking at subjects like sovereignty, will, and the social contract. This also includes reviewing different broad schools of thought on the origin of the state, from divine theory to the social contract theory in its various forms. The subject of "sovereignty" is at the heart of the discussion on the "state" and is a concept that has been written on by numerous political theorists. An early recognition of the need for a supreme or higher power than the individual featured in Aristotle's "Politics" (Merriam, 2001) and is referred to in discussions on the social contract, from Jean Bodin to Jean Jacques Rousseau.

Perspectives on the state can also be viewed through the liberal or Marxist lens, based on the approach to governance and the supposed "role of the state". The purpose of the state is closely linked to the formation of the state and subsequently

DOI: 10.4324/9781003330417-1

with the source of authority of the state to carry out its mandate. In "Liberalism, Marxism and the State" Ralph Raico discusses this difference between liberalism and Marxism in the context of the state. On liberalism, he notes that this concept was developed in response to absolute monarchies that abused their power on citizens and needed to be controlled. Marxism, on the other hand, considers the state as the tool that the ruling class use to dominate the general public, based on the ruling class' relationship with, and control over the factors of production (Raico, 1992). Raico goes on to argue that true liberalism is concerned with two things. First, the ability and requirement of civilized society to function without restraint and external influence. Second, Raico believes that liberalism should work towards restricting the powers and activity of the state (Raico, 1992). Jean Baptiste Say (1815) takes an amusing jab at the subject by pointing out that wealth is composed of what has value and value is based on utility; therefore, any members, categories, or groups in society that produce value should be considered productive and vice versa. (Un)surprisingly, Jean Baptiste Say does not include the Government and Military in this category of wealth creators (Raico, 1992). Industrial liberalists believe that society's purpose is the creation of utility – goods and services that are useful to individuals and that support individual's survival/growth. Based on this, people in a society have one of two choices – to produce wealth (utility), or to live off the wealth that has been created by others (disutility). Of this situation, Raico makes the statement that the "history of society is the history of the struggles between the classes of people producing wealth, and the classes of people living off the wealth created by others" (Raico, 1992).

These arguments contemplate the role of the state and set the scene for the broader political theory discussions that take place through history on the origin of the state, authority, and sovereignty. These differentiations and associated perspectives also influence economic interpretations of utility in the context of the state. However, there is a critical need to reflect on how states are structured, as well as well as reflect on how society creates and captures value. This need stems from the understanding that current approaches have become limited in their capacity for inclusive social and economic development. These limitations mean that populations around the world consistently lack access to financial and social systems and are marginalized from the productivity process. It is important to point out that being marginalized from the productivity process does not mean that the individual is not creating value in their immediate environment. It just means that there is no method to capture that value as it is created, and as such, that value cannot be counted as contributing to many of the now standardized economic metrics.

Current approaches to economic value which are centred around money/currency have also become limited in their current designs as a store of value and medium of exchange. This is not necessarily news. The limitations to the global financial system as well as to currency models have been expressed as far back and potentially even further back than 1997 when Shigemitsu Sugisaki, then Deputy Managing Director of the International Monetary Fund, addressed the conference on "The Global Economy: Three Worlds or One". In his statement, Shigemitsu Sugisaki notes the macro-economic importance of market confidence in a currency among other things (Sugisaki, 1997). In a more recent example from 2019, these limitations to the global financial system were again highlighted by Emily Jones and Peter Knaack who argue for a greater focus not only on financial stability but also on financial inclusion, and that this should be integrated into the mandates of standard-setting bodies (Jones & Knaack, 2019). Jones and Knaack (2019) go on to call for the creation of a standard-setting body for digital financial services. Remember the image from space and the remote village? That is the level of financial inclusion that we need to aim for. So what exactly does financial inclusion mean? According to the World Bank, it means "access to useful and affordable financial products and services that meet their needs … delivered in a responsible and sustainable way" (World Bank, 2018b). This definition largely refers to access to a store of value and means of exchange/payment/credit/savings, all of which are achieved through/with currency. This emphasis on the importance of financial inclusion, or the importance of access to an effective and well-designed currency system, further highlights the need for a rethink of social and economic value mechanisms. The silver lining is that unlike any other period in history, humanity has the right tools at its disposal to design these currency models. Even better, we have the tools to really rethink what our societies could look like, in a way that enhances inclusivity for the world's most marginalized individuals, families, communities and states.

As human interaction continues to evolve, advancements in technology also continue at an exponential pace, meaning that humanity is creating more tools, as well as combining and applying these tools in novel ways. These exponential advancements in technology also mean that we can interact with each other in more "new" ways than previously possible, while at the same time existing methods of interaction are enhanced. The COVID-19 pandemic years (or just "pandemic years") demonstrated this. The fourth industrial revolution (4IR) and digital economy capture these technological advancements and their associated impact on humanity. Understanding what this means is important because historically, human interaction was defined as a relationship primarily between citizens and a government. In contemporary societies, however, these relationships are not so monogamous and straight forward. Interaction has broadened beyond the state and individual to include a range of non-state actors like private businesses which have become central to leading the innovation process in this fourth phase of the industrial revolution. Beyond just the technological advancements, non-state actors, e.g., private businesses, are interacting with populations as much as, and even more than some governments (state's) are able to in certain instances.

Despite these technological advancements which have been alluded to (and which will be touched on in more detail later), a large percentage of the global population still lives in extreme or multidimensional poverty. While industrialized states have been able to take advantage of each subsequent industrial revolution to strengthen their economies, many others have been unable to build the necessary competitive/comparative advantage, and are, as a result, unable to realize the much needed financial inclusion that would allow their populations effectively harness and exchange value. The resulting inefficiencies mean that these economies have weakly charged interactions among citizens, among stakeholders within each economy and across economies. According to the "World Poverty Clock" an estimated 712 million people live in extreme poverty as of July 2021 (World Data Lab, 2021). In addition, as of 2018, an estimated 55% of the world's population lacked access to "social protection cash benefits" (Harris, 2021), further highlighting the relationship between money as a store of value and socio-economic development. Significant effort has gone into addressing this inequity: the sustainable development goals, formerly the millennium development goals, laid out a set of 17 targets meant to improve the state of humanity, not just as a species, but as individuals living every day on a planet with scarce resources. Together, these goals have realized some progress. According to the World Bank, the percentage of the global population living in extreme poverty fell from 36% to 10% over a 25-year period between 1990 and 2015 (World Bank, 2018a; Roser & Ortiz-Ospina, 2019).

So, we have established, albeit briefly, that we need to think differently about certain things. Some important questions then are: "What financial tools or alternative stores of value can we (humanity) use to replace or complement existing models, in a way that facilitates social and economic inclusion?" "How are social and economic interactions evolving to better reflect the roles of non-state actors?" Digital currencies have emerged as a potential solution to the first question on alternative stores of value (Lis & Urbiola, 2020; PDXCoin, n.d.). However, even though these present vast amounts of potential, there are still limitations to the current designs that have prevented them from unlocking large-scale economic value in the context of sustainable development, global financial stability, and financial inclusion. In addition, the question on how social and economic interactions are evolving has not effectively been answered. This is largely because social interactions are still viewed through the lens of the social contract as it was initially defined, without reflecting the many realities that now make up the human experience. More so, we are learning that the human experience is in fact not solely human, but, rather, a complicated web of connections with animals, the planet, and natural forces beyond our reach (for now?).

The 4IR offers humanity a unique opportunity to look beyond the 2030 target and well into the future, in response to the question, "where do we want to go?" Conquering the next century requires us to rethink our approach to value, in a way that is truly inclusive, and reflective of the opportunities that our species is now faced with.

To fully explore the subject on "re-imagining value" against the timeline of the industrial revolutions, and in the various contexts presented, we will dig into a series of sub-topics that ultimately make up the whole. First, we look at the "State and Society", before moving on to the concept of "Value", the "Digital Economy"; and ultimately "Time". Our starting point, the "State and Society", allows us to explore the concept of human interaction from one of the earliest perspectives on the subject. As we go on, we will explore the evolution of key concepts from cultural and philosophical perspectives in an attempt to paint a holistic picture.

You could think about this book as flowing like this: First, we start with a view of the "state" as well as the relationship of the "state" with the individual or "citizen". We will flow on from this to discuss the concept of "value", looking at different perspectives on value creation, to show how political economists have approached this concept throughout history. Consider this: Individuals must use resources (raw materials) from the land, land which is owned by the collective of individuals; "the state". Once we have established an understanding of "state" and "value", we will flow logically into the discussions on the digital economy, time, 4IR, and digital currencies, before ultimately pulling these together to form the basis of our new currency model.

Bibliography

Harris, R. (2021). *Progress in Poverty Reduction Over the Last Decade.* [Online] Available at: https://www.borgenmagazine.com/poverty-reduction-over-the-last-decade/ [Accessed 25 July 2021].

Jones, E. & Knaack, P. (2019). *Global Financial Regulation: Shortcomings and Reform Options.* [Online] Available at: https://onlinelibrary.wiley.com/doi/full/10.1111/1758-5899.12656 [Accessed 25 July 2021].

Lis, S. F. D. & Urbiola, P. (2020). *Retail Central Bank Digital Currencies: Means of Payment vs Store of Value.* [Online] Available at: https://www.suerf.org/policynotes/15609/retail-central-bank-digital-currencies-means-of-payment-vs-store-of-value [Accessed 3 May 2021].

Merriam, C. E. (2001). *History of the Theory of Sovereignty Since Rousseau.* Kitchiner: Batoche Books.

PDXCoin. (n.d.) *Are Cryptocurrencies Still Far Away from a Reliable Store of Value?.* [Online] Available at: https://pdxcoin.io/news/reliable-store-of-value.html [Accessed 3 May 2021].

Raico, R. (1992). Liberalism, Marxism and The State. *Cato Journal, 11*(3), 391–404.

Roser, M. & Ortiz-Ospina, E. (2019). *Global Extreme Poverty.* [Online] Available at: https://ourworldindata.org/extreme-poverty [Accessed 5 August 2021].

Sugisaki, S. (1997). *The Global Financial System: Status Report--Address by Shigemitsu Sugisaki.* [Online] Available at: https://www.imf.org/en/News/Articles/2015/09/28/04/53/sp111897 [Accessed 25 July 2021].

World Bank. (2018a). *Decline of Global Extreme Poverty Continues but Has Slowed: World Bank.* [Online] Available at: https://www.worldbank.org/en/news/press-release/2018/09/19/decline-of-global-extreme-poverty-continues-but-has-slowed-world-bank [Accessed 25 July 2021].

World Bank. (2018b). *Financial Inclusion.* [Online] Available at: https://www.worldbank.org/en/topic/financialinclusion/overview [Accessed 25 July 2021].

World Data Lab. (2021). *World Poverty Clock.* [Online] Available at: https://worldpoverty.io/headline [Accessed 25 July 2021].

Part I

Philosophy of (Human) Society

2 If God Designed the Political State... (and Human Interaction)

Our societies are divided, and we tend to pull back from discussions on the "divine". But I invite you to contemplate the role of divinity in society. Our exploration on the origin and design of the state starts at one of the earliest points for humanity, divine theory. Before science equipped us with the tools and vocabulary to better understand and describe our world, humans often attributed the "unknown" to an "external force" or "higher power" (even in societies today where science and infrastructure are limited, much is still attributed to external forces and higher powers). Take the excerpt below and the implications it had on early societies (Bible, n.d.):

> Let every soul be subject unto the higher powers. For there is no power but of God: the powers that be are ordained of God. Whosoever therefore resisteth the power, resisteth the ordinance of God: and they that resist shall receive to themselves damnation. For rulers are not a terror to good works, but to the evil. Wilt thou then not be afraid of the power? do that which is good, and thou shalt have praise of the same: For he is the minister of God to thee for good. But if thou do that which is evil, be afraid; for he beareth not the sword in vain: for he is the minister of God, a revenger to execute wrath upon him that doeth evil.
>
> (Romans 13 verses 1–4, Holy Bible, King James Version)

The passage above does not shy away from the relationship between the community and the divine. This is "divine theory" or the theory on the "divine rights of kings". You might have guessed it already from the last phrase in quotes, that divine theory focuses on the "state" as an intentional design and creation of "God". Here, the king/leader/ruler receives their authority directly from God and represents God on earth. This theory reflected the inseparable relationship between the church and state/religion and politics. Because the king represented God on earth, disobeying the king was paramount to disobeying God. This would be an important feature through which monarchies were equipped to absolutist rule over their citizens/territories. By this same logic on divine authority, the king could also only answer to God from who he received his instructions and guidance. It is important to note the intentional use of "king" here (masculine)

DOI: 10.4324/9781003330417-3

which further highlights the link with religion, many of which have historically held the male figure superior to the female, and which also reflects the patriarchal nature of early societies. In the Bible verse above, Saint Paul highlights the divine creation of the state, the vesting of the king with his authority from God (executive powers), the need to obey the laws or instructions of the king (legislative powers) and the ability of the king to punish any offenders (judicial powers). These roles and responsibilities of the God-endowed king are reiterated by King James Stuart 1 of England in "The Trew Law of Free Monarchies" (1598) (yorku.ca, n.d.). According to King James, it was without doubt that the king was ordained to rule by God and, as such, was the highest possible authority on earth (Dyke et al., 2013).

Divine theory features across the various religions and throughout history. Another example, taken here to reflect the wide-ranging representations of divine theory, is from the Manusmriti. The Manusmriti ("Laws of Manu" or "The Remembered Tradition of Manu" or "The Dharma Text of Manu") (Britannica, 1998). The Manusmriti is considered to be (one of) the most important texts in Hinduism, as it is believed to have originated from "Manu the lawgiver" in c. 100 AD. The Manusmriti, like the Christian Holy Bible or Islamic Quran, describes the laws that humanity should adhere to. Also like the other religious texts, the Manusmriti describes the state and resulting government as a specific intention of creation by God (Buhler, 1500 BCE).

While aspects of divine theory would remain part of political theory throughout history, this school of thought was not built out as extensively as other political theories on the origin of the state. This was the case because over time, in addition to more scientific theories emerging, there was also the push by political philosophers, to delink the state from religion. The attempt to separate the two emerged as states were equipped with additional laws and mechanisms to regulate the activities of citizens and institutions. These laws, which provided checks and balances of society, also limited the absolutist tendencies of governments, and ultimately led to the establishment of the state and religious organizations as two independently functioning entities. Thomas Jefferson has a famous phrase attributed to him that supposedly provides an explanation to a section of the American constitution, to explain the need for the separation between the church and the state. The phrase "wall of separation" featured in Jefferson's reply to an address from the Danbury (1802) about the section of the constitution which says that "Congress shall make no law respecting an establishment of religion" (Hutson, 1998).

In questioning the authenticity of an absolute king who represents "God" on earth with divine authority, political theorists and philosophers engaged in a critical review on the concept of sovereignty and its relationship with the state. Here, interaction is defined in the context of spirituality and religion, where a superior being, a Sovereign, presides over motives. Aspects of divine theory would emerge in different forms around the world; one such form was around morality in ancient African kingdoms.

Historians believe that a great deal of literature was produced by early inhabitants of the African continent, cataloguing important historical facts and traditions.

Unlike popular belief, these cultural facts and traditions were passed down not only through orally shared stories, but in fact also through written text. One historian who argues this is Wendy Laura Belcher, who says that African literature does not start in the 1950s as part of the colonial-era struggles, but instead can be traced back much further into history where inhabitants of the African continent engaged in intellectual feats on par with other parts of the world at the time. The challenge that Belcher points out, however, is that many of these texts have not been preserved through history, or where they have been preserved, they are yet to be translated (Belcher, 2021). Of the ancient literature that exists from the region on politics and theories of the state, there is a strong focus on morality, duty, and religion, as well as the interrelationship of these elements in the individual–state interaction.

Ptahhotep's early teachings on morality were among these pieces of literature that have survived through history. Ptahhotep (25th century BCE) was the "vizier of ancient Egypt", a high-ranking political official responsible for managing the affairs of the state. Ptahhotep wrote "The Maxims of Ptahhotep" as a guide for young Egyptian men, on; duty, respect, and morality (Britannica, 2014), and this text is considered one of the earlier philosophical discussions about morality and ethics from the African region. In the text, Ptahhotep defines the expected interactions among individuals, as well as between individuals and the state. The Maxims of Ptahhotep is laid out as a dialogue that starts with Ptahhotep describing his old age to the king, with the hope that he can be permitted to retire while his son takes his place in service (Devaud, 1916). Ptahhotep paints a grim picture of aging that is captured in the statement:

> O my Sovereign,
> Old age has struck, age has descended,
> Feebleness has arrived, weakness is here again.
> Sleep is upon him in discomfort all day.
> Eyes are grown small, ears deaf,
> Mouth silent, unable to speak,
> Heart emptied, unable to recall yesterday.
> Bones ache his whole length.
> Goodness has turned to evil,
> All taste is gone.
> What old age does to people is evil in every way.
> Nose is blocked, unable to breathe,
> how old (it feels) standing or sitting.
>
> (Devaud, 1916)

From this statement, Ptahhotep also highlights the relationship between the Vizier and the Sovereign, painting the Sovereign as one that is concerned with the welfare of its citizens. The king grants Ptahhotep's request, but would go on to say that since no one is born wise, Ptahhotep would have to teach his replacement. This text is significant to our discussion because Ptahhotep goes on to describe what the ideal behaviour should be under various circumstances and social interactions.

Importantly he does not explicitly tie morality to the existence of a higher authority such as God, but rather alludes to a sort of "natural law" or "intrinsic good" known by all. We will talk about both natural law and intrinsic versus extrinsic good in later chapters. Ptahhotep also talks about "greed" as a "levy of all evils", suggesting that everyone has their rights to resources, a view shared by many other philosophers. Ptahhotep refers to "good" in several instances; however, across the text, he reflects on "good" as something that is received or passed on from others (extrinsic good). Only at the end of the text does Ptahhotep give a clue as to what might be considered a true intrinsic good. This is reflected in the statement:

> How good is one instructed by his father,
> when he emerged from him out of his body,
> and he told him, while he was in the body, entirely,
> May what he has done be greater than what he was told.
> See, a good son, by the gift of the god,
> surpassing what he was told before his lord.
>
> (Devaud, 1916)

Ptahhotep is one of the earlier representations of morality in African philosophy. The text reflects on an age-old question around what drives individuals to take certain actions over others, what influences perspectives of right and wrong, and what is an intrinsic versus extrinsic good. Contemporary society around much of the African continent still aligns with this approach to interaction with morality at its centre. A quick search across Hofstede's cultural insights will confirm this. Most countries that have been catalogued from the African continent show a high relevance for the family, with low individualism and high-power distance. This approach to defining interaction based on morality is not exclusive to the region, and of course is not the only approach from the region.

Bibliography

Belcher, W. L., 2021 Are We Global Yet? Africa and the Future of Early Modern Studies. *Eighteenth-Century Fiction*, 33(3), 413–446.

Bible, H. (n.d.) *Romans 13:1–4*. [Online] Available at: https://www.bible.com/bible/1/ROM.13.1-4.KJV [Accessed 2 July 2021].

Britannica. (1998). *Manu-smriti*. [Online] Available at: https://www.britannica.com/topic/Manu-smriti [Accessed 24 May 2021].

Britannica. (2014). *Ptahhotep*. [Online] Available at: https://www.britannica.com/biography/Ptahhotep [Accessed 10 May 2021].

Buhler, G. (1500 BC). *Manusmriti: The Laws of Manu*. [Online] Available at: https://vedpuran.files.wordpress.com/2013/04/manusmriti.pdf [Accessed 24 May 2021].

Devaud. (1916). *Ptahhotep*. [Online] Available at: https://www.ucl.ac.uk/museums-static/digitalegypt/literature/ptahhotep.html [Accessed 10 May 2021].

Dyke, C., Martin, A., & Jones, C. (2013). *King James I: Absolutism*. [Online] Available at: https://westerncivguides.umwblogs.org/2013/12/07/king-james-i-absolutism/ [Accessed 4 May 2021].

Hutson, J. (1998). *A Wall of Separation.* [Online] Available at: https://www.loc.gov/loc/lcib/9806/danbury.html#:~:text=Thomas%20Jefferson's%20reply%20on%20Jan,from%20the%20Danbury%20(Conn.)&text=Board%20of%20Education%2C%20that%2C%20%22,separation%20between%20church%20and%20state [Accessed 24 May 2021].

Merriam, C. E. (2001). *History of the Theory of Sovereignty Since Rousseau.* Kitchiner: Batoche Books.

Raico, R. (1992). Liberalism, Marxism and The State. *Cato Journal, 11*(3) 391–404.

Yorku.ca. (n.d.) *Trew Law.* [Online] Available at: http://www.yorku.ca/comninel/courses/3025pdf/TrewLaw.pdf [Accessed 24 May 2021].

3 The Nei Ye, The Guanzi, The Analects

Managing the affairs of a population as large as that of China's requires some creativity, and Chinese philosophers have presented a colourful tapestry of theory's to achieve this. Stephen C. Angle, in *Social and Political Thought in Chinese Philosophy*, attempts a description of major Chinese philosophy through history. Angle breaks down the analysis of Chinese philosophical history to two main time periods: the classical era and the early imperial era (Angle, 2017). Under the classical era, Angle starts by exploring the Guanzi (a collection of ancient Chinese texts) as one of the first in-depth pieces of literature on politics and governance (Angle, 2017). The text below is taken from the "Nei Ye" or "Nei Yeh" which can be translated as "Inner Enterprise", "Inner Cultivation", or "Inner Development. The text states:

> Thus the Qi of the citizens:
> Is it bright?
> As though ascending to heaven.
> Is it dark and quiet?
> As though entering into an abyss.
> Is it wide and spacious?
> As though residing in the ocean.
> Is it close?
> As though residing in oneself.
> (Anonymous, 350–300 BCE)

The "Nei Ye" describes the nature of existence and highlights how human existence flows from birth until a point of self-mastery and subsequently, until a point of leadership. The above statement is an excerpt from the "Nei Ye" that highlights early contemplations on the "life force" or driving force of citizens within a state. The text goes on to describe how to build up this life force and how to manipulate it, by controlling oneself and mastering one's own existence (Linnell, 2011). According to the author who has remained anonymous through history, mastery of self is an important aspect in leadership. In the statement below, the "Nei Ye" describes a sort of natural law, by suggesting that "Dao", which could be

DOI: 10.4324/9781003330417-4

translated as "the natural way of things" (Linnell, 2011), is in people when they are born:

> That Dao is not remote,
> Citizens attain it by being born.
> That Dao does not depart,
> Citizens rely on it for understanding.
> (Anonymous, 350–300 BCE)

This is an allusion to natural law because it suggests that there is a universal understanding of the way of doing things (intrinsic) that is not derived from something else (extrinsic). An important coincidence is that almost around the same time period, Aristotle (384–322 BCE) was also making significant contributions to European philosophical perspectives on natural law. The Guanzi attempts to establish the parameters for political success, and according to Angle, the text presents two important political techniques to consider, namely, attending to the needs of the citizens and establishing appropriate standards. Angle goes on to reflect on the Mozi text by Mozi or "Mo Di" (470–400 BCE) which presents further guidelines on governance. According to Russell Kirkland, the Mozi citizens are required to care for each other, and this is the ultimate objective, making this an intrinsic good to which all other actions must build towards (Kirkland, n.d.). Like John Locke many years after him, Mozi believed that all people are equal; however, his text describes equality in the context of the political and economic state, as opposed to John Locke who described this equality first in the "state of nature". Like Hobbes, Mozi believed that people worked together to protect themselves from harm (which was the central theme in Hobbes' Leviathan, describing why people chose to leave the state of nature). Kirkland goes on to highlight that the Sovereign receives their authority from God, and furthermore takes an absolutist view to the citizens' relationship with the Sovereign. Kirkland refers to Mozi as a materialistic universalistic utilitarian who believed that actions should work towards improving the "good" for people in an equal manner (Kirkland, n.d.).

Let us continue now with Stephen C. Angle's chronology which moves on to the "Analects" (Lunyu), a collection of texts by the renowned Chinese philosopher Confucius, and his students. There is a popular belief that a large portion of the Analects were composed after Confucius death by his direct students and people who associated with his teachings. D.C Lau offers helpful context on the circumstances surrounding the discovery of the "Analects". According to D.C Lau, the "Analects" were recovered when the house of the K'ung family was demolished at the request of a king of Lu in the year 154 BCE. The house in question was believed to have been where Confucius himself lived, and the copies were discovered in the walls where they must have been hidden from being burnt. The texts (Shu-ching, Ch'un Ch'iu, Hsiao-ching, and the Lun Yu), which were written in the most ancient form of the Chinese language, were subsequently translated and published, and would go on to play a significant role in shedding light on Confucius

(551–479 BCE) teaching and theories (Lau, 1979). The "Analects" begin with a strong focus on morality by quoting Seng Tzu in saying:

> every day I examine myself on three counts. In what I have undertaken on another's behalf, have I failed to do my best? In my dealings with my friends have I failed to be trustworthy in what I say? Have I passed on to others anything that I have not tried out myself?
>
> (Lau, 1979)

This reflects the role that morality is expected to play in driving human actions as well as the central place of "love" in defining interaction between citizens. Like Ptahhotep (25th century BCE), Confucius theory lays out the ideal behaviour for the individual in relation to others and society. This ethical approach to defining human interaction extends to the state and was captured in the sentence:

> while the gentleman cherishes benign rule, the small man cherishes his native land. While the gentleman cherishes a respect for the law, the small man cherishes generous treatment.
>
> (Confucius, c. 500 BCE)

This text emphasizes the importance of education in defining the individual and is the basis upon which the differentiation of "gentleman" and "small man" are made. This emphasis on gaining knowledge as the source of one's goodness suggests that Confucius does not hold religious obligations to be the core driving force for human actions, even though the text highlights "reverence for the gods" as "wisdom". The Analects highlight four things that define goodness (referring in the text to Tzu-ch'an but representative of broader expectations of goodness from individuals), namely: respect, submission to authority, benevolence, or caring for the "common people" and "just" (Confucius, c. 500 BCE). This approach to morality also discourages violence against the state and violence against fellow citizens.

> Do not look unless it is in accordance with the rites; do not listen unless it is in accordance with the rites; do not speak unless it is in accordance with the rites; do not move unless it is in accordance with the rites.
>
> (Confucius, c. 500 BCE)

The rites mentioned here are among the key principles of Confucianism which also include the Five Relations, Rectification of Names, and Ren (Perkins, 2019).

As part of Confucianism, morality is the most important goal in life and it is supposedly from here that all else flow. On this, the Analects posit that "If he is trustworthy in word, the common people will entrust him with responsibility. If he is quick he will achieve results" (Confucius, c. 500 BCE). Reading this last quote paints a picture where benevolence is so important that it is the basis on which a people entrust the Sovereign with authority. Confucius philosophy places morality at the centre of the human experience and emphasizes that the state can only function based on this when individuals show good morality to each other, to the state and vice versa. This philosophy also holds the general good or greater good as important, as it seeks to ensure the harmony and safety of all citizens under the state (without taking an absolutist view to the relationship of the Sovereign with the state).

The next stop on this tour of Chinese philosophical history, as guided by Stephen Angle, is the "Dao De Jing" – also known as "Tao-te Ching" and previously known as "Laozi" (based on the belief that it was written by Laozi[1] (Britannica, 2019). Daodejing takes an interesting approach to the subject of value/ good in the sense that it suggests that things are good not because they have certain characteristics in them that make them good, but because they have been proclaimed as good by an individual, in comparison to something else that is bad. The text also assumes that the Sovereign's primary objective is to serve the people, and that to do this effectively, the Sovereign must get rid of desire for themselves and for the citizens under their care. In the absence of desire is simplicity, which reduces greed, contriving, and other such "evils" that go against the "Dao". The Daodejing also refers to natural law and notes that things do not "deviate from their natural and orderly places" (Laozi, 4th century BCE). You may already notice that natural law theory features prominently across the different parts of the world and throughout history, each time humanity has attempted to define the bounds of interaction. Like Confucius, Laozi also preaches "benevolence" as a core characteristic that every individual should strive for in their dealings with self and others. Laozi further presents an almost moral guide to life, urging individuals to do away with earthly desires and to focus on knowledge, benevolence, and inner peace. According to Laozi, the "Dao" or "the way" existed before heaven and earth and is the source of the two. The statement below is one of the strongest allusions in the Daodejing to natural law:

> The great man emulates the great Earth.
> The great earth emulates the great Heaven,
> The great heaven emulates the great Dao.
> The great Dao emulates the great Nature.
> (Laozi, 4th century BCE)

Similar to natural law theories from the Western world, the Laozi urges against violence and implores the Sovereign (and advisers of the Sovereign) to avoid the use of force. On the nature of government, the Laozi proposes a "laissez-faire" or non-interventionist government that focuses on providing the basic needs of the people, and also, like previous Chinese philosophers, does not believe in the absolute authority or control of the state. The philosophy of the "Dao" extends to relationships between states (foreign relations) and suggests that by following "the way" states can also reap benefits in their interactions with others. While the Daodejing provides guidance to leaders on governance and politics, it does not provide any insights into how these leaders receive their authority from citizens.

> Huizi said to Zhuangzi, "The king of Wei gave me some seeds of a huge gourd. I planted them, and when they grew up, the fruit was big enough to hold five piculs. I tried using it for a water container, but it was so heavy

> I could not lift it. I split it in half to make dippers, but they were so large and unwieldy that I could not dip them into anything. It's not that the gourds weren't fantastically big – but I decided they were of no use, and so I smashed them to pieces." Zhuangzi said, "You certainly are dense when it comes to using big things!" .
>
> (Zhou, c. 3rd century BCE)

The "Zhuangzi" is an ancient Chinese text that is believed to have been compiled during the period known as the "Warring States Period" (a period characterized by continuous conflict and military reform). Much like Laozi, Zhuangzi also emphasizes the importance of knowledge to the individual; however, for Zhuangzi, this is not necessarily knowledge of the world, but rather knowledge of the "Dao" (the way). The statement above from the opening passage reflects the tone that the Zhuangzi takes throughout the text. The way is referred to as a virtue that is not self-serving and does not seek fame, because according to the Zhuangzi, human nature becomes corrupted by knowledge and pleasures (a similarity with the Christian Bible's impurity attained from the tree of knowledge of good and evil).

The way is against human knowledge because human knowledge is subjective and limited since it is influenced by desire, pleasures, pain, loss, want, etc. These emotions tend to limit the individual's ability to think clearly and, as such, do not allow the individual to attain that level of oneness with "the way" which the Zhuangzi believes drives all existence. Human knowledge leads to comparison and competition which in turn lead people to scheming and devising, which goes against the way. In a sense, the way is similar to natural law or a natural state of existence that results in things as they should be. According to the Zhuangzi, as described in the statement below, the individual is primarily concerned with survival and, if left alone, would focus on meeting their basic needs (quite the contrary to Hobbes' state of nature. More to come on that later):

> The potter says, "I'm good at handling clay! To round it, I apply the compass; to square it, I apply the T square." The carpenter says, "I'm good at handling wood! To arc it, I apply the curve; to make it straight, I apply the plumb line." But as far as inborn nature is concerned, the clay and the wood surely have no wish to be subjected to compass and square, curve and plumb line. Yet generation after generation sings out in praise, saying, "Bo Luo is good at handling horses! The potter and the carpenter are good at handling clay and wood!" And the same fault is committed by the men who handle the affairs of the world! In my opinion, someone who was really good at handling the affairs of the world would not go about it like this. The people have their constant inborn nature. To weave for their clothing, to till for their food – this is the Virtue they share.
>
> (Zhou, c. 3rd century BCE)

Zhuangzi uses this analogy to show how human knowledge has perverted the natural order of things through history, and to emphasize the need for a "laissez-faire" type of government. This type of government would leave the people to do as they wish, with no state intervention in any form of public administration. Commentators have suggested that this stance makes the Zhuangzi completely anti-government (Hansen, 2017), a sentiment that is repeated throughout the text. In the same spirit, laws are considered unnecessary since they have only been set up based on human knowledge and to support human ideals of right and wrong.

Human beings are many, but they all are subjects of the Sovereign. The Sovereign finds his source in Virtue, his completion in Heaven. (Zhou, c. 3rd century BCE)

While recognizing that a Sovereign may exist (even though one is not necessarily needed), the Zhuangzi describes the relationship of the citizens as one of subjection and the authority of the Sovereign as coming from "heaven"/"god".

The Zhuangzi was written during the "Warring States Period" (453–221). This was a momentous period in Chinese history that chronologically came after the "Western Zhou Dynasty" and the "Spring and Autumn Period". The Warring States Period also ultimately led to the first unified Chinese empire (Song, 2021). During this period, there were seven warring states (Qin, Chu, Zhao, Wei, Han, Yan, and Qi) who had all broken off from the Zhou dynasty and whose nobles now refused to support the Zhou dynasty. The Warring States Period was a period of economic, social, political, and military reform. In order to sustain their large armies needed for the continuous wars, there needed to be systemic changes to the relationships between the individuals and the states as well as between farmers and their feudal lords. Food and natural resources had become the most important resource, and so farmers gained a more prominent role in society thanks to their ability to provide for these needs (Indiana University, 2010). At the same time, the method of fighting changed from chariot-based armies to infantry-based armies, and as such, there was a need to find leaders who could command such large armies. This meant a cultural shift away from elite-led armies to armies led by intelligent and strategic leaders.

These drastic events and changes explain the tone of the text as being anti-government and anti-knowledge. It was human knowledge and the associated feelings that led to competition and led states to believe that they were better than each other. It was human knowledge and its associated corruptions on the natural order of things, according to the Zhuangzi, that led to an imbalance in "the way" and led the governments at the time to interfere in the activities of the state to the point of war. Considering the realities present in China during the time of the Zhuangzi, it is understandable that the philosophy seeks to minimize the impact and even existence of government and seeks to engage citizens in as little political reflection as possible, to potentially avoid what it sees as the root causes of conflict.

The perspectives presented here also reflect the role of morality in defining interaction. This is complemented by allusions to a natural law that straddles a fine line between the divine approach and the natural law theories as will be discussed in greater detail later. In addition, these perspectives reflect the growing importance of resource management in defining how and why humans interacted at a point in history.

Note

1 The true author of the Laozi is contested as certain historians believe the text to be a compilation of various authors as opposed to the works of single philosopher. Alan Chan, among others, believes that the *Laozi* text was attributed to *Lao Dan* based on his reputation (Chan, 2018).

Bibliography

Chan, A., 2018. *Laozi*. [Online] Available at: https://plato.stanford.edu/entries/laozi/ [Accessed 2021].

Angle, S. C. (2017). *Social and Political Thought in Chinese Philosophy*. [Online] Available at: https://plato.stanford.edu/entries/chinese-social-political/ [Accessed 11 May 2021].

Anonymous. (350-300 BC). *Guanzi 49: Study of Inner Cultivation*. [Online] Available at: https://www.gutenberg.org/files/38585/38585-pdf/38585-pdf.pdf [Accessed 11 May 2021].

Britannica. (2019). *Tao-te Ching*. [Online] Available at: https://www.britannica.com/topic/Tao-te-Ching [Accessed 12 May 2021].

Confucius. (n.d. c. 500 BC). *Lun Yu*. s.l.:s.n.

Hansen, C. (2017). *Zhuangzi*. [Online] Available at: https://plato.stanford.edu/entries/zhuangzi/#pagetopright [Accessed 16 May 2021].

Indiana University. (2010). *The Warring States Period (453-221)*. [Online] Available at: https://scholarworks.iu.edu/dspace/bitstream/handle/2022/23445/2.1-Warring_States-2010.pdf?sequence=2&isAllowed=y [Accessed 16 May 2021].

Kirkland, R. (n.d.) *The Book of Mozi (Mo-Tzu)*. [Online] Available at: https://faculty.franklin.uga.edu/kirkland/sites/faculty.franklin.uga.edu.kirkland/files/MOTZU.pdf [Accessed 11 May 2021].

Laozi. (n.d. 4th Century BC). *Daodejing*. Republished 1868 ed. s.l.:s.n.

Lau, D. (1979). *The Analects: Sayings of Confucius*. s.l.: Penguin Classics.

Linnell, B. R. (2011). *Guanzi, Number 49 : Study of Inner Cultivation*. [Online] Available at: https://www.gutenberg.org/files/38585/38585-pdf/38585-pdf.pdf [Accessed 11 May 2021].

Perkins, M. (2019). *Confucianism Beliefs: The Four Tenets*. [Online] Available at: https://www.learnreligions.com/confucianism-beliefs-the-four-tenets-4779927 [Accessed 12 May 2021].

Song, C. (2021). [Online] Available at: https://www.chinahighlights.com/travelguide/china-history/warring-states-period.htm [Accessed 16 May 2021].

Zhou, Z. (n.d. c. 3rd century BC). *Zhuangzi*. 2013 ed. New York: Columbia University Press.

4 Sovereignty and Natural Law

To provide as much diversity as possible in presenting historical perspectives on the origin of the state, and indirectly human interaction, we turn next to Western philosophy. Before we start, a quick clarification on the term "west". According to William H. McNeil, the term "West" in relation to an ideology and region of the world has its roots as far back in history as 480 and 479 BCE (McNeil, 1997). In McNeil's account on the origin of the term, it is possible to point out the centrality of Europe in defining this term. McNeil, however, notes that as an ideology, the "West" would be defined rather subjectively given that it could be seen as competing with other perspectives. Here, we will use the term "west" to refer to geographically located western countries, primarily referring to Europe and North America. This chapter hops between the usual suspects of Western philosophy about the state, but it is an important reflection for the bigger picture.

***

Jean Bodin on Sovereignty

Jean Bodin (1529/30–1596) trained as a lawyer, economist, historian, political theorist, and philosopher who is famous for works including *The Six Books of the Commonwealth* (Les Six livres de la République, 1576), *Method for the Easy Comprehension of History* (Methodus ad facilem historiarum cognitionem, 1566), *European Humanism's Ars historica*, and *Colloquium of the Seven about Secrets of the Sublime* (Colloquium Heptaplomeres de rerum sublimium arcanis abditis, 1683) (Turchetti, 2018).

For Bodin (1530–1596), feudalism, religious reformation, and war were the main features of his world; we can safely assume that these features influenced his world view.[1] Jean Bodin offers a relatively straightforward definition of the state at the start of "The Republic" which he describes, "an aggregation of families and their common possessions, ruled by a sovereign power and by reason" (Dunning, 1896). With this definition, Bodin makes a few points clear about his position on the state and sovereignty. He highlights the important role of the family, the role of "will" and the need for a supreme power for coordination. He goes on to define a citizen as "a free man who is subject to the sovereign power of another" (excluding slaves). Paternal references and a perspective on family feature prominently in the

DOI: 10.4324/9781003330417-5

author's work. For Bodin, this approach means that there are only two categories of people within the state, namely, the Citizen and the Sovereign. Bodin describes the Sovereign as

> Master or Sovereign the most high, absolute, and perpetual power over the citizens and subjects in a Commonwealth: which the Latins call Majesty, the Greeks akra exousia (extreme power), the Italians Signoria, and the Hebrews tomech shévet, that is to say, The greatest power to command.
>
> (Lindfors, 2021)

An implication of Bodin's definitions is that the Sovereign is bound by the laws of nature and is answerable to God, while the citizens, on the other hand, are subject to the Sovereign and must answer to the Sovereign. While Bodin uses this approach to define the relationship between the Sovereign and the citizens in the state, he is cautious not to lay the foundation for tyranny and goes on to clarify with the statement that "the omnipotence of a prince is only imperium and not dominatus". In Latin, the word "imperium" could mean Government, while dominatus could be taken to mean mastery. This differentiation highlights Bodin's belief that the Sovereign is meant to serve the people and not be "master" over them as would be the case in slavery (note here another differentiation between the title master and position of master). These distinctions on what the Sovereign can and cannot do are captured in "natural law" which a Sovereign is bound by. For the state, Bodin believes that there are laws which the Sovereign cannot tamper with. While he does not state this clearly, the text suggests that he is referring to the constitution. According to Dunning (1896), Bodin fails to make a distinction between the constitution-making Sovereign and the ordinary law-making superior. The failure to make this distinction results in confusion about the differences between law and customs. Bodin concludes by saying that law is enforceable and can overwrite customs, while the reverse is not always the case. Edward Andrew, in his review of Bodin's work, elaborates further on the distinction between law and custom. Andrew points out that customs come into force gradually while laws on the other hand come into effect immediately, and that customs tend to be introduced softly while laws come as commands to the citizens (Andrew, 2011).

Bodin goes on to discuss the types and characters of state, pointing out that the character of a state is different from the way a state is governed. This means there is a difference between "state" and "government". For Bodin, as highlighted by Dunning, the character or structure of a state is determined by the number of people who make up the Sovereign, while the form of government is determined by the way the Sovereign exerts their power and authority (Dunning, 1896). This authority, Bodin believed, was either all in the control of the people as would be the case in a democracy, or in the hands of a small group of people as would be the case in an aristocracy, or the authority would be in the hands of one person in which case this would be classified as a monarchy (Andrew, 2011). Bodin, like Aristotle, lists these three categories as the types of states, namely, monarchy, aristocracy, and democracy, further noting that it is possible for a state to have one character and to be governed in another manner. This feature or possibility is reflective of contemporary societies which have both royal heads of government and elected heads of state. This notion, the separation of powers, will remain an important element of political theory throughout history and is at the core of Bodin's thinking (Fairlie, 1923).

Bodin's central idea is that sovereignty must be absolute (total in its implementation), perpetual (never ending in its application), and undivided (whole in its form). In defining the nature of sovereignty, however, he draws a limit on the Sovereign's ability to take from the private property of citizens. On this subject, unlike Hobbes' approach, Bodin believes that the Sovereign cannot tax the citizens without their consent. Bodin also believes that the Sovereign cannot claim or reclaim any property owned by a citizen. This is contrary to Hobbes, who believed that although a citizen could restrict other citizens from their private property, that right of restriction did not extend to the Sovereign (Andrew, 2011). All of these concepts come together to form Bodin's ideal definition of the term "sovereignty" and what it means to be sovereign. In his text, Jean Bodin notes that sovereignty is the "supreme power over citizens and subjects, unrestrained by law" (Lindfors, 2021).

Bodin's approach to sovereignty suggests that in order for the Sovereign to be effective in delivering on their mandate, they must be placed above the law and must respond only to a higher calling or authority: God. This approach ties in morality, religion, and politics in defining the relationship between authority and sovereignty.

***

Johannes Althusius on the State: Association, Sovereignty, and Federalism

Considered the father of modern federalism, Johannes Althusius (1557–1638) was a German political theorist, professor, and philosopher who was also a strong advocate of the concept of popular sovereignty. Althusius spent time living in Germany and Switzerland where he was strongly influenced by Calvinism. This influence will go on to be reflected in his works and play an important role in defining his political philosophy. Some of his notable literary contributions include "Politica methodice digesta atque exemplis sacris et profanis illustrata" 1614; and "Dicaeologica libri tres, totum et universum Jus", 1618 (On Law and Power, Politica) (Duignan, 1998).

In his work "Politica", Althusius makes two important statements that reflect his political inclinations. The first statement is "Politics is the art of associating men for the purpose of establishing, cultivating, and conserving social life among them. Whence it is called symbiotics" (Coffey, 2004).

The second statement is:

> Truly, in living this life no man is self-sufficient, or adequately endowed by nature. For when he is born, destitute of all help, naked and defenceless ... he is cast forth into the hardships of this life, not able by his own efforts to reach

> a maternal breast, nor to endure the harshness of his condition.... Nor in his adulthood is he able ... to provide by his own energies all the requirements of life.... As long as he remains isolated and does not mingle in the society of men, he cannot live at all comfortably and well while lacking so many necessary and useful things. An aid and remedy for this state of affairs is offered him in symbiotic life. He is led, and almost impelled, to embrace it if he wants to live comfortably and well, even if he merely wants to live.
>
> (Coffey, 2004)

Both statements highlight the importance that Althusius places on association, as well as the role that he believes that association plays in both political theory and the (natural) human needs for self-preservation, survival, and growth. Althusius was trying to establish a link between interaction and value. From both statements, interaction enables us to create value, which would mean that value was extrinsic to the interacting parties. In defining the origin of the state, Althusius goes on to identify five essential types of association that logically flow from each other. This starts with the family, friendships formed through voluntary association, community, province, and finally the state. The family unit is described as the first real level of association because it is the point where the individual comes into the world. This unit, for the new-born, is involuntary and comes with its peculiarities. From the family, the individual makes associations with friends of like mind and interest. This association of like minds varies in size and purpose, and just like in the case of a family, Althusius believes that there is always a leader from among the participants. So far, we have looked at two associations: family and friends (keep in mind that the friends here represent other families). Building on this is the understanding that these friends and families would live within a community. Practically, this is a collection of other friends and families living in proximity. Multiple communities within a region would form the provinces, and multiple provinces within a larger region would form the "state". This chain is meant to show how association builds out from the family unity and ultimately continues to flow until it turns into the state. Althusius believes that each of these associations and all of them as a whole, while independent and unique in their own rights, are held together by different social contracts that are inalienable. Through this approach, Althusius describes a federal (decentralized) system where sovereignty is held by the people through the various groups and levels of association. As part of this federal system, Althusius believed that cities and communities should have a relative degree of autonomy. This was meant to protect them from potential dominance by a central state authority. Althusius can be considered a liberal thinker in his approach to the purpose of the state.

"Politica" by Johannes Althusius was the first book to go into detail on a full theory of federalism, although Althusius was careful not to claim this as the very first account of federalism. For him the Bible was the "first grand federalist design" and was the ideal system based on the principles that it set out for the citizens and communities it spoke of. Althusius describes the Bible's design as federal in three ways (Althusius, 1614):

i Based on a network of covenants between God and humanity – this covenant also describes the relationship between humans;
ii A biblical commonwealth set around the tribes of Israel;
iii The biblical "end of days" era which Althusius believes presents a world confederation.

"Polity", according to Althusius, had three main meanings, of which political theory is concerned:

- Citizenship – the communication of right,
- Government – the form of administering the commonwealth, and
- Law – the constitution of the commonwealth that guides the actions of citizens.

Althusius describes a communion that brings the different citizens together and through which decisions are made on the roles and responsibilities of each citizen as part of the community. This communion is essential to the functioning of society. Althusius describes the communion of right as the law of association and symbiosis (lex consociationis et symbiosis), or the symbiotic right (jus symbioticum) as is made up primarily of self-sufficiency, order, and discipline (Althusius, 1614). Althusius calls this common law because it defines the relationship between individuals but also defines the relationship between the "rulers" and the "citizens". He goes on to describe the relationship between Adam and Eve as one of subjection, all of which is ultimately subject to God's authority. Again, the relationship between religion and politics surfaces. This relationship is emphasized in the statement "be subject to one another in fear of the Lord" (Althusius, 1614). Politica continues by describing the need for communication as ordained by God, noting that it is God who has distributed talents among humanity such that humans have need for each other. This mutual dependence is what drives individuals together to build communities and work together. Like Locke and Rousseau, Althusius notes that people come together based on a need for self-preservation and driven by an inner virtue, unlike Hobbes' account where people come together to escape the nasty, brutish state of nature.

Politica emphasizes that when citizens give their "consent" and "agreement", when they seek "fellowship" and "happiness" from each other as a collective, these are the binding forces behind political association. Althusius provides a detailed explanation of how communication and agreement influence the nature of the family, friends, cities, provinces, and states, as well as how this interaction impacts the relationship of superiors with inferiors. His perspective holds that the ultimate goal of interaction and communication is to promote peace. The statement "whatever cultivates love among the citizens and conserves the common good is to be nurtured, and the causes of discord among citizens and neighbours are to be guarded against" suggests that pleasure is the intrinsic good and all actions (extrinsic) should lead towards achieving the pleasure of unity among citizens. This suggests that Althusius had utilitarian, and some might even say hedonist, views on utility and value. Importantly, however, Althusius does not mix the pleasure of attaining social peace, with sensual pleasures and explains his position by making the statement "Might also leads to wealth, … to the pursuit of sensual pleasures, and so to everything corrupt" (Althusius, 1614).

Bodin described sovereignty and the characteristics that define it. For Bodin, sovereignty must be absolute (total in its implementation), perpetual (never ending in its application), and undivided (whole in its form). Building on the concept of sovereignty, Althusius describes the state as a series of associations that build up from the micro units until the federal system of connected sovereignty's vested within the small groups. For Althusius, absolutism was to be avoided at all costs. Much like Bodin, Althusius draws interesting parallels between human interaction and value creation. Yes, the definition of value might differ slightly for both thinkers, but the origin of that value remains the same.

***

Hugo Grotius on Natural Law: Influences and Contributions to the Theory

Natural law theory is a part of ethics and philosophy that has influenced broader thinking from politics to economics. The core idea behind natural law theory is that the concepts of "right" or "wrong" exist independent of human thought/perspective, and that humans can ascertain which from which by an internal force, as opposed to being told which from which by a set of human-made laws. Hugo Grotius (1583–1645) was a Dutch politician, lawyer, and philosopher, who was already writing at an early age and was recognized for his intelligence. This intelligence and the experiences that came with it saw him serve in several governments, including the Dutch, French, and Swedish. The circumstances of Grotius' life would also have a significant influence on his political views and theories. Among his famous works were "Pontifex Romanus", a collection of political essays; editions of the "Phaenomena", and Martianus Capella's "Handbook of the Seven Liberal Arts". He also published "Annales et Historiae de Rebus Belgicis"; "De Jure Praedae Commentaries" (Commentary on the law of prize and booty, also shorted as D.I.P); "De Jure Belli Ac Pacis" (DIB); and "Mare Liberum" (On the freedom of the seas) (Miller, 2021).

Max Salomon Shellens claims in "Aristotle on Natural Law" that while Aristotle (384–322 BCE) is considered as the father of natural law, he was not the first to coin the term, which was already popular thanks to the Sophists (Shellens, 1959). Sophists were ancient Greek teachers who were considered experts or sages on various topics (Taylor & Mi-Kyoung, 2011). Aristotle makes a differentiation between "natural law" or "natural justice" and "legal law", noting that the two are not always the same and that "natural law" exists whether people recognize its existence or not. Aristotle goes on to highlight the different between particular and general laws, noting that particular laws are concerned with a specific community and have been created by the community for its own particular needs. The second category of laws, general laws, are laws which are accepted by all but not created by any. This second category is akin to natural law in the sense that it is accepted by all but owned by none (however Aristotle still emphasizes that it is not exactly natural law).

> Insofar as law is not 'by nature' but is merely human enactment it is not the same everywhere. It is not even the case with regards to constitutions that they are everywhere the same, though there is only one constitution which is – by nature – everywhere the best.
>
> (Shellens, 1959)

From this statement, Aristotle highlights the role of natural law in justice, as well as the superiority of natural law to constitutional and other laws which have been created by humans. Max Salomon Shellens takes this a step further to suggest that through this statement, Aristotle believes that natural law should judge the laws that are in place at the time (Shellens, 1959).

St. Thomas Aquinas (1224/25–1274 CE) also had certain influences on Hugo Grotius' thinking on natural law. For Aquinas, it was impossible to separate natural law and religion. Aquinas' perspective was that natural law was indeed a subset of the ecclesiastical, and that by adhering to natural law, humans were playing their part in the divine interaction. C.S Lewis supports this by saying that

> according to the religious view, what is behind the universe is more like a mind than anything else we know … it is conscious and has purposes….. There is a "something" which is directing the universe, and which appears to me as a law urging me to do right.
>
> (Investopedia, 2020)

Natural law principles also feature in economics, with theories from economists like John Locke and Adam Smith building on the principles described by many as natural law principles.

In the book titled *On the Law of War and Peace*, Hugo Grotius makes a compelling case against wars, and attempts to establish the principles under which wars must be conducted in the circumstances where they cannot be avoided. Before setting out these principles however, Grotius goes into detail to emphasize the need for peace and the need for leaders (princes) to err on the side of caution when deciding on wars. His account includes a review on the justifications that parties use in seeking out wars. Cicero was one of the major thinkers that influenced Grotius' thinking, and as such, it was Cicero's definition of war that featured first in the text. According to Cicero, war is "a contention by force" (Grotius, 1625). Grotius builds on this definition to say that war is indeed not an action that happens suddenly, but rather is state of affairs characterized by contention (Grotius, 1625). Grotius breaks down the contention to say that this represents a misunderstanding between two parties, based on what each of them believes is right or "just". This therefore means that there must be principles that define what is right or wrong, or principles upon which the parties must base their perspectives of what is "just". The individual's well-being is placed at the centre of what is "just" in Grotius account, and this is reflected in his statement, "now anything is unjust, which is repugnant to the nature of society, established among rational creatures". Again, Grotius quotes Cicero to further highlight the centrality of humanity in the moral question on right and wrong, "to deprive another of what belongs to him, merely for one's own advantage, is repugnant to the law of nature" (Grotius, 1625). Continuing on the subject to emphasize the need for peace, Grotius compares individuals in society to the different parts of the body (much like Hobbes' Leviathan which sees all of society come together to create the one individual: The Leviathan). The purpose of this analogy is to say that as all parts of the body would work in unison for the good of the body as a whole, so as well should all individuals in society work together for the benefit of society as whole, even if they do not always agree. Furthermore, "right" is defined in two contexts – one right established for the individual and their claims to their property, and the other right established for the state and state's "right" to all property for the public good.

The moral question on what is "right" and "just" is an important question when considering the interactions of individuals within the state as well as the interactions of the state with its citizens. Authors like John Gay highlight the obligations that drive human action to include consequence, civil law, religious obligations, and inner ethical prescriptions (Driver, 2014). This is where Grotius differs and believes that instead a set of natural laws drive human action, further stating that even the power of God cannot change natural laws. Unlike some of his contemporaries and other philosophers before him, Grotius does not believe religious law is the highest authority. These natural rights, for Grotius, are the basis on which society is built. Just like Adam and Eve had the right to possess all that was in the world given to them, so also did humans in nature have the right to possess the resources at their disposal as long as it did not prevent others from possessing these rights. For most philosophers who have considered natural law, they would agree to a few central elements on this theory. One of these elements is the intrinsic nature of natural laws in the sense that these laws are not derived from anything else. This includes an individual's right to access the resources around them, according to Grotius. This economic right to resources has far-reaching implications on utility and value in the context of the citizen and the state. At the same time, *On the Law of War and Peace* uses the argument of natural law to highlight the rights due to all individuals (citizens), and to emphasize the need to protect these rights in avoiding war.

Bodin described sovereignty as absolute; Althusius took a different path to emphasize the need for decentralization. Grotius talks about the intrinsic attitude of natural law and its existence outside of human control.

> If you were the only one on a distant human outpost on a moon deep in space, and you told a lie, would it be a bad thing?

***

Note

1 Analysts draw similarities between the conditions surrounding Hobbes' life at the time of his work, and the conditions surrounding Jean Bodin. Both philosophers developed their core ideas at times of civil unrest and dissent.

Bibliography

Althusius, J. (1614). *Politica.* 1995 ed. Indianapolis: Liberty Fund.

Andrew, E. (2011). Jean Bodin on Sovereignty. *Republic of Letters: A Journal for the Study of Knowledge, Politics and the Arts, 2*(2), 75–84.

Coffey, J. (2004). *Johannes Althusius.* [Online] Available at: https://www.jubilee-centre.org/blog/johannes-althusius [Accessed 7 May 2021].

Driver, J. (2014). *The History of Utilitarianism.* [Online] Available at: https://plato.stanford.edu/entries/utilitarianism-history/

Duignan, B. (1998). *Johannes Althusius.* [Online] Available at: https://www.britannica.com/biography/Johannes-Althusius [Accessed 7 May 2021].

Dunning, W. A. (1896). Jean Bodin on Sovereignty. *Political Science Quarterly, 11*(1), 82–104.

Fairlie, J. A. (1923). The Separation of Powers. *Michigan Law Review, 1*(4), 393–436.

Grotius, H. (1625). *On the Law of War and Peace.* 2001 ed. Kitchener: Batoche Books.

Investopedia. (2020). *Natural Law.* [Online] Available at: https://www.investopedia.com/terms/n/natural-law.asp#:~:text=Natural%20law%20is%20a%20theory,by%20society%20or%20court%20judges. [Accessed 9 May 2021].

Lindfors, T. (2021). *Jean Bodin (c. 1529—1596).* [Online] Available at: https://iep.utm.edu/bodin/ [Accessed 5 May 2021].

McNeil, W. H. (1997). *Western Civ in World Politics: What We Mean by the West.* [Online] Available at: https://www.fpri.org/wp-content/uploads/2016/07/WH-McNeil-What-We-Mean-by-the-West.pdf

Miller, J. (2021). *Hugo Grotius.* [Online] Available at: https://plato.stanford.edu/cgi-bin/encyclopedia/archinfo.cgi?entry=grotius [Accessed 8 May 2021].

Shellens, M. S. (1959). *Aristotle on Natural Law.* [Online] Available at: https://scholarship.law.nd.edu/cgi/viewcontent.cgi?article=1039&context=nd_naturallaw_forum&source=post_page [Accessed 9 May 2021].

Taylor, C. & Mi-Kyoung, L. (2011). *The Sophists.* [Online] Available at: https://plato.stanford.edu/entries/sophists/ [Accessed 9 May 2021].

Turchetti, M. (2018). *Jean Bodin.* [Online] Available at: https://plato.stanford.edu/entries/bodin/ [Accessed 6 May 2021].

5 And Now the (First) Social Contract

The social contract theory is one of the important theories defining human interaction and the structure of society. In this chapter, we explore this theory from the perspectives of Thomas Hobbes, John Locke, and Jean Jacques Rousseau. Thomas Hobbes (1588–1679) was an English political philosopher, who made significant contributions to multiple fields, including history, physics, and ethics, among others. Throughout his life, Hobbes would take several trips to the European continent, where he would be influenced by Aristotle (whose theories he would challenge), Thucydides, and Euclid (Long, 1962). Euclid's geometry influenced Hobbes so much that Hobbes would go on to use a model similar to a geometric proof in his methodology of laying out the Leviathan. Using this model, each chapter of the Leviathan builds on a conclusion from the previous chapter, making each subsequent conclusion irrefutable since the foundation it is built on has already been proven. John Locke (1632–1704) was born in Wrington in England and has been referred to as one of the greatest philosophers in European history for his contributions to philosophy, politics, and medicine. Shortly after his birth, England was thrown into conflict among the Protestants, Catholics, and Anglicans; the resulting political landscape and associated events would go on to influence Locke's perspectives of government and state. Jean Jacques Rousseau was born in Geneva in 1712. His father was a watchmaker named Isaac Rousseau and was married to Suzanne Bernard. His diverse background benefitted from training to be a Catholic priest, musician, and schoolteacher. Rousseau spent time in Geneva, Bossy, Turin, Paris, and Venice, all of which would contribute to shaping his views of the world. In 1744, he moved back to Paris, where he would spend time working on music and contributing to the encyclopaedia of Diderot and d'Alembert. Throughout his life, Rousseau's work sought to protect human freedom, given the constraints of daily life and the heavy dependence that humans have of each other. He believed that human nature was inherently good, but that it is the interactions in and of society that corrupt the individual. He also believes in self-preservation as a critical aspect of human nature, and this is a part of why the social contract can exist (Bertram, 2020).

In every instance of the social contract defined by the authors, the world starts off at a blank state, or the "state of nature" where individuals roam on their own with no government, no laws, and no "civil reasoning". While each author defines

DOI: 10.4324/9781003330417-6

this "state of nature" with their various nuances, a central theme emerges across all three contributions. This theme is survival and hardship, since everyone must fend for themselves and against each other. To leave the "state of nature", the individuals must enter into two agreements (Laskar, 2017):

1 Pactum **Unionis** – through this agreement, individuals hoped to protect themselves from harm. This is the primary agreement that forms the state since it is the first instance where the individuals agree to come together as a collective.
2 Pactum **Subjectionis** – through this agreement, individuals agree to obey a central authority by giving up their freedoms to this authority who would in turn act on their interests and protect their freedoms.

By going into both agreements to form the state and equip it with the authority to function, the individuals give up the rights they had in the "state of nature" which would have allowed them to act as they chose and potentially in harm of others, for the actors' own personal gain. Thomas Hobbes, John Locke, and Jean Jacques Rousseau have emerged over time as the most prominent philosophers on the subject, and many have already commented in depth on their work, so I will not go into a lot of detail here.

Hobbes' first mention of the theory of the Social Contract came in his 1651 book the *Leviathan* which was published during the Civil War in Britain. His definition of the "state of nature" may have been the harshest of the three philosophers and was captured in the statement:

> Whatsoever therefore is consequent to a time of Warre, where every man is Enemy to every man; the same is consequent to the time, wherein men live without other security, than what their own strength, and their own invention shall furnish them withall. In such condition, there is no place for Industry; because the fruit thereof is uncertain; and consequently no Culture of the Earth; no Navigation, nor use of the commodities that may be imported by Sea; no commodious Building; no Instruments of moving, and removing such things as require much force; no Knowledge of the face of the Earth; no account of Time; no Arts; no Letters; no Society; and which is worst of all, continuall feare, and danger of violent death; And the life of man, solitary, poore, nasty, brutish, and short.
>
> (Hobbes, 1651)

Hobbes believes that self-preservation is an important aspect of "human nature", and as such, the individual would tend towards opportunities to protect themselves. This need for protection is what Hobbes believes drives the individual into the social contract, where we willingly give up a portion of our freedoms to this greater authority, in exchange for protection. In Hobbes' Leviathan, he describes all the individuals coming together to create one large individual, the Sovereign. This Sovereign becomes the authority figure/ruler/Monarch who is charged with leading the collective. Hobbes (a supporter of absolutism) goes on to suggest that citizens, once they give authority to the Sovereign, have no right to go against the Sovereign. This, of course, results in a degree of controversy seeing as Hobbes expects the notion to apply even when the Sovereign goes against the will of the people. He, however, believes that the Sovereign is bound by a moral obligation to act in the interest of the citizens or towards the greater good. Remember here that the greater good is the "general will" which is believed to be in everyone's best interest. Hobbes further believed that the Sovereign, charged with authority, was free to use force in delivering the requests of the citizens, and further believed that civil law was the truest form of law since it was enforced by the Sovereign. These beliefs were embodied in the statement "law is dependent upon the sanction of the Sovereign and the Government without sword are but words and of no strength to secure a man at all". Hobbes posits that the individual needs to be subjected to a central authority; otherwise, the state of nature is chaotic. This is unlike Rousseau and Locke who believe that the state's reason for existence is to "preserve and protect the natural rights of its citizens". Rousseau and Locke believe that if the state should fail to protect its citizens, then the citizens have a right to rebel.

Hobbes' approach to human nature suggests that humans will always only focus on their own self-interest and self-protection. This act is what he believes drives the individual to make decisions and furthermore, that the individual will try to maximize their own good or interest.

John Locke's theory of Social Contract takes a different and softer approach to defining the "state of nature" and the factors that drive the individual into that contract that forms the state. An important distinction in John Locke's definition of the "state of nature" is captured in the statement "reasonably good and enjoyable, but the property was not secure" (Locke, 1689). Locke notes that the "state of nature" is calm and collaborative and that "men had all the rights which nature could give them" (Locke, 1689), going on to say that all individuals in the "state of nature" were equal. These definitions and distinctions are important not only in political theory, but also in economic theory where economists seek to understand the factors that influence decision-making towards consumption and production. Locke's state of nature allowed individuals to carry out their lives as best as they see fit but does not give the individual a licence to harm others. Even though the "state of nature" had no laws or authority or government to control the affairs of the individuals and to punish offers, it was still a state of existence with a moral code.

Locke's approach to the "state of nature" makes it a "state of liberty", where individuals can seek out their interests without fear or interference. The use of the word "fear" here being a key deviation from Hobbes' state of nature which was specifically characterized by the fear of individuals. For Locke, the act of the individual working to process the raw materials in nature within their space is what creates "property"; however, there are limits on how much property one can own, and limits to how much of the natural resources that an individual can use. This need to define property among the individuals in the "state of nature" is what Locke believes to drive the need for a social contract. Furthermore,

Locke emphasized that property is not secure in the state of nature for the following reasons (Locke, 1689):

1 Absence of established law;
2 Absence of impartial Judge; and
3 Absence of natural power to execute natural laws.

As part of this contract, it is believed that "man did not surrender all their rights to one single individual, but they surrendered only the right to preserve/maintain order and enforce the law of nature". The individual, however, does not lose their other rights such as the "right to life, liberty and estate because these rights were considered natural and inalienable rights of men". Through this process of forming a collective, individuals that have now left the "state of nature" have gained:

- Laws – to define the affairs of the collective,
- judges – to preside over the laws,
- executive powers – to enforce the laws.

According to Locke (1689):

> the purpose of the Government and law is to uphold and protect the natural rights of men. So long as the Government fulfils this purpose, the laws given by it are valid and binding but, when it ceases to fulfil it, then the laws would have no validity and the Government can be thrown out of power.
>
> (Locke, 1689)

Locke furthermore believes that a Sovereign should not have absolute authority, unlike Hobbes' view, because for Locke, this goes against natural law, further suggesting the principle of "a state of liberty; not of license". Locke and Hugo Grotius would agree on the approach to natural law and protecting citizen rights as the purpose of government. John Locke would go on to make "life", "liberty", and "property", the three cardinal rights, which greatly dominated and influenced the Declaration of American Independence, 1776.

Jean Jacques Rousseau also takes a slightly different approach to the theory of the social contract but defines his "state of nature" closer to Locke's theory. For Rousseau, "the life in the State of Nature was happy and there was equality among men" (Rousseau, 1998). Rousseau believes that as populations increased, it became harder for individuals to satisfy their needs as they would have previously done. This phenomenon is what Rousseau believes inspired the formation of communities, division of labour, collaboration, and so on. Rousseau believes that over time, individuals which became families and communities started to invent things to improve their ways of living. Furthermore, over time, communities started to develop value systems, concepts around trade, wealth, and, most importantly, "property". For Rousseau, the invention of property is the point where "humanity falls from grace out of the state of nature" (Rousseau, 1998).

Rousseau talks about the "wills"; the General Will is "that State and Law were the product of General Will of the people" (Rousseau, 1998). If a government and the laws of a state go against the General Will, they will naturally be disregarded since they do not go in line with the greater good.

***

Understanding the origins of the state has been important to establish the nature of interaction between individuals, as well as the nature of interaction between individuals and the resources within the state. The last four chapters have offered insights into the multitude of perspectives on social interaction around the world. One central theme that emerged from all of these perspectives regardless of cultural context was the fact that interaction happens in the context of resources and value. Economics is concerned with the science of choice and resource management, and so before flowing into the discussion on economic value, it was necessary to establish an understanding of the context in which economic value is created. Humans interact with each other and with nature to create value. In contemporary society, individuals and groups are valued based on their contributions to their communities. The reality, however, is that not all states function through a proper social contract. Despite this, despite the fact that individuals and communities are left out of the social contract, this does not stop them from interacting. Because not all states function through a proper social contract, the Sovereign or Leviathan cannot meet the needs of all its citizens. The result, as we saw earlier on, is that populations do not have access to social services and financial systems. One concrete translation of this is the large percentage of the world's population currently operating in the informal economy. These individuals, families, and communities interact every day, and create value every day.

Bibliography

Bertram, C. (2020). *Jean Jacques Rousseau.* [Online] Available at: https://plato.stanford.edu/entries/rousseau/

Hobbes, T. (1651). *Leviathan.* London: Andrew Crooke.

Laskar, M. E. (2017). Summary of Social Contract Theory by Hobbes, Locke and Rousseau. *SSRN Electronic Journal*, 21 October.

Locke, J. (1689). *Two Treatises of Government.* London: Awnsham Churchill.

Long, J. A. (1962). *Thomas Hobbes's "Leviathan": A study in interpretation.* [Online] Available at: https://scholarworks.umt.edu/cgi/viewcontent.cgi?article=6625&context=etd [Accessed 6 June 2021].

Rousseau, J. J. (1998). *The Social Contract.* Hertfordshire: Wordsworth.

Spark Notes (n.d.) *Leviathan.* [Online] Available at: https://www.sparknotes.com/philosophy/leviathan/summary/ [Accessed 6 June 2021].

Part II

Economic Philosophy of Human Interaction

6 Value (i)

Socially Intrinsic?

In Part 1, we discussed a range of historical perspectives on the origin of the state and political society across various philosophical and geographic contexts. The objective of those discussions was to present a foundation for human interaction by highlighting how states are formed through a social contract which involves individuals coming together to form a group/collective. Those discussions also highlighted how resource management is one of the driving factors behind individuals entering the social contract. Building on that understanding, we will now discuss resource management (economic value) to understand how this is defined and measured.

In short, the first part of the book focused on politics; now the second part will focus on economics. This approach is important because it is difficult and impractical to attempt to separate politics and economics in the real world. Tejvan Pettinger, in the article "The Relationship between Economics and Politics" (Pettinger, 2020), explains the relationship between the two in simple terms. From the balance of fiscal (government) versus monetary (central bank) policies, to the taxation and political campaigns, politics and economics go hand in hand in defining the nature of interaction and resource management within the state or across state structures.

A central theme that emerged from Part 1 of the book was that the state or civil society brings individuals together to form a community that is primarily concerned with improving the status of the individual and managing the scarce resources that all individuals must share. In Hobbes' account, this was managing human resources and protecting against danger; in Locke's account, this was protecting property and effectively dividing this up. According to the Zhuangzi on the other hand, the state and active governance are unnecessary since "the way" which is described as a sort of natural law is sufficient to guide human resource management. In all instances, whether the philosopher in question agreed with the necessity of the state/government or not, resource management is at the heart of individuals coming together to form a society. Resource management is the core tenet of economics and further emphasizes the need for a symbiotic relationship between politics and economics.

***

DOI: 10.4324/9781003330417-8

Value theory dates as far back as Aristotle (384–322), who believed that "value" is based on need and that it is from this "need" that exchange takes place (Fogarty, 2021). This early thinking on value took a subjective approach to the concept in the sense that it considered value in relation to the utility received by the consumer. Early approaches to value theory also heavily considered "value for use" versus "value for exchange". This distinction on the nature of value is captured in the argument on intrinsic vs extrinsic value. In thinking about value for use, this is related to the utility or good that a commodity offers to a consumer from the direct consumption of that commodity. This concept on utility, the usefulness of a good or service, will go on to remain a central theme in value theory throughout history. An example of this case is cooked food which provides nourishment to the consumer, or clothing which provides cover from the elements. In thinking about value for exchange, consider the example of money. Fiat currency or cash is valuable not because of the paper it is printed on, but because the money/cash can be used to exchange for other goods and services. In simple terms, intrinsic value could be said of something that has value in itself as with the example of food above, and extrinsic value would be defined as all other cases. Arriving at a definition of what is intrinsic versus extrinsic value has been the subject of much philosophical discourse, and so it is important to consider some of this.

In their extensive article "Intrinsic vs Extrinsic Value" Michael J. Zimmerman and Ben Bradley highlight how, historically, the question of "what has intrinsic value" has preceded the question on "what is intrinsic value" (Zimmerman & Bradley, 2019). Let us start with the question on "what is intrinsic value", with the belief that defining intrinsic value will flow logically into understanding what has intrinsic value. Here's an illustration from Aristotle's Nicomachean Ethics:

> You ask someone whether it is good to help others in time of need and they would most likely answer that "yes, it is". If you ask again why helping people in time of need is a "good" act, they might respond saying that it is good to help others in time of need because it is good that their needs are satisfied. If you then ask why it is good that people's needs are satisfied, the person might respond saying "It just is". Another person might seek to respond further and say that that it is good that people's needs are satisfied because this brings them pleasure. You can take it a step further and ask again, "what is good about people being pleased?". At this point you could get the response again saying that "it just is good that people are pleased". Depending on who is responding, you the person could try to justify the need for human pleasure based on something else that they deem to be "good".
>
> (Zimmerman & Bradley, 2019)

Aristotle believes that at some point it would be difficult to further justify why something is good, because the individual will reach a point of realizing that not everything derives its goodness from something else. The philosopher believed that at some point, the individual arrives at something that "just is" good in its own right and which causes other things to be good. This point is intrinsic goodness. This approach defines intrinsic good as anything whose good or whose value is not derived from something else. It is important to note, however, that while intrinsic good is non-derivatively good, non-derivative good does not equal intrinsic value.

One of the early authors on the subject was George Edward Moore (G.E Moore) (1873–1958) in the book *Principia Ethica*. In this book, Moore contemplates three questions which he believes are essential to theories on ethics:

- "What is good?"
- "What things are good or bad in themselves?" and
- "What is good as a means?"

Moore is first concerned with defining what exactly is "good" and emphasizes the difficulty in defining this term. Moore was not wrong in contemplating the difficult of defining "good". In this book, the word "good" is used multiple times and under multiple contexts. There is just as much liberal and diverse use of the word among philosophers and historians. While the subject will be touched on at various points later, it is important to highlight in summary here some of the definitions of the term by prominent philosophers and in various contexts. In the study of ethics, good is given a moral connotation (the-philosophy.com, 2021) and is a fundamental normative concept. In economics, good refers to tangible items/commodities/products or other physical items of economic interest, i.e. property and capital.

Various thinkers have also defined the word (the-philosophy.com, 2021); Aristotle says "the good is that toward which it tends in all circumstances". For Spinoza, good is "any kind of joy, all that fills the wait". For John Locke, good is "everything in us pleasure". For Descartes,

> "the highest good of all men is a whole heap of all property, both the soul and the body of capital, which may be in some men but that of each individual is in anything else, and it consists only of a determination to do well, and contentment". For Immanuel Kant, "the virtue and happiness are the highest good".

Moore goes on to discuss what things are good or bad in themselves and agrees that "pleasure is good in itself but is not the only intrinsically valuable thing". Moore's final question explores "what is good as a means" which is concerned with duty and action. In *Principia Ethica*, he dives into the question on intrinsic good with the aim of breaking this concept down to its core components. To do this, the author considers what things, if isolated, would have their existence judged as good and notes that this approach will truly help humans in understanding what has value.

So far, philosophers have agreed on the general approach to defining intrinsic good as good that exists in and of itself, that is, good or value that is not derived from something else. Logically, with an understanding that some things have value in themselves, it should be easy for the individual to understand what commodities, goods, services, or things have this type of non-derivative value or good in themselves. This question is important from an economic perspective because of the relationship of economic utility with consumer decision-making.

In **Protagoras** by Plato (428–347 BCE), the philosopher concludes that pleasure and pain are good in themselves regardless of the consequences they result in. Everyone has a perspective on whether pleasure is the ultimate good, or whether pleasure is the only intrinsic good. This latter view is what we now commonly refer to as hedonism; a concept that is as old as the time of philosophers like Epicurus (341–271 BCE). Most known commentators on this subject have, however, not been hedonists and have instead believed that other aspects of life are capable of holding intrinsic value.

William Frankena (1973) (Zimmerman & Bradley, 2019) has proposed a good list on this subject:

> life, consciousness, and activity; health and strength; pleasures and satisfactions of all or certain kinds; happiness, beatitude, contentment, etc.; truth; knowledge and true opinions of various kinds, understanding, wisdom; beauty, harmony, proportion in objects contemplated; aesthetic experience; morally good dispositions or virtues; mutual affection, love, friendship, cooperation; just distribution of goods and evils; harmony and proportion in one's own life; power and experiences of achievement; self-expression; freedom; peace, security; adventure and novelty; and good reputation, honour, esteem, etc.

Philosophers have through history largely agreed that the intrinsic value or intrinsic good of a thing is a natural quality of that thing; however, there are a few who disagreed with this perspective, such as Thomas Hobbes (1588–1679) and David Hume (1711–1776). Both philosophers believed that the intrinsic value of an object or commodity was based on the consumers' perspective, noting that a commodity was valuable only if there was someone there to consider it valuable. Zimmerman and Bradley summarize some of these perspectives by noting that for Panayot Butchvarov, it is the "properties" of things that have intrinsic value; for Chisholm, it is the "state of affairs" of things that have the intrinsic value; and for Ross, it is "facts" that hold intrinsic value (Zimmerman & Bradley, 2019). Extrinsic value, on the other hand, could simply be described as derived good, or, good that is good because of something else other than itself.

Intrinsic value is closely linked with foundationalism: the idea that intrinsic value lays the foundation for other value to build on; in other words, intrinsic value is the foundation that other value is derived from. Contemporary authors like James Harold attempt to dissect the concept of intrinsic versus extrinsic value from a different perspective. In "Between Intrinsic and Extrinsic Value" published in the *Journal of Social Philosophy*, Harold argues for mutual dependence as a form of value justification that should be considered important (Harold, 2005). Harold starts by taking a moral view to value, referring to this in the context of personal goals, principles, and ideals. While many other philosophers have only a moral inclination to their descriptions of value, Harold's approach is unique in that it starts off strongly with this, as opposed to starting to approach value from the perspective of a commodity (good or service). Harold also looks at the concept of value from the consumers' standpoint, or subjectively, like Hobbes and Hume.

Value theory can be broadly classified into three categories, namely, ethical theory, theories on value justification, and value theory. Ethical theory focuses on what is right or wrong, good, or bad, evil, or good. This is a heavily moral approach influenced by several factors, all of which are concerned with humanity in a sense. Theories of value justification take a different approach and focus on showing the extent or circumstances under which something is considered good. Value justification leans towards ethical theory because it brings in perspective and extent, in its determinations. Value theories focus on "the good" and try to answer the question on what is good and why it is considered to be good.

Harold notes that in value justification, there are internal and external elements. For him, the value itself would serve as the internal element while external elements would include things like sentiments, beliefs, and natural properties (Harold, 2005). Harold, like Christine Korsgaard, distinguishes between intrinsic/extrinsic value and final/instrumental value. Harold believes that with intrinsic/extrinsic value, it is about the circumstance that the subject considers the thing to be valuable. On final/instrumental value, Harold believes this concerns the value that a thing has in itself (final), or the value that a thing is used to achieve in something else (instrumental). Other authors have considered final and instrumental values as defined by Harold, to be the same as intrinsic versus extrinsic value, Zimmerman and Bradley would be among this group. In building out the concept on value justification, Harold compares beliefs to values. For some philosophers, the justification of belief is based on truth, and by this logic, the justification of values should also be based on truth. For others, however, this basis on truth is not necessarily the case in justifications of belief. Other theories of foundationalism were proposed by authors like W.D. Ross' system of prima facie duties and Nagel's theory of objective reasons. In the discussion, Harold believes that not all values are strictly intrinsic or extrinsic and suggests that attempting to classify all values under only these approaches is limiting. The author goes on to note the challenge with foundationalist theorists not acknowledging that value such as happiness, humility, and integrity is mutually dependent and mutually supporting (Harold, 2005). Harold uses the example of nature to explain from his perspective, why intrinsic and extrinsic values are not the only approaches to understanding value. As in the case of nature, imagine a forest untouched and untapped by humans. You could argue that this forest has value for existing in itself; you could also argue that this forest has value because of what it could offer to humans and animals. This forest has value because it is home to multiple species, but also because it is a resource to humanity. Harold believes this is an example of a mutual dependence that cannot be defined too strictly in intrinsic versus extrinsic terms. The whole point of challenging the foundationalist approach to value is to show that the relationship is not a one-way relationship and to show that there are instances when things typically considered intrinsic value are influenced by factors outside of the values themselves.

Harold ends by presenting coherence theory, noting that in here, it is possible for every value to contribute to justifying other values, without being justified independently of those other values. This theory, however, faces certain challenges which Harold believes any coherent theorist must aim to address. These challenges according to him are (Harold, 2005):

- Regress/circularity – here there is the risk of running into a justification loop where there is no real starting point to base the justification of value on.
- Isolation – here, Harold considers the need to gain knowledge on the nature of the world.
- The basing relation – Harold believes that this is concerned with justifiable versus justified beliefs and asks the question whether a person being able to justify a belief is enough to make said person adopt the belief.

The point emphasized by Harold and highlighted above is an important notion in this book. Value is as dynamic and free-flowing as human intention. This is important as we are considering value in the context of interaction, and because we now understand, from previous chapters, the relationship between interaction and value. You see, until more recently in human history, economic and political systems have done a decent job in coordinating interactions in society. By providing policy and building out financial systems for the exchange of value, we have ensured some semblance of stability. But this stability has been contingent on the existence of central authorities to facilitate the interaction. As we saw with the discussion on the state, philosophers are divided on just how central this authority should be. As we see from contemporary society, centralization is not always the best option. This is true for those many economies with persistent social and economic crises. We have also seen the close relationship between value and interaction. The indications so far are that humanity is inching closer to a hybrid, decentralized type of society. In this new social contract;

- Many reasons pull individuals out of the state of nature,
- Many stakeholders become the leviathan, like the private sector and international organizations who can sometimes reach citizens in the state of nature better than failed governments,
- Value is created and exchanged every day, everywhere, even when the central authority is not available to coordinate this,
- Technology can help us to create a platform for the transfer of that decentralized value, in a way that allows us to effectively link multiple ecosystems to form a larger whole.

***

Bibliography

Fogarty, M. (2021). *A History of Value Theory*. [Online] Available at: https://www.tcd.ie/Economics/assets/pdf/SER/1996/Martin_Fogarty.html

Harold, J. (2005). Between Intrinsic and Extrinsic Value. *Journal of Social Philosophy*, 36, 85–105.

Pettinger, T. (2020). *The Relationship Between Economics and Politics*. [Online] Available at: https://www.economicshelp.org/blog/11298/concepts/the-relationship-between-economics-and-politics/ [Accessed 12 June 2021].

The-philosophy.com (2021). *The Good: Philosophical Definition*. [Online] Available at: https://www.the-philosophy.com/good-philosophical-definition [Accessed 4 May 2021].

Zimmerman, M. J. & Bradley, B. (2019). *Intrinsic vs. Extrinsic Value*. [Online] Available at: https://plato.stanford.edu/archives/spr2019/entries/value-intrinsic-extrinsic/

7 Value (ii)

Economically Extrinsic?

"Value" in economics attempts to measure how important a good or service is relative to a consumer, whether individual, group, community, business, or state. This concept has evolved throughout history, with several economists taking different approaches to defining, measuring, capturing, storing, and transferring economic value. In this book, I argue that given the evolution of social interactions, the evolution of value through history, and the current state of global technology, it is time to re-visit our understanding of social and economic value, or at least re-visit the tools and systems that we use to measure, capture, and transfer this. This position is supported by the question from J.M. Clark in "the Concept of Value" which asks, "how long will the definition of value survive social and economic reform?" (Clark, 1915). Yes, I know that question was asked a long time ago, but it applies very much today (currently May 2022). This question is critical in contemporary society and economics. J.M. Clark touches on the approaches of various economists such as John Stuart Mill, the English philosopher and political economist who argued that it is impossible to have a "general rise or fall in values". Mill's belief is that values are not absolute or isolated, but rather are in relation to each other; for example, the value of commodity A is determined in relation to the value of commodity B. General F.A. Walker, an American economist, on the other hand, presents the counter argument that it is not possible to measure a ratio or relation. Frank William Taussig, also an American economist, argues that the value of a commodity is expressed in terms of its ability or "power" to command other commodities in exchange. In response to General Walker, Professor Nixon Carver, also an American economist, positioned that to measure the relation or ratio between two commodities, both commodities would need to have a common attribute or common quality which would serve as the base for measurement. This common quality is expected to serve as the "value", and the exchange ratio between these commodities is meant to vary based on how much of the common quality is present in each commodity. This final point from Professor Carver on the common attribute (common denominator) is an important one to remember and will come up again later.

The variations between economists continue through history and go into greater detail in what is expected to constitute value, as well as what metrics should be applied in its measurement. In all definitions of value, however, it is important

DOI: 10.4324/9781003330417-9

to remember the consumer and the commodity as the central pillars or focal points around which the discussions take place. Broadly speaking, and based on the research till date, there are two categories of value theory, namely, the objective and the subjective theories (McLure, 2014).

Objective value theory is primarily concerned with classical political economy, labour theory of value, and the Piero Sraffa revival of classical value theory in the 20th century. This category of value theory was widely acknowledged during the time of Karl Marx, the German philosopher and economist, and David Ricardo, the British political economist. Furthermore, objective value theory focuses on the conditions of production of commodities and less on the circumstances surrounding the exchange of these commodities. Karl Marx highlighted that the "conditions of production" are made up of three elements (Harvey et al., n.d.):

- human labour: personal conditions of production
- the environment: natural or external conditions of productions
- urban infrastructure: general, communal conditions of production

Subjective value theory is concerned with neoclassical economics and its emphasis on marginal utility, equilibrium, marginal productivity, and enhancements to utility analysis. This category of value theory, which is still used today, gained relevance after 1870, and was driven by economists like William Stanley Jevons, Leon Walras, and Carl Menger. Subjective value theory focuses on the preferences of consumers and is not concerned as much with the conditions under which the commodities for these consumers are produced. At first look, subjective value theory aligns well with our previous discussions on the link between interaction and value, given that it focuses on the consumer (and not on the conditions of production). However, a good number of humans also understand that the conditions of production are important if we are to live harmoniously and sustainably with the environment.

In *The Wealth of Nations*, Adam Smith took three approaches to measuring value (O'Rourke, 2007):

1 Labour embodied theory
2 Adding-up theory (which considers the sum of the land, labour, and capital employed in producing value)
3 Value determined by the work, effort, and energy put in by the producer

The third approach proposed by Adam Smith somewhat aligns with David Ricardo's "Labour Theory of Value" which suggests that a commodity's value is proportional to how much labour was required to produce it. In *Principles of Political Economy*, John Stuart Mill continues on the importance of context in understanding measuring value and even today, the role of context cannot be overstated. Mill uses the analogy of water, air, and gold, highlighting how important water and air are compared to the conventionally perceived value of gold. In this analogy, context here refers to what the consumer can do with water or air versus gold.

This analogy ties into Frank William Taussig's notion that the value of a commodity is tied to the rate at which that commodity can be exchanged for others. Air and water, while essential to human survival, cannot currently be exchanged for other commodities in the same way that gold can be and has been done for centuries. Whether in the future air and water will be exchangeable in the same way that gold is in contemporary society is a discussion for another day. The discussion on the utility of air and water ties into subjective approach to value theory which looks to understand consumer utility in measuring value.

In *Value and Capital* (Hicks, 1939), Hicks notes that Alfred Marshal's main argument asks how a consumer will divide his income when presented with an option of commodities. Since income is often limited for the average consumer, the consumer is forced to split his income among a basket of goods and will make decisions on quantity and quality based on what that consumer perceives as most important. This is the typical dilemma that we all (well, most of us) face when grocery shopping.

Now, let's talk about utility. Utility has been present throughout the history of ethical theory but was most clearly articulated first in the 19th century (Read, 2004). There are different approaches to defining utility. One definition says that "the morally right action is the right action". This approach brings in concepts like morality and consequentialism because actions are viewed and understood in relation to their outcomes or consequences. Utilitarian theorists believed that a consumer needs to maximize total "good" or "happiness". Classical utilitarian theorists like Jeremy Bentham and John Stuart Mill believed that the consumer ought to maximize the good or "bring the greatest amount of good for the greatest number of people". This approach to defining utility posits that everyone's happiness or good has the same weight, and that everyone within a given population would normally promote the overall good because everyone else was doing so. Before the classical approach to utilitarianism took over, Jeremy Bentham (1748–1832) developed the first "systemic account" of the subject, stating that morally appropriate behaviour will not harm others but will increase happiness or utility. Other early thinkers on the subject include Cumberland, Shaftesbury, Hutcheson, Gay, and Hume (Raphael, 1969). Another perspective is that of James Harold, who believes in utilitarianism as the ultimate theory in foundationalism. This assumption is based on the consideration that utilitarianism seeks happiness as its ultimate goal (foundational value) on which all other values are built. The key thing about this is that happiness is considered the intrinsic good, while all actions that seek to enhance/increase/create happiness are extrinsic seeing as these secondary actions are not good in themselves but rather are bringing about good (Harold, 2005).

Richard Cumberland (1631–1718) and John Gay (1699–1745) related human happiness to religion and noted that human happiness is approved by God. Gay goes on to talk about the ways that humans come under "obligations" or the way that humans are motivated to act (Driver, 2014). For him, we act based on, or are driven by:

- what the individual or actor perceives as the natural consequences of their actions
- civil obligations and laws

- the need to be "virtuous"
- the authority of God – which Gay believes is the most important source of obligation and the one through which other forms flow

Relating happiness to God's will is an important aspect of the theological approach to utilitarianism, which would be further developed by William Paley.

Anthony Ashley Cooper (1671–1713) was an early moral-sense theorist who believed we have an inner guidance system to judge between good and evil, right, and wrong (Cooper, 1711). Francis Hutcheson and David Hume (1711–1776) would go on to develop this concept further. Hume takes a slightly different approach from Gay by suggesting that moral positions are subject to perception. Hume makes the comparison to colour and states that discrimination is only discrimination based on how it is perceived, and if an act is not perceived as discrimination, then it cannot be referred to as such. This approach is the opposite in a sense of the theologians (Hume, 1738).

The classical approach built out the concept of utilitarianism and featured key contributions like Jeremy Bentham (1748–1832). Bentham was influenced by Thomas Hobbes' account of human nature and Hume's account of social utility. Bentham believed that humans are ruled by two Sovereigns: pleasure, and pain. Bentham further believed that humans act according to these, to promote pleasure or social good, and to reduce pain or social harm. Bentham's approach suggests that an action is not wrong because of the action, but rather because of its effects (Bentham, 1789). John Stuart Mill (1806–1873) also investigated these differentiations of pleasure and pain, as well as the nuances around these in the context of utility (Mill, 1843).

Henry Sidgwick (1838–1900) argues in *The Methods of Ethics* (1874) that utilitarianism is the higher principle that humans use to resolve fundamental conflicts between values or rules. Sidgwick goes further to suggest the need for greater average utility and the need for larger populations to the point where society can maximize the product of the population and the average happiness.

Under ideal utilitarianism, G.E. Moore did not agree with the "pleasure central" value theory which was the focus of classical theorists, and which sought primarily to maximize the consumers' pleasure. Moore believed strongly in value being an independent element of any pleasure gained by the consumer. He uses beauty as an example and suggests that an object is beautiful whether someone is there to say it is beautiful or not. Moore also suggested "organic unity" or "organic whole", saying that the sum of value of the part of a body is not the same as the intrinsic value of the body as a whole (Driver, 2014).

Understanding utility helps us to understand the consumers' behaviour in relation to changes in market conditions. Building on this understanding of utility, because the consumer must manage scarce resources, it is believed that the consumer will try to maximize their utility/total good/total happiness. Marshal suggests that to maximize total utility, the marginal utility of commodities must be equal to their prices. Unlike Marshal, Pareto looked at the relationship/interaction of multiple commodities.

Hicks argues to replace certain concepts in utility or happiness. He starts with marginal utility and suggests that this be replaced with marginal rate of substitution, because total utility or total happiness is an arbitrary number that is assigned by whoever is doing the calculation. Marginal rate of substitution, on the other hand, is meant to look at the interchangeability between commodities and focuses more on the ratio of this interchangeability. This approach from Hicks looks at value in relation to the price of the commodity, that is, in relation to the commodity's exchange value. The second concept that Hicks suggests should be replaced is diminishing marginal utility which is suggested to become diminishing marginal rate of substitution. This approach relates the value of a product, i.e. the utility or happiness that the product offers, to its price, which in turn is then related to the consumer. By the same logic, an individual's economic value could be determined in relation to their utility to others and to the economy/society. Hicks notes that economic theories are formed with reference to economic assumptions that are meant to reflect the state of reality. He asks how these assumptions came to be and notes that often economic theories tend to ignore all other variables from the ones they consider. How then can these theories still hold in societies and economies with so many more variables interacting? This research suggests that any real calculation of utility should try to factor in as many variables as possible and this is where the application of technology comes in. According to Hicks, "there are distinct advantages to be gained from having a theory of value in which the relations of demand, price and income are all made quite clear" (Hicks, 1939).

Tired, excited, confused, intrigued? We are not done yet. It is important to reflect on the variety of perspectives here. Doing this will allow us together to rethink what value means now and into the future. Research till date suggests that value is determined by several factors both internal and external to the commodity or good in question. Consumer disposition and preference are among these factors which philosophers and political economists have considered in understanding value. In this regard, Hicks looks at the effect that price changes and income changes have on consumer behaviour. This approach relates the value of a good or commodity, to the income of the consumer, with inferior goods losing value as income rises. An inferior good is an economic term that is used to describe goods whose demand falls when the consumers' incomes rises and whose demand rises when the consumers' income falls (Corporate Finance Institute, n.d.). Hicks explains this phenomenon by highlighting two things that happen when prices fall. First, the fall in prices increases the real income of the consumer and makes the consumer better off. Second, the fall in prices changes the relative price of other commodities because the commodity whose price fell is likely to be substituted for other commodities. The combination of both tendencies is the total effect on demand. This does not include luxury goods which tend to act outside of the typical laws of demand; here value is influenced heavily by the factors of production as well as by perception, and not necessarily by functionality. The impact of price changes on these two potential actions, is referred to as the income effect and substitution effect. In the income effect, if the consumer was buying a large quantity of a good relative to their income when the price falls, then the consumer is much better off. If the consumer was buying a small quantity of a good, the consumer gains only a little when the price falls and the income effect is overcome by the substitution effect. The substitution effect always tends to increase demand when the price falls. Several other factors come into play when determining the value of a product to a given consumer. The income and substitution effects flow naturally into complementarity and competition between goods and services, including how the value of these is perceived. As part of the consumption process, certain products will be consumed together, while for other goods or services, the inverse might be the case. Goods and services can be said to be complementary when an increase in the supply of X (Y constant) increases the marginal utility of Y. In other words, an increase in the quantity of X would increase the consumers' happiness for Y. Conversely, goods and services can be said to be competitive when an increase in the supply of X (Y constant) decreases the marginal utility of Y, or, as seen earlier, decreases the consumers' happiness with Y. Consider the example of petrol. A can of petrol on its own might be of little value to a consumer. If the consumer gets a car, then the can of petrol gains utility, or value. Now consider adding multiple other elements to this scenario. Say that the consumer has the can of petrol in a community where there are many cars, but there is a scarcity of petrol. The utility of the petrol could change for the consumer even though they don't have a car themselves. Instead, the utility of the petrol in this scenario would be based on the petrol's recently gained exchangeability or exchange value. Equilibrium considers this exchangeability from the demand and supply perspectives, by looking at the optimum point where both demand and supply for the product are aligned.

Pricing in itself is a potentially sensitive subject given its impact on consumer behaviour, demand, and supply (Conover, 1984). Hicks highlights that very often the current supply of a commodity depends on the past prices that the commodity has achieved, and not on the current price (Hicks, 1939). This approach to demand and supply that factors in "time" is referred to as dynamic theory. For the Austrians, the stationary state concept suggests that tastes, techniques, and resources remain constant, and as such, entrepreneurs do not expect prices to change and so supply stays the same. This is almost never the case. Stationary state theorists believe that reality is generally tending towards stationariness. The consumer rarely has specific price expectations; instead, they have a range within which they would be willing to pay for a bundle of services.

Hicks goes on to highlight how prices would be set in a new market, using the example of a market starting on day 1, Monday. This example assumes that by the start of the day 1, all information available is taken as "given" and as such cannot be changed. Hicks posits that traders will bargain throughout the day and will try setting the price by trial and error, before finally arriving at a price by the end of the day which would be the market price (Hicks, 1939). Hicks uses this analogy to relate value to price, and to describe how price is naturally adjusted by the consumers and producers over time. Jevons (1871) describes this relationship of price through the arrangement:

> Cost of production determines supply,
> Supply determines final degree of utility,
> Final degree of utility determines value.
>
> (Jevons, 1871)

The American economist Dr Irving Fisher takes a more mathematical approach to defining value, noting that for utility to be an effective economic concept, it needs to be calculable in mathematical terms. In his thesis "Mathematical Investigations in the Theory of Value and Prices", submitted to Yale in 1891, Fisher starts by urging economists to shy away from psychological theories and to focus on facts in any attempt to understand "utility". For Fisher, economists should not be focusing on whether pain and pleasure are the sole determinants of consumption decisions, adding that "utility" or "happiness" and "consequence" are not the only factors that influence consumer decisions. This approach, unlike early utilitarians, tries to move away from the subjective elements of how the consumer feels, to more tangible and measurable concepts and inputs.

Fisher posits that desire is what leads people to make decisions; however, he did not believe that pleasure brought about desire, or whether fear or duty bring about desire. The concept of linking fear to desire is in line with consequentialist thinking. Fisher believed that all of these nuances and variations are topics for psychologists to debate and askes economists to focus simply on the fact that individuals act based on desire. The mathematical approach to value looks at the concept of utility as a quantity, meaning the quantity of good or quantity of happiness that the consumer gains from an action. This approach to utility as a quantity posits that:

- For a given consumer at a given time, the utility of A units of a commodity (a) is equal to the utility of B units of commodity (b), if the consumer does not want to exchange one for the other.
- If the consumer prefers A to B, then the utility of A is higher than the utility of B to the consumer.
- The ratio of two infinitesimal utilities is measured by the ratio of two infinitesimal increments of the same commodity respectively equal in utility to the two utilities whose ratios are required, provided these increments are on the margin of equal finite quantities.

Jevons' *Theory of Political Economy* (Jevons, 1871) goes into some depth on the subject and starts by saying that the science of political economy is based on utility, wealth, value, commodity, labour, land, and capital. Jevons believes that individuals are driven by motives and feelings, and that it is difficult to measure how one feeling in person A is felt in person B. Fisher would agree with this statement on the difficulty of measuring feelings, choosing not to dwell on the psychology of human feelings and emotions. For Jevons, economics should be considered as a science and economists, when approaching decision-making, should attempt to measure as inputs all the phenomenon influencing the consumers' decision-making process. Accounting for all inputs into the consumption process is a particularly difficult task; however, this is not an impossible task, especially with advancements in technology. Jevons and Gay would both agree (as would potentially many utilitarians) that the object of economics is to "maximise happiness by purchasing pleasure at the lowest cost of pain". This approach which Jevons presented clearly, ultimately, ties pleasure to wealth and purchasing power, which some philosophers may not agree with.

Utility has so far been referred to by several political economists as good and happiness, two broad and subjective terms. Definitions until now have focused on utility in terms of commodities as goods and services. Jevons, however, takes this a step further to suggest calculating utility is about calculating the good that comes from satisfying basic human wants and needs such as feeding and shelter, which Bentham suggested are driven by pleasure and pain. According to Bentham, an individual would determine for themselves how much value they gain from a commodity or situation based on the following (Jevons, 1871):

- The intensity of the stimuli concerned, whether from consuming a good or service;
- The duration of the stimuli and whether this is extended or short-lived;
- The certainty or uncertainty of the stimuli;
- The propinquity or remoteness of the stimuli.

Bentham goes on to further identify three circumstances that relate to the results of any act or feeling:

- Fecundity – its ability to replicate or reproduce more of the feeling,
- Purity,
- Extent – meaning how many people are affected by the act or feeling.

You might already notice that all seven points mentioned above are relatively straightforward data points that can be measured and fed into a calculation on utility. In every case described by Bentham and Jevons, the length of time and the intensity play a role in defining the value whether as pleasure or pain. This also applies when you introduce the "time" context. "Anticipated feeling", as Jevons calls it (Jevons, 1871), causes the individual to expect pleasure or pain in the future, from an action happening in the present. Jevons believes that this is also an important factor in decision-making, further noting that individuals seldom ever make decisions based on the moment, but rather make decisions taking inputs from the past, and expectations for the future. In this regard, the intensity of present anticipated feeling must be some function of the future actual feeling and of the intervening time between both.

Before going into the discussion on utility, Jevons compares pleasure and pain to positive and negative figures in algebra. He says that like drawing a graph, it is possible to consider pleasures as numbers on the positive side of the axes, and pain on the negative side, and that all actions would tend to move the graph further into the positive side. James Harold would consider Jevons' approach to pleasure as foundational in the sense that all other actions (extrinsic goods) are focused on achieving pleasure (intrinsic good). The approach to pleasure and pain adopted here requires any calculations of the two to be done on the same scale, such that an increase in pleasure reduced pain and an increase in pain reduces pleasure. Jevons believes that utility is not an inherent or intrinsic value of a commodity, but rather a quality that is derived based on the circumstances surrounding the commodity's interaction with an individual. Utility is further broken down into three distinctions which Jevons believes must be considered (Jevons, 1871):

- actual utility – this refers to commodities, goods, and services that are immediately useful to someone. Take the example of a raw material. When this raw material is being used to create a commodity for consumption, it has utility in the moment. This is actual utility as it is the actual good that the raw material is offering.
- prospective utility – prospective utility refers to commodities, goods, and services that would be useful once they are in the hands of someone who has a use for them. Continuing on with the example of raw materials, a raw material would be prospectively useful if it was in a market waiting to be bought by a consumer for use.
- potential utility – with the example of a raw material, potential utility considers the raw material while it is still buried in the ground. This raw material has the potential to be useful and offers a potential good.

This review on the subject of value has touched on multiple definitions and approaches, each influenced by a multitudinous array of factors. Jevons points out the ambiguity in this term and offers up a definition which he believed reflected his thoughts on the subject. For Jevons, value "expresses the circumstances of its (/a commodities) exchange in a certain ration for some other substance" (Jevons, 1871). Measuring the value of a good or service is not an arbitrary action. By looking at the utility of that product or service in the context of the individuals' immediate surroundings, and factoring market conditions, it becomes possible to calculate value with a new level of precision previously impossible. Again, this is where technology comes in.

Bibliography

Bentham, J. (1789). *An Introduction to the Principle of Morals and Legislation*. Oxford: Clarendon Press.

Clark, J. (1915). The Concept of Value. *Quarterly Journal of Economics, 29* 663–673.

Conover, J. F. (1984). Price Effects on Consumer Behavior: a Status Report. *A - Advances in Consumer Research, 11*, 633–635.

Cooper, A. A. (1711). *Inquiry Concerning Virtue or Merit*. Raphael: s.n.

Corporate Finance Institute (n.d.) *Inferior Goods*. [Online] Available at: https://corporatefinanceinstitute.com/resources/knowledge/economics/inferior-goods/

Driver, J. (2014). *The History of Utilitarianism*. [Online] Available at: https://plato.stanford.edu/entries/utilitarianism-history/

Harold, J. (2005). Between Intrinsic and Extrinsic Value. *Journal of Social Philosophy, 36* 85–105.

Harvey, D., O'Connor, J., & Engels. (n.d.) *Conditions of the Working Class in England*. [Online] Available at: http://www.columbia.edu/~lnp3/mydocs/ecology/harvey_oconnor.htm#:~:text=The%20%22conditions%20of%20production%22%20require,%2C%20communal%20conditions%20of%20production%22

Hicks, J. (1939). *Value and Capital*. Oxford: Clarendon Press.

Hume, D. (1738). *A Treatise of Human Nature*. Oxford: Oxford University Press.

Jevons, W. S. (1871). *Theory of Political Economy*. London: Palgrave Macmillan UK.

McLure, J. K. A. M. (2014). *History of the Concept of Value*. [Online] Available at: https://www.business.uwa.edu.au/__data/assets/pdf_file/0004/2478883/14-06-History-of-the-Concept-of-Value.pdf

Mill, J. S. (1843). *A System of Logic*. London: Harper & Brothers Publishers.

O'Rourke, P. J. (2007). *On 'The Wealth of Nations'*. [Online] Available at: https://www.nytimes.com/2007/01/07/books/chapters/0107-1st-orou.html [Accessed 7 May 2021].

Raphael, D. (1969). *British Moralists*. London: Clarendon Press.

Read, D. (2004). *Utility theory from Jeremy Bentham to Daniel Kahneman*. [Online] Available at: http://eprints.lse.ac.uk/22750/1/04064.pdf [Accessed 10 May 2021].

8 Deep Dive

Origin of Contemporary States and Influence on Economic Perspectives of Value

Until now we have discussed various concepts from their theoretical perspectives, but how do these apply in the real world? This case study takes a critical look at the origin of two states and attempts to situate the factors that have influenced the origin of both states, within political theories and philosophy. In doing so, the case study seeks to analyse and understand real-world examples of state formation, as well as real-world applications of political theory on the state and public administration. This approach will shed light on elements of the state such as sovereignty and authority. The case study starts with the history on the formation of the states in question, in relation to political theories. The study then goes on to highlight major periods of political thought, and the impact that these periods have had on shaping contemporary social and economic administration. The study ends with a comparison of both states as well as a critical analysis on the concept of value.

The State-Nation Paradigm

Before going into the discussions and analysis on the state, it is important to address the state-nation paradigm. Simply put, according to the Matt Rosenberg (Rosenberg, 2020), the state is "a territory with its own institutions and populations".

> sovereign state is a state with its own institutions and populations that has a permanent population, territory, and government. It must also have the right and capacity to make treaties and other agreements with other states.
>
> (Rosenberg, 2020)

> the nation is a large group of people who inhabit a specific territory and are connected by history, culture, or another commonality.
>
> (Rosenberg, 2020)

> nation-state is a cultural group (a nation) that is also a state (and may, in addition, be a sovereign state).
>
> (Rosenberg, 2020)

The fact that both terms seem close in definition, and tend to (wrongly) be used interchangeably, has opened the concepts of state and nation up for debate and

DOI: 10.4324/9781003330417-10

interpretation throughout history. The Pontifical Academy of Social Sciences (PASS), an institution within the Vatican City, also agrees that there is no single definition of the "nation", but highlights that "peoples with common ethnic roots, language, religion, historical memory and the explicit desire to act as a political unity make up a nation" (Pontifical Academy of Social Sciences, 2019). According to PASS, the term "nation" has taken on multiple connotations to include both that group of people who are together because of culture and identity, and political connotations for states looking to unify their citizens based on identity. The debate on the state versus the nation continues into which precedes which, and what this means. One author that believes that the natural emergence of the nation is impossible is Samuel Pinheiro Guimarães. In *Nation, Nationalism, State*, Samuel P.G. notes that this natural emergence is impossible because of the "ignorance of the masses" whom he believes could not recognize the common features that bound them together (Guimarães, 2007). Samuel P.G. goes on to highlight his perspective on the origin of the state as one driven by competition for scarce resources and ultimately survival. According to him, the state was needed to manage the conflicts that arose from this competition, and to establish the laws needed to guide the conduct of citizens (who by definition lived or originated in the territory). Furthermore, Samuel P.G. notes that as populations grew, states were forced to absorb surrounding territories which meant absorbing cultures that were not necessarily the same or necessarily collaborating with each other. The resulting non-alignment has been the cause of numerous conflicts even until today.

Origin of the Country of Nigerian and Relations to Political Theory

Toyin Falola and Matthew M. Heaton, in *A History of Nigeria*, provide an excellent chronology of the evolution of the state of Nigeria. This case study leverages the structure provided by this chronology in the discussion on the formation of the Nigerian state and Nigerian political economy. Nigeria has remained a global dilemma since its formation. The country boasts of Africa's largest population at home, as well as a sizeable diaspora that brings the total population to staggering figures. Nigeria's population is estimated at 219,463,862 as of July 2021, with over 250 ethnic groups dominated by the Hausa (30%), Igbo (15.2%), and Yoruba (15.5%), also including the Fulani (6%), Tiv (2.4%), Kanuri/Beriberi (2.4%), Ibibio (1.8%), Ijaw/Izon (1.8%), and others (24.7%) (CIA World Fact Book, 2021).

Falola and Heaton (Falola & Heaton, 2008) start their chronology in 9000 BCE/BC[1] to highlight evidence that the south-western region of Nigeria was inhabited by indigenous people as far back. By 600 BCE/BC, evidence suggests that the Nok civilization (close to present-day Abuja) was already using iron technology as part of their daily lives. The Nok culture was around in the area known today as Nigeria between 500 BC and 200 AD and is regarded as one of the earliest known organized societies in the Western Africa region (Natinoal Geographic, 2020). According to Falola and Heaton, major states such as Benin, Borno, Oyo, Ife, and Kanem emerged during the 1000–1500 AD period, around which time Islam was also introduced into the Savana and Sahel region of present-day Northern

Nigeria. The period from 1300 to 1600 also saw a lot of the trans-Saharan trade in gold, slaves, and other commodities which headed out of the region and up towards Northern Africa, Europe, and the Middle East. Other accounts extend this period to include from 1100 to 1600, and also highlight the high levels of scholarship that accompanied the period (Fauvelle, 2020). According to these and several other accounts, this period was significant not only because of the volume and diversity of trade, but also because of how far trade from the region spread across the globe. The activities between AD 1450 and 1850 would play a significant role on the subsequent social structures in the region and would go on to lay a foundation that would be almost impossible to change throughout the country's political history. According to Falola and Heaton, 1804 marked the beginning of the Islamic revolution that ultimately led to the creation of the Sokoto Caliphate in the northern part of present-day Nigeria. The expansive Sokoto Caliphate was founded by Usman dan Fodio and deserves a review of its own for its influence in regional politics. In 1807 the British had abolished the slave trade, and by 1833,[2] the Oyo Empire had fallen, leading to conflict and instability among Yoruba states. Between 1841 and 1846, Christian missionaries began active efforts to spread the religion deeper into present-day Nigeria. This was an important period in Nigeria's history because it would mark a turning point in the interactions between Christianity and Islam which, until that point, may not have necessarily had to interact in the context of that specific territory. In 1861, the British annexed Lagos as a Crown Colony. This was followed over the next 50 years by events including the subsequent amalgamation of Nigeria in the year 1914 (Falola & Heaton, 2008). This amalgamation is largely acknowledged as the creation of the Nigerian state as it is known today. Unlike the examples and circumstances presented in political theory, the citizens of this territory (who are now called Nigerians) did not exist together in a state of nature, and, as such, were not driven out of this "state of nature" by the same events that philosophers on the subject have presented, such as fear and the need for the protection of property. Instead, one could argue that the elements of fear and protection of property existed on the British side, hence the need to amalgamate the regions and consolidate their political control. It is important to note, however, that the circumstances are different for the many sub-nations that inhabited the territory prior to the Nigerian state.

As seen in earlier chapters, entering into the social contract was typically preceded by human existence with little to no "civil reasoning". According to Hobbes, this state of nature was characterized by a life that was solitary, poor, nasty, brutish, and short. In Hobbes' account, it was a need for self-preservation that drove the individuals out of the state of nature and into the social contract. This need for self-preservation did not apply in the case of early Nigerian citizens. According to John Locke's own approach to the social contract, the "state of nature" was "reasonably good and enjoyable, but the property was not secure". As such, individuals were driven out of the state of nature and into the terms of the social contract in order to protect their property. This need to protect property was not present in the case of early Nigerian citizens and, as such, was not a characteristic binding enough for people to respect the terms of this social contract that they had now become a part of. According to Jean Jacques Rousseau, the state of nature was about happiness and equality for all, but as a result of increasing competition for scarce resources, individuals were driven out of the state of nature and into the social contract in order to have their needs met.

The process of forming the Nigerian state (one example of many) has deviated from the social contract philosophies. This is primarily because the citizens did not enter the two agreements: **Pactum Unionis** to create the state, and **Pactum Subjectionis** to give the state the authority it needs to function.

Falola and Heaton's chronology of Nigerian history continues: Between 1914 and 1918, Nigerian troops aid the British as part of the First World War. From this period onwards, various pockets of agitation emerged to oppose British colonial rule, growing in strength over the next 40 years. Notable events that featured in this period of agitation were the 1929 Aba Riots; the 1936 formation of the Nigerian Youth Movement; 1944 establishment of the National Council of Nigeria and the Cameroons by Nnamdi Azikiwe; the 1946 Richards constitution; the 1949 formation of the Northern People's Congress by Tafawa Balewa, Aminu Kano, and Ahmadu Bello; the 1951 MacPherson Constitution and the formation of the Action Group by Obafemi Awolowo in the same year; the 1954 Lyttleton Constitution and the discovery of petroleum in the Niger delta region in 1956.

While it is possible to argue that prior to the formation of the Nigerian state, early inhabitants in the region did not have the opportunity to experience or exit the state of nature at their own volition, it is also possible to argue that Nigeria in its early stages (early post-independence years) had become that state of nature. This claim could be backed up by the agitations for identity, protection of property, fear of harm, and other such elements that featured during the years just described. Between 1957 and 1959, regional self-governments were attained around the country. The years immediately leading up to and following the 1960 independence featured a coup d'état in 1966, and the declaration of the secessionist state of the sovereign Republic of Biafra in 1967. This declaration would lead to the 1967–1970 civil war until the surrender of Biafra on 12 January 1970 (Falola & Heaton, 2008), and the subsequent reintegration of the region with the rest of Nigeria. From a philosophical perspective, it could be argued that this broad period was Nigeria's state of nature because of the fear of harm and the limited protection of property as part of the war. It could also be argued that by ending the war at the time, this was an agreement by all parties to enter into a new social contract to remain one country of their own volition. Whether this contract has been implemented effectively or not is a subject on its own.

All through this time, the discovery of oil in Nigeria continues to influence the country's relationships with the international community. By 1973, rising oil prices represent a significant economic opportunity for Nigeria, which were, however, hampered by the 1975 coup d'état by General Murtala Mohammed. Following further events including reforms and an additional unsuccessful coup, political power is handed over to a civilian government under President Alhaji Shehu Shagari. The political turmoil, military coups, and economic hardship continue until a civilian government is elected again in 1999 under President Olusegun Obasanjo, who oversaw the first (albeit controversial) civilian transfer of power in the country's history.

This notion that the Nigerian state (whose situation was similar to others in the region) and the Nigerian citizens did not get the proper chance to enter into the social contract may explain why it has remained difficult for the parties to understand the terms and ramifications of the contract. The formation of the state and the responsibilities of the state are closely linked. Ralph Raico approaches this subject from the perspectives of liberalism and Marxism, noting that liberalist views are concerned with limiting the powers and authority of the state while Marxist views considered the state as a mechanism through which the citizenry is exploited (Raico, 1992). In the case of Nigeria, the "role of the state" came before the "natural origin of the state" in the sense that the "Nigerian State" did not come together through a natural process in response to the needs of individuals (and later citizens). The origin of the Nigerian state also does not align with divine theory which posits that the state was created through an act of God. Divine theory, on the other hand, while not leading to the origin of the state, was used as a form of justification for the authority of early Nigerian leaders, whether pre-independence or in the years since.

States that have had similar historical challenges, balancing out the nation-state paradigm, tend to appear as absolutist. This rationalization is opposed to the theory presented by Jean Bodin, who, while believing sovereignty to be absolute (whole), expects the 'Sovereign" or "ruler" to serve the people. The place of authority in the Nigerian state has also varied through history. Because initial interactions between individuals and communities were guided by religion and because religion played an important role in the events that ultimately led to Nigeria's amalgamation (the role of religious exploration and the missionary visits exploring the Niger area region), religion continues to be a strong influence as a source of political authority. This is as opposed to the source of political authority coming from the sovereignty or freedoms which the people give up in exchange for order as part of the social contract. The Nigerian case in relation to the social contract has not been helped by the presence of multiple nations within the single state territory. This phenomenon has resulted in ethnic clashes between the nations who over time have continued to refuse the terms of their social contract. This is not unique to Nigeria, and there are several other cases around the world, some more famous than others.

Origins of the Country of Switzerland and Relations to Political Theory

As in the chronological example on the formation of the Nigerian state, it is important to also take a chronological approach to understanding the origin of the state of Switzerland. The chronology presented here forms the core structure of this analysis, in an attempt to show clearly the factors and elements that ultimately built on each other in contribution to the origin of the Swiss state. The chronology presented here is taken from the official account of the Federation of Switzerland (Federation of Switzerland, 2020).

The chronology starts in 100,000 BC with early traces of *Homo erectus* in what is present-day Switzerland and goes on to trace settlement in the region up to 200 and 100 BC when the first "Helvetians" settle in the region and are subsequently conquered as part of the Roman Empire. According to this chronology, the regions in the area of Switzerland converted to Christianity between the 4th and 7th centuries (early introductions of religion to the region). Between the 5th and 6th centuries, as a result of migrations and the settlement of Alemannic and Burgundian tribes, the Germanic-Romance languages are introduced to the region. Between the 6th and 9th centuries, the region falls under Frankish rule and in the 10th century is then ruled by a German-speaking emperor. A key moment in Swiss history comes up in 1291 following the agreement for peace between Schwyz, Unterwalden (Nidwaledn) and Uri; an agreement that would later be referred to as the Federal Charter through which Switzerland was created. The "Federal Charter" or "Letter of Alliance" was necessary between the three parties to establish a relationship of mutual protection, mutual aid and support, and collective justice. The charter would also define the collective approach to subjects ranging from criminal punishment to the settlement of disputes among the parties (Federation of Switzerland, 2017). This charter was a critical step in protecting the "Forest States" from external influence and control, considering that the region at the time was surrounded by much larger states looking to expand their territory including the Germans and Habsburgs. This point in history, prior to the 1291 charter, could be considered as the point when the smaller groups and regions consciously made the decision to bind together for their own safety. This approach to viewing the origin of the Swiss state aligns with Hobbesian theory which suggests that the state of nature was nasty and brutish, and as such, the individual gives up their sovereignty to form the Leviathan. It is important to note that one of the core proponents of social contract theory was indeed the Swiss philosopher Jean Jacques Rousseau, who described the state of nature as "happy" and suggested that individuals come out of this state of nature as populations grew and demand for scarce resources increased.

It is not possible to talk about the Federal Charter without mentioning any of the controversies surrounding its authenticity; however, it is important to note that these controversies do not take away from the core argument on the origin of the Swiss state in relation to the conscious decision by citizens to bind together. According to Albert Winkley, in "The Federal Charter of 1291 and the Founding of the Swiss State" several discrepancies exist to dispute the authenticity of the document and its true role in founding the Swiss State. Winkley highlights some of these to include the fact that the 1291 charter was not referenced in a later piece signed between Zurich, Uri, and Schwyz in October of 1291, two months after the Federal Charter was supposedly agreed to in August of the same year (Winkley, 2014). Winkley also notes other discrepancies in the format of the text, the dating of the original parchment on which it was written, and the lack of supporting information such as seals and dates, to back up the document. Winkley also refers to other instances in the history of the region that suggest that alliances were in place that ultimately served as the origin of the Swiss state. One reference is to an agreement signed between Fribourg and Bern in 1243. According to Winkley, this 1243 agreement also refers to the renewal of an older agreement (Winkley, 2014). All of this goes to show the central agreement held by historians and political philosophers that the origin of the Swiss state happened through the enactment of a (social) contract driven by the interests of the citizens for protection, resource management, and value. According to the chronology of the Federation of Switzerland (Federation of Switzerland, 2020), between 1351 and 1353, these alliances had grown to include Bern, Glarus, Luzern, Schwyz, Uri, Unterwalden, Zurich, and Zug. Over the next 500 years, the Swiss federation will continue to grow to include additional cantons. Notable dates within this period include Solothurn and Fribourg joining the Confederation in 1481; Basel and Schaffhausen (1501); Appenzell (1513); recognition of the confederation in international law (1648); formation of the Helvetic republic (1798); creation of St. Gallen, Graubünden, Aargau, Thurgau, Ticino, and Vaud (1803); Neuchâtel and Geneva (1815); establishment of the Federal State (1848); approval of the Federal Constitution (1874); and adoption of the revised Federal Constitution in 1999 (Federation of Switzerland, 2020). The origin of Switzerland as a state very closely aligns with social contract theory and would no doubt have influenced Jean Jacques Rousseau's thinking on the subject.

Reflecting on the Origins of the Nigerian and Swiss States

Nigeria and Switzerland emerged as "states" through very different processes, and this has ultimately affected the evolution of both states into their contemporary forms. For one, the regions of both present-day Nigeria and present-day Switzerland were shown in the chronology to have been inhabited for a long time in upright human history (9000 BC and 200 BC). In both instances, these historical habitations would leave long-standing traces of cultures and traditions.

In the philosophical context, the formation of the Nigerian state does not align with any major political theories on what "drives man into civil and organized society". Switzerland, on the other hand, very closely aligns with social contract theory and is a clear example of groups coming together under a contract to improve their living conditions and enhance their communal protection. Both countries have strong religious histories. With Nigeria, the religious history is reflected in the introduction of Islam and Christianity in the early Northern and Southern protectorates respectively, and the subsequent religious-ethnic lines around which political camps have since been drawn. In Nigeria, religion has been used as a cause for conflict, while at the same time, religious leaders hold a strong position of significance among their followers. In "Religion, Leadership and Struggle for Power in Nigeria:

A Case Study of the 2011 Presidential Election in Nigeria", Danoye Oguntola-Laguda presents multiple definitions of religion in order to properly reflect on its impact in the Nigerian political context. Oguntola-Laguda starts off with Milton Yinger's description of religion as the belief system that people use to get through life, and continues on to the Marxist approach that believes that religion is a tool used by the elite to control the masses (Oguntola-Laguda, 2015). According to Oguntola-Laguda's analysis of the 2011 presidential election in Nigeria, several aspiring political leaders built their campaigns around religious symbols which they quickly abandoned when these symbols got in the way of their secular interests.

Oluwaseun Olawale Afolabi in "The Role of Religion in Nigerian Politics and Its Sustainability for Political Development" agrees with Oguntola-Laguda's assessment that religion has been used as a negative tool in Nigeria's political evolution; however, Afolabi goes on to suggest that religion can play a positive role if it is used to improve morality, sense of duty, and respect for authority among the populace (Afolabi, 2015). With Switzerland, the impact of religion in its history is as early as with the Reformation movement and the role that this played in Swiss politics (Federal Department of Foreign Affairs, n.d.). The reformation movement was a point in history that would separate receiving salvation with God, from loyalty to the Church as an institution whether led by the pope or any other of the Christian religious leaders. The resulting differences from this separation, and the allegiances that were formed as a result, meant that in Switzerland, religion served as a cause for conflict at points in its history. This complex history of conflict has led Switzerland to take a practical approach to managing the interactions between politics and religion, based on an understanding that the two cannot be completely de-linked in the real world. According to Jean-Nicolas Bitter and Angela Ullmann, four elements make up Switzerland's political culture. These four elements are critical to defining how Switzerland approaches its governance, how it handles conflict, and how it manages the interaction between religion and politics, given the influence that both have had on the country's history. These four characteristics on which Swiss political culture is built are identified by Bitter and Ullmann as direct democracy, federalism, subsidiarity, and concordance (Bitter & Ullmann, 2018). In addition, these characteristics have been crucial to fostering dialogue, entrenching pragmatism, and ensuring participation in the governance process.

Both countries are made up of multiple national identities. In Nigeria, there are over 250 ethnic groups which all form unique and distinct nations (or sometimes combine to form small nations). Among these are three large nations: the Igbo, Hausa, and Yoruba's. Switzerland is similar in the sense that it is made up of the French-speaking Swiss, the German speakers, the Italian speakers, and the Swiss Romandie.

Implications of the Origin of the State on Political Economy and Economic Value

The origin of the state defines its political structure and defines how the people come together to manage resources, which is influenced by how the people measure and capture value. If a state emerges through divine theory for example, with a leader such as a monarch who believes that they receive their authority from God, such a state is likely to have an economic system where all economic activity is focused on meeting the demands or needs of the monarch and monarchist state. In this instance, satisfying the monarch would be a direct response to God's will and would be considered as a "good thing to do" since it pleases God. This would make meeting the monarch's demands and intrinsic good, while all other activities would be considered as extrinsic goods if they are not directly pleasing God. Such an economic system is likely to have limited competition since all resources are owned or controlled by the state. Furthermore, such a system with limited flexibility for the factors of production is likely to focus on production methods that maximize output. This focus on the factors and conditions of production in relation to economic value is aligned with the objective theory of value. This is not to say that monarchist states do not exist that defy this approach. On the other hand, if a state emerges through social contract theory, such a state is more likely to have a distributed approach to value creation, since all parties to the contract would agree to contribute to upholding the contract and utilizing the resources at their disposal for everyone's collective good. Such a state would encourage competition and more likely focus on the needs of those signatory to the contract, that is, the population. This approach, which focuses on the needs of the population and seeks to maximize utility for the population, would be considered a subjective approach to value theory.

A state's core structure has direct links with its approach to economic policies. As shown in the example of Nigeria, the state was not created in line with any political theories on the formation of the state. As a result, the inhabitants have not determined of their own volition how to collectively manage and utilize the resources at their disposal. This has meant that Nigeria is able to neither agree on the methods of enhancing the production environment nor agree on the best ways to maximize utility for the consumer. This has unfortunately created a loose economic system subject to political abuse. With Switzerland, the situation is quite different. As indicated, Switzerland emerged through an inclusive and participatory process. This meant that all parties to the social contract consciously agreed to use the resources at their disposal to everyone's benefit. In the case of Switzerland, this has resulted in both an enhancement of the conditions of production and a focus on maximizing utility for the consumer.

The relationship between the origin/structure of a state and its economy is far more nuanced than presented here. In summary, the origin and/or structure of the state determine its approach to managing the resources under its care, which ultimately determines how the factors of production are engaged, as well as to what end they are engaged.

In earlier chapters, we discussed extensively the role that interaction plays in defining economic value and resource management. We also discussed value from the utility perspective and in the context of interaction. This chapter brought these theories and philosophies into the real world by identifying how they have applied in real states. A driving force behind this book is the reality that not every government is able to meet the terms of the social contract and, as such, is not always able to cater to the needs of its citizens. Evolving societies therefore require an evolved social contract, one that recognizes that other entities are already participating in bringing individuals out of the state of nature. Going into the future, interaction will continue to evolve, as will the state structure. The digital economy will be a key tool in these states of the future. Given the participation of new stakeholders in an evolving social contract, as well as the trend towards decentralization, the participation of new stakeholders in an evolving role of the state in public administration, the task of bringing individuals out of the state of nature will no longer be the strict responsibility or task of the government. This will be discussed later on when we consider the role of the private sector.

Notes

1 Note that "BCE" refers to "Before Common Era" or "BC" which represents "Before Christ" (McClure, 2020).
2 Various accounts exist on the actual date of the fall of the Oyo Empire, with some sources referencing 1838.

Bibliography

Afolabi, O. O. (2015). The role of religion in Nigerian politics and its sustainability for political development. *Net Journal of Social Sciences, 3*(2), 42–49.

Bitter, J.-N. & Ullmann, A. (2018). *Swiss Experiences in Addressing Religion in Conflict*. CSS Analyses in Security Policy, June.

CIA World Fact Book. (2021). *Nigeria*. [Online] Available at: https://www.cia.gov/the-world-factbook/countries/nigeria/#people-and-society [Accessed 19 May 2021].

Falola, T. & Heaton, M. M. (2008). *A History of Nigeria*. Austin: Cambridge University Press.

Fauvelle, F.-X. (2020). *Africa's Medieval Golden Age*. [Online] Available at: https://www.historyextra.com/period/what-was-africa-like-middle-ages-medieval-golden-age-culture/ [Accessed 19 May 2021].

Federal Department of Foreign Affairs. (n.d.) *Reformation*. [Online] Available at: https://www.eda.admin.ch/dam/PRS-Web/en/dokumente/die-reformation_EN.pdf [Accessed 29 May 2021].

Federation of Switzerland. (2017). *The Federal Charter of 1291*. [Online] Available at: https://www.admin.ch/gov/en/start/federal-council/history-of-the-federal-council/federal-charter-of-1291.html [Accessed 25 May 2021].

Federation of Switzerland (2020). *Chronology*. [Online] Available at: https://www.eda.admin.ch/aboutswitzerland/en/home/geschichte/uebersicht.html# [Accessed 25 May 2021].

Guimarães, S. P. (2007). *Nation, nationalism, State*. [Online] Available at: https://www.scielo.br/pdf/ea/v22n62/en_a10v2262.pdf [Accessed 18 May 2021].

Natinoal Geographic (2020). *The Nok Culture*. [Online] Available at: https://www.nationalgeographic.org/encyclopedia/nok-culture/ [Accessed 19 May 2021].

Oguntola-Laguda, D. (2015). Struggle for Power in Nigeria: A Case Study of The 2011 Presidential Election in Nigeria. *Studia Historiae Ecclesiasticae, 41*(2), 219–233.

Pontifical Academy of Social Sciences (2019). *Nation, State, Nation-State*. [Online] Available at: http://www.pass.va/content/scienzesociali/en/events/2019-23/nations.pdf [Accessed 18 May 2021].

Raico, R. (1992). Liberalism, Marxism and The State. *Cato Journal, 11*, 391–404.

Rosenberg, M. (2020). *Differences between a Country, State, and Nation*. [Online] Available at: https://www.thoughtco.com/country-state-and-nation-1433559#:~:text=A%20state%20is%20a%20territory%20with%20its%20own%20institutions%20and%20populations.&text=A%20nation%20is%20a%20large,%2C%20be%20a%20sovereign%20state [Accessed 18 May 2021].

Winkley, A. (2014). *The Federal Charter of 1291 and the Founding of the Swiss State*. [Online] Available at: https://scholarsarchive.byu.edu/cgi/viewcontent.cgi?article=2825&context=facpub [Accessed 25 May 2021].

9 The Money We Value, the Value We Monetize

Take a moment to consider the concepts that were presented in the previous chapters. The first section of this book sought to understand the origin of the state. Those early chapters identified the factors that drive individuals out of the state of nature into civil society. The analysis showed that a key factor that facilitated the move to civil society was the collective need for better resource management in the economic context of scare resources. The discussion in the subsequent chapters naturally flowed into the subject of 'value' since value can be determined by utility which in turn influences resource management. Continuing with this line of thought, the next question is, "what happens after 'value' has been defined?" Building on the understanding of economic value presented in earlier chapters, and how this subject has evolved through history, the next phase of discussions will look at the different ways that economic value has been stored. A store of value is defined by the Corporate Finance Institute as an "asset, currency, or commodity that maintains its value over a long period" (Corporate Finance Institute, 2021). Other definitions exist that go into a greater amount of detail in describing what a store of value is such as any object that retains (or increases) its assigned value over time.

Several objects have held historical significance for their use as a store of social and economic value; most recently in human history, paper money has played this role (IBNS, n.d.). For early societies, it became necessary to find ways to store value as more and more individuals in society needed a means to trade (interact) among themselves. With growing populations, scarce resources, and an increasingly complex mix of goods and services to trade, the barter system, which had worked for so long through history, was starting to lose relevance. It had become necessary to identify convenient objects (assets, currency, commodities) that could be collectively agreed on as stores of value and used in the trading process (used to facilitate interaction). An equally important factor in the rise of the importance of money and other stores of value was the issue of "coincidence of wants". A coincidence of wants is a situation within a barter economy where two or more consumers need the same item and also had the same item to trade (Berentsen & Rocheteau, 2000). This problem would quickly become a limiting factor in trade where more than one person needed the same thing at the same time. Today, money is the most widely used store of value; however, this was not

DOI: 10.4324/9781003330417-11

always the case. At different points in time, different items served as forms of money. According to Susanne König, for an object to serve as money, it had to have some intrinsic value of its own and had to be widely accepted (König, 2001).

Moving on from the barter system and to these objects that helped early societies capture value led to the introduction of cattle (livestock) as a store of value. This was particularly prominent between 9000 and 6000 BC, given the intrinsic value that cattle offered whether as food, labour for agriculture, or for secondary resources like their leather and wool. By 1200 BC, cowrie shells had come into use and by 1000 BC metal and coins had started to emerge in a rudimentary form. These included bronze and copper in China at the end of the Stone Age, as well as other metal objects that were considered valuable at the time (PBS, 1966). James Surowiecki presents a history of paper money in the article "A Brief History of Money" which starts in 13th-century China with Emperor Kublai Khan (Surowiecki, 2012) who had ordered that paper money be introduced to replace coins. Prior to this point, however, Surowiecki identifies the use of coins as far back as in the 7th century BC (700–500 BC) in Lydia, present-day Turkey. "Electrum", a gold–silver alloy, is believed to have emerged in Lydia as a coin for trade. At around the same time as the Chinese were experimenting with paper money, Surowiecki notes that the "Bill of Exchange" was also invented in Europe and would lay the groundwork in the region for paper money. By 118 BC, leather money was being used in China. China would go on to introduce what are likely to have been the first bank notes in 806 AD. By 1816, England made gold the standard of value, although a de facto gold standard was already in place by 1717 (Cooper, 1982). This de facto standard was a result of a calculation error by Isaac Newton who inadequately depreciated the value of gold against silver such that newly minted silver coins were sought outside of England, leaving only the old silver and overvalued gold coins available for trade (Cooper, 1982). It was not until 1900 that the gold standard was adopted in the United States. By the 1930s, following the Depression, the gold standard entered a slow decline around the world, to make way for fiat currencies which dominated money for the coming decades until current times (PBS, 1966). Until this point in history, stores of economic value had been commodity based, that means backed by commodities such as gold and other precious metals/objects. François R. Velde suggests that some of the reasons why commodity money was so widely adopted included the fact that it offered some protections against price fluctuations. Authors like Simon Brown, however, dispute the notion that gold is a stable store of value, citing significant price fluctuations throughout history (Brown, 2001). Other authors like Pradeep Dubey, John Geanakoplos, and Martin Shubikeven go as far as comparing gold to commodities like tobacco to suggest that gold is not a good store of value (Dubey et al., 2003). The decline of the gold standard paved the way for a new type of money, fiat money/currency. A simple definition of a fiat currency is offered by IG Bank as "a national currency that is not backed by any commodity or does not have its price pegged to the price of a commodity such as gold or silver" (IG Bank, 2021). Fiat currencies allow a level of centralization and control of monetary systems since they have historically been controlled by governments. Fiat currencies, not backed by any commodities, also mean in principle that governments and central banks can print more notes in line with national monetary policies.

Regardless of its form, money is meant to serve three primary functions (König, 2001):

a **A medium of exchange** – Money serves as a medium of exchange since it allows trade in goods and services outside of the barter system. As a medium of exchange, money makes it possible for consumers to capture and represent the value of the goods and services which they want to trade, in an efficient manner. Money also solves the problem of the coincidence of wants.

b **A unit of account** – The use of money as a unit of account means that money standardizes value and allows multiple individuals and groups to take a standardized approach to measuring value.

c **A store of value** – money as a store of value means that purchasing power is transferred from the present to the future" (König, 2001).

König goes on to present three reasons why consumers seek to hold money, as first presented by economist John Maynard Keynes (König, 2001):

a For **Transaction** – in this instance, money is held as a means of exchange for goods and services.

b As a **Precaution** – in this instance, money is held as potential protection against future needs, as a store of value to be able to trade future goods and services.

c Our of **Speculation** – in this instance, money is held when consumers speculate future market conditions like interest rates or future economic values (Figures 9.1–9.3).

Money has emerged as the most prominent store of value since it has allowed humanity to facilitate trade, economic interaction, and resource management. Consider money in the context of value theory; money allows the consumer to quantify the utility they receive from a good or service and trade this utility for other goods and services.

Until now, we have looked at economic value from the perspective of utility, resource management, and money, against the backdrop of money as the most commonly used store of value in contemporary society. The objective here was not to get lost in any complex calculations, but rather to lay a foundation for understanding how value is stored.

Figure 9.1 People and institutions hold money for transactions.
Design by Margaryta Pugach.

Figure 9.2 People and institutions hold money as protection against an uncertain future.
Design by Margaryta Pugach.

Figure 9.3 People and institutions hold money as part of speculation on future market conditions.

Design by Margaryta Pugach.

Bibliography

Berentsen, A. & Rocheteau, G. (2000). *The Role of Money in Double Coincidence of Environments.* [Online] Available at: https://www.unil.ch/de/files/live/sites/de/files/working-papers/00.18.pdf [Accessed 26 June 2021].

Brown, S. (2001). What is a Store of Value. *Finweek*, 11 June.

Cooper, R. N. (1982). *The Gold Standard: Historical Facts and Future Prospects.* [Online] Available at: https://www.brookings.edu/wp-content/uploads/1982/01/1982a_bpea_cooper_dornbusch_hall.pdf [Accessed 26 June 2021].

Corporate Finance Institute. (2021). *Store of Value.* [Online] Available at: https://corporatefinanceinstitute.com/resources/knowledge/valuation/store-of-value/ [Accessed 25 June 2021].

Dubey, P., Geanakoplos, J., & Shubik, M. (2003). Is Gold an Efficient Store of Value?. *Economic Theory*, *21* (4), 767–782.

IBNS (n.d.) *A History of Printed Money.* [Online] Available at: https://www.theibns.org/joomla/index.php?option=com_content&view=article&id=251&limitstart=2 [Accessed 10 May 2021].

IG Bank. (2021). *Fiat Currency definition.* [Online] Available at: https://www.ig.com/en-ch/glossary-trading-terms/fiat-currency-definition [Accessed 26 June 2021].

König, S. (2001). *The Evolution of Money.* [Online] Available at: http://www.ww.uni-magdeburg.de/fwwdeka/student/arbeiten/009.pdf [Accessed 26 June 2021].

PBS. (1966). *The History of Money.* [Online] Available at: https://www.pbs.org/wgbh/nova/article/history-money/ [Accessed 26 June 2021].

Surowiecki, J. (2012). *A Brief History of Money.* [Online] Available at: https://spectrum.ieee.org/at-work/innovation/a-brief-history-of-money [Accessed 26 June 2021].

Part III

Digital Economy and the Fourth Industrial Revolution

10 We're Live, We're Digital

We started off by defining the origins of human interaction, before going on to define value. First, we looked at how the state is formed, and explored the central theme of resource management (value creation) in bringing individuals out of the state of nature and into the social contract. Now, we will look at the digital economy to understand what this is, how it has evolved over time, and what role it plays in unlocking social and economic value. The world that we live in is digital, and this will be truer than ever before, the older this book gets. On average, an individual spent 90 minutes online in 2012, compared to 145 minutes in 2020 (Tankovska, 2021). By 2019, within each minute, an average of 59.7 million texts were sent either as SMS or over WhatsApp and/or Facebook messenger; over $900,000 was spent online and an average of 347,222 people were scrolling through Instagram (Ranzetta, 2019).

Take a moment to think about the parameters that define your human experience. Humanity is spending a lot of time online and we are able to do more in the digital space (we all saw this during the COVID-19 pandemic years). In 2020, individuals were spending up to 145 minutes (2.4 hours) a day on social media sites (Tankovska, 2021); this number went up significantly if you include all other online activity. But as we saw earlier, this upward trend has been going on for a while now. For example, in 2018, Americans spent over six hours actively online each day (Brynjolfsson & Collis, 2019). With so much time and resources being spent online, and with every aspect of our lives being influenced by digitalization, it is imperative to understand how the digital economy works. One definition of the digital economy that captures this very phenomenon is that "the digital economy is the economic activity that results from billions of everyday online connections among people, businesses, devices, data, and processes" (Deloitte, 2021). Authors like Dieter Ernst argue that the digital economy should be considered as part of a long evolutionary process made up of several elements including tangible and intangible inputs and outputs (Ernst, 2001). Erik Brynjolfsson and Avinash Collis, in the *Harvard Business Review* article "How Should We Measure the Digital Economy", argue that despite the amount of time spent online and interacting with the digital economy, because GDP is based on what people pay for goods and services, GDP calculations do not effectively capture the vast amounts of value that are created and transferred in the digital economy (Brynjolfsson & Collis, 2019).

DOI: 10.4324/9781003330417-13

Brynjolfsson and Collis furthermore argue that for governments to start planning more effectively for their economies, humanity needs to be able to measure the value of more elements in society such as, but not limited to, the free goods and services present in the digital economy. Brynjolfsson and Collis make the distinction between consumer spending – which is reflected in GDP– and consumer surplus which is currently not reflected in GDP but in reality reflects a significant amount of information since it shows consumer benefits. Brynjolfsson and Collis, along with the Erwin Diewert, Felix Eggers, and Kevin Fox, have developed an alternative method that is proposed to use to measure the value of the digital economy. This measure is called GDP-B that is aimed at effectively "quantifying contributions to consumer well-being from free goods" (Brynjolfsson & Collis, 2019).

Let us adopt the definition of the digital economy as all the economic activity and social interaction that takes place on or is facilitated by the internet and related digital technologies. The digital economy is humanity's digital presence and is as important a factor in daily interactions and the global economy. The digital economy is fundamentally underpinned by key elements which according the UNCTAD are "semiconductors, processors, … computers, telecommunication devices and … the internet and telecoms networks" (UNCTAD, 2019).

Rumana Bukht and Richard Heeks also present a definition of the digital economy as "part of economic output derived solely or primarily from digital technologies with a business model (that is) based on digital goods or services" (Bukht & Heeks, 2017).

Our lives will only get more digital going forward, and so it makes sense that as many interactions as possible can benefit from digitalization. If we agree, based on previous chapters, that interaction is driven by the need to manage economic value, then we would agree that this digitalization must apply to how we manage economic value. This notion is not new, and is already driving fintech solutions around the world, from digital and cryptocurrencies to payment gateways and transfer platforms. When I say value here, I remind you of the discussions we have had on utility. Digitalization must be applied to how we manage utility, from measurement to capture and transfer (Figure 10.1).

Okay so now we understand just how much happens in the digital economy and we agree that digitalization could filter into every aspect of our lives, or at least you agree with me that it should apply to how we manage utility. In order to fully grasp the possibilities for a digital future, it is important to understand our digital history. Looking to a history of the digital economy, Carlota Perez provides an overview in her 2002 book titled *Technological Revolutions and Financial Capital: The Dynamics of Bubbles and Golden Ages*. In this text, Perez lists out the periods as (Mennis, 2003):

- The Industrial Revolution – 1771
- The Period of Steam and Railways – 1829
- The Period of Steel, Electricity and Heavy Engineering – 1875
- The Period of Oil, the Automobile and Mass Production – 1908
- The Period of Information and Telecommunications – 1971

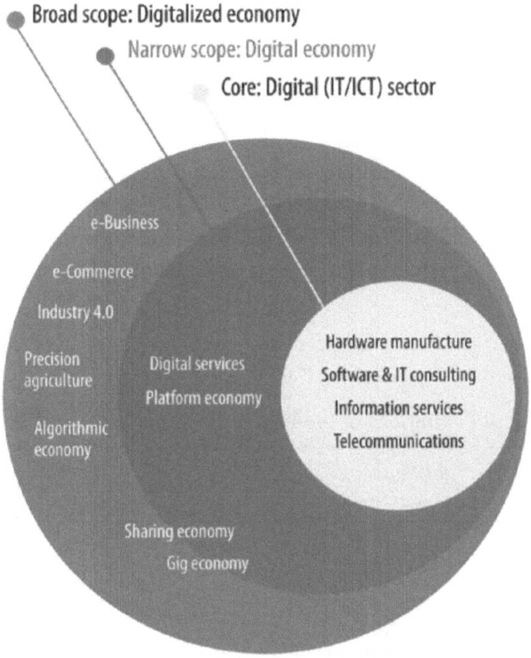

Figure 10.1 Visual Representation of the Digital Economy (Bukht & Heeks, 2017).

Perez further notes that each period lasts approximately 60 years and is further broken down into two sub-periods of 20–30 years, each of which is first an installation period and second a deployment period (Wladawsky-Berger, 2017). According to Wladawsky-Berger's summary of Perez, the installation period is the period when the new technology has emerged, and entrepreneurs set out to take advantage of its opportunities. The influx of businesses, capital, and competition ultimately lead to a financial bubble and crash which paves way for the deployment period. This deployment period is where the established businesses flourish; this is where according to Perez and several interpretations of her work, the technology has become mainstream and is widely adopted. It is important to note that Perez's breakdown of the historical periods of advancement in the digital economy is loosely linked with the early industrial revolutions or the different "phases" of the industrial revolution.

The historical evolution of the digital economy can also be considered from the perspective of the advancements in data transfer that have taken place in the 30 years between 1992 and 2022. According to an UNCTAD report, global internet protocol traffic grew from 100 GB per day in 1992 to 100 GB per second in 2002, to 46,600 GB per second in 2017 and to 150,700 GB per second by 2022 (UNCTAD, 2019).

Another important way to look at the historical evolution of the digital economy would be to look at how definitions of the term have evolved through different points in history. Bukht and Heeks (2017) present a summary of definitions of the digital economy, as well as the key themes that each definition focuses on. This approach helps to show how the core components of, and approach to, the subject have changed over time. Let us look at some of these definitions (Bukht & Heeks, 2017) (Table 10.1):

The evolution of these definitions through history shows how the digital economy has gone from a focus on technology to the impact of this technology. This only makes sense as naturally we would focus on what we can use a tool to do, instead of focusing on the tool itself. That being said, in order to make a tool fit-for-purpose, the design process would need to focus on the tool's purpose, its users and their context.

Table 10.1 Summary of Definitions of the Digital Economy (Bukht & Heeks, 2017)

Source of Definition	*Definition*	*Focus of Definition (according to Bukht & Heeks)*
Don Tapscott (1995) "The Digital Economy: Promise and Peril in the Age of Networked Intelligence" (Tapscott, 1995)	"age of networked intelligence … not only about the networking of technology … but networking of humans through technology … that combine intelligence, knowledge, and creativity for breakthroughs in the creation of wealth and social development".	This definition focuses on new relationships and interactions with technology for business and consumers.
Erik Brynjolfsson and Brian Kahin (2002) "Understanding the Digital Economy: Data, Tools, and Research" (Brynjolfsson & Kahin, 2002)	"the recent and still largely unrealized transformation of all sectors of the economy by the computer-enabled digitization of information".	This definition approaches the digital economy from various angles such as macroeconomics and labour.
Economist Intelligence Unit (2010) "Digital Economy Rankings 2010" (Economist Intelligence Unit, 2010)	"the quality of a country's ICT infrastructure and the ability of its consumers, businesses and governments to use ICT to their benefit".	This definition looks at the underlying technologies, platforms, and stakeholders that enable the digital economy.
European Parliament (2015) "Challenges for Competition Policy in a Digitalized Economy" (European Parliament, 2015)	"A complex structure of several levels/layers connected … by an almost endless and always growing number of nodes. Platforms are stacked on each other allowing for multiple routes to reach end-users and making it difficult to exclude certain players, i.e., competitors".	This definition focuses on regulations for the digital economy.

(*Continued*)

Table 1.1 (Continued)

Source of Definition	*Definition*	*Focus of Definition (according to Bukht & Heeks)*
Carl Dahlman, Sam Mealy and Martin Wermelinger (2016) "Harnessing the Digital Economy for Developing Countries (OECD)" (Dahlman et al., 2016)	"The digital economy is the amalgamation of several general purpose technologies (GPTs) and the range of economic and social activities carried out by people over the Internet and related technologies … infrastructure that digital technologies are based on, the devices that are used for access, the applications they power and the functionality they provide".	This definition looks at the potential that the digital economy can contribute to sustainable development.

Bibliography

Brynjolfsson, E. & Collis, A. (2019). How Should We Measure the Digital Economy?. *Harvard Business Review, 97*(6), 140–148.

Brynjolfsson, E. & Kahin, B. (2002). *Understanding the Digital Economy: Data, Tools, and Research*. 1 ed. s.l.: MIT Press Books.

Bukht, R. & Heeks, R. (2017). *Defining, Conceptualising and Measuring the Digital Economy*. [Online] Available at: https://papers.ssrn.com/sol3/papers.cfm?abstract_id=3431732 [Accessed 11 July 2021].

Dahlman, C., Mealy, S., & Wermelinger, M. (2016). *Harnessing the Digital Economy for Developing Countries*. Paris: OECD.

Deloitte, 2021. *What is Digital Economy? Unicorns, Transformation and the Internet of Things*. [Online] Available at: https://www2.deloitte.com/mt/en/pages/technology/articles/mt-what-is-digital-economy.html [Accessed 2 July 2021].

Economist Intelligence Unit. (2010). *Digital Economy Rankings 2010*. [Online] Available at: https://eiuperspectives.economist.com/technology-innovation/digital-economy-rankings-2010/white-paper/digital-economy-rankings-2010 [Accessed 5 August 2021].

Ernst, D. (2001). *The Evolution of a Digital Economy: Research Issues and Policy Challenges*. [Online] Available at: https://www.files.ethz.ch/isn/101705/2001_07_The%20Evolution_of_a_Digital.pdf [Accessed 2 July 2021].

European Parliament. (2015). *Challenges for Competition Policy in a Digitalized Economy*. [Online] Available at: https://www.europarl.europa.eu/RegData/etudes/STUD/2015/542235/IPOL_STU(2015)542235_EN.pdf [Accessed 5 August 2021].

Mennis, E. A. (2003). *Technological Revolutions and Financial Capital: the Dynamics of Bubbles and Golden Ages*. [Online] Available at: http://www.carlotaperez.org/downloads/reviews/Mennis_review_newv2.pdf [Accessed 2 July 2021].

Ranzetta, T. (2019). *How Much Money is Spent on the Internet Every 60 Seconds?*. [Online] Available at: https://www.ngpf.org/blog/question-of-the-day/qod-how-much-money-is-spent-on-the-internet-every-60-seconds/ [Accessed 2 July 2021].

Tankovska, H. (2021). *Daily Social Media Usage Worldwide 2012–2020*. [Online] Available at: https://www.statista.com/statistics/433871/daily-social-media-usage-worldwide/ [Accessed 2 July 2021].

Tapscott, D. (1995). *The Digital Economy: Promise and Peril In The Age of Networked Intelligence*. 1 ed. s.l.: McGraw-Hill.

UNCTAD. (2019). *Digital Economy 2019 – Value Creation and Capture: Implications for Developing Countries*. Geneva: UNCTAD.

Wladawsky-Berger, I. (2017). *A Historical Perspective on the Digital Economy*. [Online] Available at: https://blog.irvingwb.com/blog/2017/12/a-historical-perspective-on-the-information-economy.html [Accessed 2 July 2021].

11 Remember the State, Well Now It's Digital

The living-breathing organism, that is the state (as a country), has evolved just as every other living organism has. Today, the state is hybrid, with digital representations of itself, just like we all have social media accounts.

In 1999, Don Tapscott and David Agnew used the article "Governance in the Digital Economy" to explore what role the government would play in what they referred to as an unfolding digital revolution. That article highlighted the exponential growth in the digital economy as well as the opportunities that this presented for businesses (Tapscott & Agnew, 1999). Tapscott and Agnew highlight key trends for businesses as part of this unfolding digital revolution which included large-scale private sector transformations; growing consumer empowerment; fast-paced business interactions; knowledge as the core asset; and transparency as a market enabler. In addition to these trends, Tapscott and Agnew note that success for businesses going into the digital revolution will mean true partnership that takes a community approach to value creation (Tapscott & Agnew, 1999). These trends are in principle the same for the state. Tapscott and Agnew do not stop there, and go on to share some ideas on governance in the digital age. Their thinking (already 23 years ago from when this book was written) highlights a shift from industrial governance to digital governance where the lines between government, market, and civil society are continually blurred by advancements in technology. According to them, governments will face a set of key challenges going forward, which they must address creatively in order to remain relevant. These challenges are (Tapscott & Agnew, 1999):

- Fiscal and performance issues – governments face continued pressure for improved social services and public infrastructure, as well as a need to manage costs and debt.
- Digital citizens – technology is enabling a tech-savvy citizenry
- New networks created by new technologies
- Competition spurred by globalization – technology is blurring the lines between conventional state structures and making it possible for citizens to sell and benefit from services across wider.

Technology, in particular the internet, is reducing the need for conventional intermediaries between the consumer and the products and services that they

DOI: 10.4324/9781003330417-14

need (Levin, 2011). Technology is also increasing accountability of governments. While this challenges the conventional role of the state, Tapscott and Agnew argue that the state must take advantage of advancements in technology to improve interaction with the citizenry beyond just elections. Furthermore, they argued at the time of the article in 1999 that technologies matured in the new millennium would bring about greater community governance.

Nineteen years later, in 2018, in the article "The Role of the State in the Digital Age", Nagy Hanna reviewed this relationship between the state and the citizenry in the context of the digital economy. That article makes a case that is captured by the statement: "the digital economy has become disconnected from the analog economy and from its keeper, the state" (Hanna, 2018). This statement highlights the influence that technology has had on economic relationships, but also importantly highlights the fact that large-scale resource management (value creation) is no longer monopolized by the state. Furthermore, it highlights the slowly, but surely growing, trend of decentralization. The question then is, how do we build out this new, decentralized society and what will (if any) the role the state be?

One might assume that these statements place the burden of value creation solely on the state, but that is not the case. Mariana Mazzucato notes that value is also not created solely within the private sector to be redistributed by the state, and goes on to point out the need for balance in the narrative in order not to isolate non–private sector value creators (Mazzucato, 2018). Hanna goes on to emphasize the need for an entrepreneurial state as a solution to the rapid evolution of tech-enabled human interactions. Historical examples of entrepreneurial states are cited such as the United States, and the investments in technologies like the internet and GPS which, according to Hanna, have contributed to enabling innovations like the iPhone (Hanna, 2018). Other states like Singapore and Estonia would no doubt make this list for the investments and successes that they have realized as entrepreneurial states.

According to Hanna, there are key roles for the state in the digital economy that demonstrate the state's entrepreneurial character and position it to create effective digital economies. These roles include but are not limited to:

a) Establishing policies for digital enhancement that are aligned with a national development plan – developing national development plans which outline the strategic process of improving the lives of citizens has remained a core function of government throughout history. As the digital age advances, governments are expected to develop policies that capture the nuances of digitization as well as policies that create the enabling environment for innovations to flourish. This role of governments is also highlighted in the WTO's World Trade Report 2020 (WTO, 2020).
b) Supporting research and development – research and development is important, and while this may not be a core function of a government, it is important that the state support research efforts, especially if these are in line with the national context and have the potential to support achieving the targets that are set out in a national development plan. In a 2021 publication, the

OECD reiterates this role of governments in supporting business research and innovation (OECD, 2021).

c) Supporting the growth of the telecom sector and overall telecom infrastructure – telecom infrastructure is a core service/technology that is needed to support digital innovations. State support to the telecom sector will ensure that service providers have the confidence and stability to expand and cover more portions of the population. Again, the OECD weighs in by presenting a perspective on the evolving role of the telecom sector in society and the impact on national telecom policy (OECD, 1995).
d) Investing in human resources and institutional learning – it is important that the population/citizens understand how to use digital tools and understand the importance of these tools in improving society and the economy. The state is expected to invest in making sure citizens have access to affordable internet, and that they have the relevant skills needed to effectively leverage digital tools.

In essence, Hanna's proposal on the role of the state in the digital economy is summarized as investing in the supporting ecosystem for digital transformation which critically includes (Hanna, 2018):

- Enabling policies and institutions tailored to and focused on the digital economy,
- Human capital to ensure knowledge and skills competence,
- ICT and data industry growth,
- Digital infrastructure investments,
- Digital transformation applications across industries and with a grassroots approach.

This new digital state recognizes it can outsource aspects of public administration to more effective entities, allowing it to focus on the critical tasks of national philosophy, ideology, social cohesion, and the holistic advancement of society. That is not to say that a state cannot develop and maintain the technological capabilities that our decentralized futures are tending to. Importantly, this new digital state can be driven by a digital social contract, one where technology developed and deployed by private entities is used to bring individuals out of the state of nature.

Bibliography

Hanna, N. (2018). A Role for the State in the Digital Age. *Journal of Innovation and Entrepreneurship*, 7(5), 1–16.

Levin, J. D. (2011). *The Economics of Internet Markets*. [Online] Available at: https://www.nber.org/system/files/working_papers/w16852/w16852.pdf [Accessed 2 August 2021].

Mazzucato, M. (2018). *Capitalism's Greatest Weakness? It Confuses Price with Value*. [Online] Available at: https://www.weforum.org/agenda/2018/05/capitalisms-greatest-weakness-it-confuses-price-with-value/ [Accessed 5 August 2021].

OECD. (1995). *The Changing Role for Telecommunications in the Economy: Globalisation and its Impact on National Telecommunication Policy*. [Online] Available at: https://www.oecd-ilibrary.org/docserver/237551337570.pdf?expires=1628190408&id=id&accname=guest&checksum=932281AD1B0C84F6E41C59B6B654F5F1 [Accessed 5 August 2021].

OECD. (2021). *Government Support for Business Research and Innovation in a World in Crisis*. [Online] Available at: https://www.oecd-ilibrary.org/sites/7a7891a5-en/index.html?itemId=/content/component/7a7891a5-en [Accessed 5 August 2021].

Tapscott, D. & Agnew, D. (1999). *Governance in the Digital Economy*. [Online] Available at: https://www.imf.org/external/pubs/ft/fandd/1999/12/pdf/tapscott.pdf [Accessed 4 July 2021].

WTO. (2020). *World Trade Report 2020: Government Policies to Promote Innovation*. Geneva: World Trade Organization.

12 The Fourth Industrial Revolution

Tech This, Tech That!

Depending on when you are reading this, it is not so farfetched to think about visiting Mars, or to think about implanting a microchip to help your brain either with memory issues or overcoming physical disabilities. It is also not so crazy to think that a swarm of robots could crawl and fly through the wreckage of a natural disaster looking for survivors; or that a computer far away could execute a terrorist without needing human permission (of course based on some predetermined criteria). This is just the tip of an almost endless iceberg of opportunities that will be unlocked during the fourth industrial revolution. Unique to this industrial revolution is that we are presented not only with individual cutting-edge tools, but also with the possibility to combine these tools in more ways than ever possible. In the context of the fourth industrial revolution and evolving economic value, we will focus on blockchain technology, big data analytics, artificial intelligence, and cloud computing as key technological advancements that should be combined to unlock value in the digital economy. The objective is not to take away from the other technologies that will contribute to advancing society, which, according to the United Nations Conference on Trade and Development's (UNCTAD) report "Digital Economy Report 2019 - Value Creation and Capture: Implications for Developing Countries", also include 3D printing/ additive manufacturing, artificial intelligence, robots and automation, and internet of things (UNCTAD, 2019). In the report "Industry 4.0: Building the Digital Enterprise" (2016), Geissbauer et al. present a framework for industry 4.0 and the technologies that make this up.

1 Blockchain

As far as buzzwords go, blockchain takes the crown at the time of writing this book. From cryptocurrencies to non-fungible tokens, the technology has been presented as the tool for both the protagonists and antagonists of social evolution. Blockchain-based systems have gained prominence in the decade leading up to 2020 (Deloitte, 2017; Gupta, 2017), and with good cause. A blockchain is a system with elements which are distributed over a network of computers communicating and storing information among themselves. Dylan Yaga, Peter Mell, Nik Roby,

DOI: 10.4324/9781003330417-15

and Karen Scarfone, in the paper "Blockchain Technology Overview", describe a blockchain as:

> distributed digital ledgers of cryptographically signed transactions that are grouped into blocks. Each block is cryptographically linked to the previous one (making it tamper evident) after validation and undergoing a consensus decision. As new blocks are added, older blocks become more difficult to modify (creating tamper resistance). New blocks are replicated across copies of the ledger within the network, and any conflicts are resolved automatically using established rules.
>
> (Yaga et al., 2018)

Blockchains can be classified based on who has access to them and who can create new blocks in the chain, making them either permissioned or permissionless (101blockchains, 2020). While blockchains started to gain popularity in 2008 and 2009, spurred by the launch of the Bitcoin cryptocurrency, the science behind this technology dates from further back. Leslie Lamport created the Paxos protocol in 1989 and published a paper titled "The Part-Time Parliament" in 1998 which described an approach to reaching consensus on a network (Yaga et al., 2018). The Part-Time Parliament starts with an overview of the problem in relation to the Island of Paxos and the part-time parliamentarians on the Island. For the Island of Paxos, it was important for parliamentarians to be able to both trade and perform their civic duties, but as they were frequently in and out of parliament, it became necessary to find a way to agree on the current state of the world across the parliament. Each parliamentarian kept a ledger where they recorded the most recent information they had received in parliament (in this case, the ledger would say the most recent decree number and decree which the parliament had passed). In order to ensure that parliamentarians in fact passed and recorded decrees, and to ensure that they also did not leave the ledgers blank, the Paxos devised an arrangement to say that

> If a majority of the legislators were in the Chamber and no one entered or left the Chamber for a sufficiently long period of time then any decree proposed by a legislator in the Chamber would be passed, and every decree that had been passed would appear in the ledger of every legislator in the Chamber.
>
> (Lamport, 1998)

This approach was applied to computer science and to distributed networks to ensure that networks can reach decisions regardless of faults in their nodes (Lamport, 1998). Key components of distributed systems are the nodes which represent processes, and the message channels that message across the network. Distributed systems have various properties (Yaga et al., 2018):

- The distributed nature serves as a safeguard against nodes failing and information being lost,

- Having concurrent components that allow the system to process information simultaneously,
- Each node has its own clock and, as such, the system does not run on a single clock.

Like in the case of the Paxos parliament, the systems on the network need to communicate among themselves and for this to happen, these systems need to agree on the most recent status of the system. Consensus mechanisms "enable a group of mutually distrusting users to work together" (Yaga et al., 2018). Consensus mechanisms are a key element of blockchains and must meet the following requirements to be considered effective (Seibold & Samman, 2016):

- Decentralized governance – this means that no one entity can validate a transaction,
- Quorum structure – this means that messages may move according to a set path,
- Authentication – makes it possible to verify participant identities,
- Integrity,
- Nonrepudiation – makes it possible to verify message senders,
- Privacy,
- Fault tolerance – this ensures that the network stays operational even if there is a faulty node,
- Performance – this ensures liveness, scalability, and latency of the network.

In addition to the above-mentioned characteristics, consensus mechanisms need to possess the following (Bushkov & Guerraoui, 2015):

- Validity – any value decided by the network must be proposed by one of the processes (one of the nodes on the network),
- Agreement – this means that all working nodes on the network must agree on a value,
- Termination – this means that all working nodes will eventually decide on a value.

Validity and agreement are safety features of a consensus mechanism, while termination is a liveness feature. Safety features ensure that the system functions as it should, while the liveness features ensures that the system does not stay dormant or inactive without a reason. This feature ensures that the system will eventually take an action and will eventually agree on a value. In addition, there are other principles that guide the functioning of distributed systems. CAP theorem (referring to **C**onsistency, **A**vailability, and **P**artial tolerance) states that a system must have any two (and only any two) of the following properties at each point in time (IBM, 2019):

- Consistency – every node when called up will always provide the most recent state of the system,

- Availability – every node can feed input into the system and every node can receive input from the system,
- Partial tolerance – system works despite partitions in the network. This means that if nodes in the system are blocked off or disconnected, the system should still work.

2 Consensus Mechanisms

Jake Frankenfield describes consensus mechanisms as "fault-tolerant mechanisms used to achieve the necessary agreement on the state of the network among distributed processes or multi-agent systems" (Frankenfield, 2020). Picture this, you and a group of your friends need to go watch a series of movies. Each movie is chosen by a different friend but to see each movie, you all have to agree on the time to see the movie. In a blockchain, you would use a consensus mechanism to decide the timings, so that each time a movie was chosen, you could all apply this mechanism to choosing the time. The idea behind this is, of course, that you can achieve reliability, consistency, and trust in the decision-making processes by digitalizing it. There is a growing suite of consensus mechanisms already in application:

a) **Proof of work** – this model requires systems to prove that they have performed a pre-requisite activity in order to successfully publish the next block on the chain. In the famous example of Bitcoin, this is task is solving a mathematical equation. In general, the puzzle that needs to be solved is a computationally heavy process that requires a level of commitment from miners; however, the process of verifying the work done is much easier, so that systems can easily verify claims. Blocks that are validated by the network are added to the chain and blocks that are not validated are rejected (Yaga et al., 2018). Blocks are easily verifiable thanks to hash algorithms, another ingenious mechanism.
b) **Proof of burn** – this consensus mechanism requires miners to burn coins as a way of reaching consensus. In principle, the more coins that a miner can burn, the more computing power they show they have to the network. Proof of burn is similar to proof of stake in the sense that both consensus mechanisms require users to commit coins; however, in proof of burn the coins are erased permanently from the network once they are burnt (CoinMarketCap, 2021b; Karantias et al., 2019).
c) **Proof of stake** – in this consensus mechanism, the systems which are assigned as validators on the network are stakeholders whose voting power is proportional to the economic stake or native currency of the system which they lock into the system. In essence, the more coins that a user has on the network, the more likely the user is to add a block to the chain (Gong, 2018). In addition, it is expected that the more stake a user has in the network, the less likely it is that the user will attempt to sabotage or subvert the network (Yaga et al., 2018).
d) **Proof of space** – this consensus mechanism requires users to show that they have allocated unused space on their systems for the network to use in storage (Chia, 2021).

e) **Proof of elapsed time** – under this mechanism, each node in the system sends a request for a randomly generated time from within their individual system. On receiving the time, the nodes go idle for the stipulated period. The first node to "wake up" publishes a block to the chain (Yaga et al., 2018). At this point the other nodes wake up and the process repeats.

f) **Proof of authority** – the proof of authority approach sees users stake their identities and reputations in the network as opposed to staking coins in the proof of stake model (Binance Academy, 2018). Proof of authority depends on "reputable validators to produce blocks" and that means a select number of validators serve as moderators for the system (CoinMarketCap, 2021a).

Consensus mechanisms have their limitations and need to be contextualized to each use case.

3 Scaling Blockchains in the Real World

Blockchains have so far tended to require a high amount of computing power and capacity. As such, it has been difficult applying blockchain-based solutions at scale across industries. One of the core reasons for this is consensus mechanisms and ensuring that a network, no matter its size, can function as expected and agree on values. To this end, there are three challenges facing blockchain scalability, known as the scalability trilemma (Seba Bank, 2020):

- **Security** – ensures protection of data on the network, as well as prevents against double spending.
- **Decentralization** – this ensures that no small group of nodes or systems on the network can control the entire network.
- **Scalability** – this refers to the ability of the blockchain to process a high volume of transactions.

Michael Zochowski, however, argued in 2018 that the scalability trilemma was misunderstood, and that scalability was indeed possible. His arguments are that sharding is not the only solution to scalability and that the term "scalability trilemma" furthers this confusion (Zochowski, 2018). Our focus here is not on the debate around the viability of the scalability trilemma, but, rather, on the dynamic thinking and creativity that are needed to apply blockchain solutions in real-world contexts. Another important reason why we consider the scalability trilemma is because it reflects the realities of human interaction which require security/trust, which happen everywhere, and which happen at scale. In addition to consensus mechanisms which allow blockchains to agree on the status of the network, nodes on the network need to be able to verify that a task was completed, without necessarily knowing the details of the task itself. This feature in real-world application would allow blockchain systems to validate information without the use of a central authority, supporting the key founding principle of decentralization in blockchains. To achieve this, blockchains adopt "zero knowledge proofs" which are a way to prove knowledge without revealing the knowledge (Alameda, 2021).

4 Big Data Analytics and Artificial Intelligence

As more people come online and technology is applied in more aspects of our societies, more data is going to be created. Harnessing and actioning this data will be a critical component of smart societies, enabling interaction and resource optimization at ever-new levels. Big data analytics as a tool takes large data sets and leverages advanced techniques to make sense of the data. According to IBM, big data analytics "use advanced analytic techniques against very large, diverse data sets that include structured, semi-structured and unstructured data, from different sources, and in different sizes" (IBM, 2021). Peter Ghavami in the book *Big Data Analytics Methods: Analytics Techniques in Data Mining, Deep Learning and Natural Language Processing* (2019) makes an important distinction between big data and business intelligence to highlight the unstructured nature of the inputs process through big data analytics (Ghavami, 2019). Wesley Chai in the article "Big Data Analytics" adds an important element to the definition by saying that big data analytics "examines large data sets to uncover information such as hidden patterns, correlations, trends" (Chai, 2021). Ghavami goes on to say that big data analytics attempts to answer three important questions to understand what happened in the past (retrospective analysis), what is going on in the present (real-time analysis), and what could happen in the future (prospective analysis) (Ghavami, 2019).

In the year 2001, Doug Laney defined three important characteristics of big data which would go on to be referred to as the 3 Vs. which were summarized by Rob Kitchin and Gavin McArdle in their 2016 journal article as (Kitchin & McArdle, 2016):

- **Volume** – this refers to the quantity of the data in question.
- **Velocity** – this refers to the speed at which new data is produced/collected.
- **Variety** – this refers to whether the data is structured or un-structured.

Chai (2021) notes that data must be collected, processed, cleansed, and analysed. A set of tools exist for this, as well as to manage and run big data analytics, and have been defined by Chai (2021) to include the following non-exhaustive list (Chai, 2021):

Chai (2021) goes on to identify some key benefits of big data analytics as the ability to quickly analyse large data sets and the influence that this has on decision-making, as well as the potential improvements in productivity and outputs based on efficiencies realized from optimized decision-making (Chai, 2021). These are, however, not without their challenges which according to Chai (2021) include quality maintenance, the accessibility of collected and stored data, ensuring the security of data as well as ensuring that data is processed using the right tools.

So we have collected the data and will store it in the cloud but it needs to be processed in real time. It is impossible for any individual to manually process these ultra-large data sets, but under the right circumstances, this is straightforward for a computer program. Cue artificial intelligence. Artificial intelligence includes the simulation process of human intelligence by machines and special computer systems. This simulation often includes everything from learning and reasoning to self-correction. We are still a few years away from supercomputers that can perfectly simulate cognition; despite this, the AI systems at our disposal today are quite impressively well advanced and are already finding life in various industries.

When you consider the opportunity for peer-to-peer trade, and the need for a currency to measure a vast and constantly changing array of metrics in real time, big data analytics and artificial intelligence are indispensable tools.

5 Cloud Computing

Where do we process and/or store all of this data generated from all of these interactions among humans, objects, resources, and nature? This is where cloud computing and cloud storage come in. The National Institute of Standards and Technology at the US Department of Commerce defines cloud computing as:

> a model for enabling ubiquitous, convenient, on-demand network access to a shared pool of configurable computing resources ... that can be rapidly provisioned and released with minimal management effort or service provider interaction.
>
> (Mell & Grance, 2011)

Cloud computing allows services and products to be offered and/or accessed over a network without needing to be stored locally such as on a user's desktop (Harris, n.d.). According to BCS, the Chartered Institute for IT in the book *Cloud Computing: Moving IT Out of the Office* (2012), cloud computing is made up of three unique types of services which are (BCS, T. C. I. for I., 2012):

- **Software as a service (SaaS)** – in this instance, the consumer can access and use services and applications from the cloud service provider (Carstensen et al., 2012),
- **Platform as a service (PaaS)** – here, the consumer is able to deploy services or applications which they have created or bought, unto the cloud platform (Carstensen et al., 2012),
- **Infrastructure as a service (IaaS)** – here, the consumer has access to computing resources like storage, processing, and network capabilities (Carstensen et al., 2012).

According to the BCS T. C. I. for I. (2012), clouds are:

- **Public** – here services are available over the internet to the public,
- **Private** – these are typically private networks,
- **Hybrid** – this allows hosting on both a server and cloud,
- **Community** – here, a group of customers share infrastructure based on a set of similar requirements.

The BCS T. C. I. for I. (2012) goes on to identify a set of important advantages of cloud computing which include but are not limited to the following.

It is important to note, however, that there may be more benefits based on the context of application:

- **Access to resources** – cloud computing offers access to the computing power of remotely located systems. This is particularly useful for the large-scale deployment of any digital currency, tool, or platform.
- **Accessibility** – users are able to access services and applications from multiple locations, which presents a further benefit whether you consider centralization or decentralization.
- **Scalability and storage capacity** – services and payment bundles for capacity can easily be increased (or reduced) as needed,
- **Data security**
- **Cost savings** – as cloud storage and computing resources are typically paid for, businesses/organizations do not have to invest in the hardware and physical servers; instead, they can pay for resources based on their needs. For a government or entity deploying digital tools, assets, or platforms, this presents a degree of flexibility that ultimately increases efficiency.
- **Maintenance and support from the supplier**
- **Improved environmental impact compared to multiple organizations storing multiple servers on-site**.

By combining all of these technologies, each unity of currency that is generated and traded can leverage measurable and clearly defined data points to reflect the true conditions of the market. Current currency models do reflect market conditions, but largely at a macro level. Digital currencies (not just digital representations of a fiat currency) can take this a step further by integrating the right data metrics into their designs and adjusting in real time to truly reflect the value it is meant to represent.

Bibliography

101blockchains. (2020). *Permissioned Vs Permissionless Blockchains*. [Online] Available at: https://101blockchains.com/permissioned-vs-permissionless-blockchains/ [Accessed 1 August 2021].

Alameda, T. (2021). *Zero Knowledge Proof: How to Maintain Privacy in a Data-Based World*. [Online] Available at: https://www.bbva.com/en/zero-knowledge-proof-how-to-maintain-privacy-in-a-data-based-world/ [Accessed 4 July 2021].

BCS, T. C. I. for I. (2012). *Cloud Computing: Moving IT Out of the Office*. Swindon: BCS, The Chartered Institute for IT.

Binance Academy. (2018). *Proof of Authority Explained*. [Online] Available at: https://academy.binance.com/en/articles/proof-of-authority-explained [Accessed 4 July 2021].

Bushkov, V. & Guerraoui, R. (2015). *Safety-Liveness Exclusion in Distributed Computing*. [Online] Available at: https://infoscience.epfl.ch/?ln=en [Accessed 4 July 2021].

Carstensen, J., Morgenthal, J., & Golden, B. (2012). *Cloud Computing: Assessing the Risks*. Ely: ITGP.

Chai, W. (2021). *Big Data Analytics*. [Online] Available at: https://searchbusinessanalytics.techtarget.com/definition/big-data-analytics [Accessed 10 July 2021].

Chia. (2021). *What is Chia?*. [Online] Available at: https://www.chia.net/faq/ [Accessed 4 July 2021].

CoinMarketCap. (2021a). *Proof of Authority*. [Online] Available at: https://coinmarketcap.com/alexandria/glossary/proof-of-authority-poa [Accessed 4 July 2021].

CoinMarketCap. (2021b). *What is Proof of Burn?*. [Online] Available at: https://coinmarketcap.com/alexandria/glossary/proof-of-burn-pob [Accessed 4 July 2021].

Deloitte. (2017). *The Blockchain (R)evolution – The Swiss Perspective*. [Online] Available at: https://www2.deloitte.com/content/dam/Deloitte/ch/Documents/innovation/ch-en-innovation-blockchain-revolution.pdf [Accessed 5 August 2021].

Frankenfield, J. (2020). *Consensus Mechanisms (Cryptocurrency)*. [Online] Available at: https://www.investopedia.com/terms/c/consensus-mechanism-cryptocurrency.asp [Accessed 4 July 2021].

Ghavami, P. (2019). *Big Data Analytics Methods: Analytics Techniques in Data Mining, Deep Learning and Natural Language Processing*. Vol. 2. Berlin: De Gruyter.

Gong, C. (2018). *5 Types of Blockchain Consensus Mechanisms*. [Online] Available at: https://www.logicsolutions.com/5-types-blockchain-consensus-mechanisms/ [Accessed 4 July 2021].

Gupta, V. (2017). *A Brief History of Blockchain*. [Online] Available at: https://hbr.org/2017/02/a-brief-history-of-blockchain [Accessed 14 July 2021].

Hanna, N. (2018). A Role for the State in the Digital Age. *Journal of Innovation and Entrepreneurship*, 7(5), 1–16.

Harris, T. (n.d.) *Cloud Computing*. [Online] Available at: https://www.torryharris.com/downloads/Cloud-Computing-Overview.pdf [Accessed 5 August 2021].

IBM. (2019). *CAP Theorem*. [Online] Available at: https://www.ibm.com/cloud/learn/cap-theorem [Accessed 4 July 2021].

IBM. (2021). *Big Data Analytics*. [Online] Available at: https://www.ibm.com/analytics/hadoop/big-data-analytics [Accessed 10 July 2021].

Karantias, K., Kiayias, A., & Zindros, D. (2019). *Proof-of-Burn*. [Online] Available at: https://eprint.iacr.org/2019/1096.pdf [Accessed 4 July 2021].

Kitchin, R. & McArdle, G. (2016). What Makes Big Data, Big Data? Exploring the Ontological Characteristics of 26 Datasets. *Big Data & Society*, *3*, 1–10.

Lamport, L. (1998). The Part-Time Parliament. *ACM Transactions on Computer Systems*, *16*(2), 133–169.

Levin, J. D. (2011). *The Economics of Internet Markets*. [Online] Available at: https://www.nber.org/system/files/working_papers/w16852/w16852.pdf [Accessed 2 August 2021].

Mazzucato, M. (2018). *Capitalism's Greatest Weakness? It Confuses Price with Value*. [Online] Available at: https://www.weforum.org/agenda/2018/05/capitalisms-greatest-weakness-it-confuses-price-with-value/ [Accessed 5 August 2021].

Mell, P. & Grance, T. (2011). *Cloud Computing*. [Online] Available at: https://nvlpubs.nist.gov/nistpubs/Legacy/SP/nistspecialpublication800-145.pdf [Accessed 10 July 2021].

OECD. (1995). *The Changing Role for Telecommunications in the Economy: Globalisation and its Impact on National Telecommunication Policy*. [Online] Available at: https://www.oecd-ilibrary.org/docserver/237551337570.pdf?expires=1628190408&id=id&accname=guest&checksum=932281AD1B0C84F6E41C59B6B654F5F1 [Accessed 5 August 2021].

OECD. (2021). *Government Support for Business Research and Innovation in a World in Crisis*. [Online] Available at: https://www.oecd-ilibrary.org/sites/7a7891a5-en/index.html?itemId=/content/component/7a7891a5-en [Accessed 5 August 2021].

Seba Bank. (2020). *The Blockchain Trilemma*. [Online] Available at: https://www.seba.swiss/research/the-blockchain-trilemma [Accessed 4 July 2021].

Seibold, S. & Samman, G. (2016). *Consensus: Immutable Agreement for the Internet of Value*. Delaware: KPMG.

Tapscott, D. & Agnew, D. (1999). *Governance in the Digital Economy*. [Online] Available at: https://www.imf.org/external/pubs/ft/fandd/1999/12/pdf/tapscott.pdf [Accessed 4 July 2021].

UNCTAD. (2019). *Digital Economy 2019 - Value Creation and Capture: Implications for Developing Countries*. Geneva: UNCTAD.

WTO. (2020). *World Trade Report 2020: Government Policies to Promote Innovation*. Geneva: World Trade Organization.

Yaga, D., Mell, P., Roby, N., & Scarfone, K. (2018). *Blockchain Technology Overview*, Maryland: National Institute of Standards and Technology, U.S. Department of Commerce.

Zochowski, M. (2018). *Everything You Know about the Scalability Trilemma is Probably Wrong*. [Online] Available at: https://medium.com/logos-network/everything-you-know-about-the-scalability-trilemma-is-probably-wrong-bc4f4b7a7ef [Accessed 4 July 2021].

13 Digital Economy and Economic Value

We have summarized the definition of the digital economy as all the economic activity and social interaction that takes place on, or is facilitated by, the internet and related digital technologies. We have also summarized the definition of economic value in the context of "utility". Building on these, we looked in previous chapters at the technologies that will be instrumental in measuring and capturing this utility based value, i.e. key technologies that form the core of the digital economy in the context of the fourth industrial revolution. Now let us explore the relationships between the digital economy and economic value, to understand how technologies in the digital economy are unlocking social and economic value. Our starting point is the United Nations Conference on Trade and Development's (UNCTAD) Digital Economy 2019 Report. It is important to note that this report in 2019 was the first time UNCTAD had produced a digital economy report, as a replacement to the preceding "Information Economy Report" (UNCTAD, 2019). This change in narrative reflects the growing importance of the digital economy for social and economic value.

The UNCTAD report starts by identifying the key stakeholders in the economy which are grouped under producers, consumers, and the government. These stakeholders, according to the report, have a main objective to produce goods and services (driven by utility). The report goes on to highlight two factors driving value creation in the digital economy as the "platformization" and "monetization" of digital data (UNCTAD, 2019). According to UNCTAD (2019), digital platforms and digital data are at the centre of value creation and value capture in the digital economy. Digital platforms create value by connecting producers and consumers as well as by creating network effects. These platforms collect critical data that allows them to improve their offerings to both producers and consumers. Personal data collected from consumers, for example, is used to improve targeting for advertising to consumers, and used to improve product design for producers. The UNCTAD (2019) report highlights that availability of data alone is not enough to effectively create value; instead, it is what is done with the resulting intelligence from the data that is most important. Again, we no longer focus solely on the tool but, rather, what we can achieve by applying the tool, or resource in this case. The report highlights the complex nature and types of data, from personal or non-personal data to instant and historic data or structured and

DOI: 10.4324/9781003330417-16

unstructured data. UNCTAD makes an important comment in this report: All of this data has an economic value that can be monetized depending on how the data is used. We are already seeing this in the monetization of consumer data as mentioned earlier.

The UNCTAD (2019) report highlights some of the challenges to measuring value in the digital economy and identifies the lack of universally agreed definitions for either the digital "economy" or "value" as being among the limitations. One thing is clear from the report: It shows that the subject on the digital economy can be approached from many angles, each influencable by context.

David Nguyen and Marta Paczos, in the report "Measuring the Economic Value of Data and Cross-Border Data Flows: A Business Perspective", which was published by the OECD, also emphasize data monetization as the basis for realizing value in the digital economy (Nguyen & Paczos, 2020). The authors go on to present the data categories first presented in ISO/IEC Standard 19944, in a bid to highlight not only the economic value of various types of data, but also to highlight the data privacy for users. As in the case of UNCTAD's report, Nguyen and Paczos reflect on value in the digital economy from the context of the data generated in/by/through the digital economy. Their work focuses on the economic value that can be realized from monetizing this data and as a result, for which they present the following approaches to measuring data's economic value (Nguyen & Paczos, 2020) (Figure 13.1):

- Valuing data based on market prices,
- Data as a knowledge-based asset,
- Valuing data based on revenue.

In the article "Releasing Trapped Value Is Key to Success in the Digital World" published by the World Economic Forum, Vedrana Savic and Alison Kennedy argue that to unlock value in the digital economy, stakeholders should "rethink the whole idea of value creation and innovate to create more value for others than they can capture for themselves" (Savic & Kennedy, 2019).

Much of the literature that exists looks at value in the digital economy in the context of revenues that can be generated from applying digital tools and new technologies to the production and consumption process. In the examples mentioned in this chapter, the approaches to value in the digital economy reflect the vast variety of potential data sources that could be monetized. As discussed in earlier sections, these approaches would qualify as extrinsic goods. The question then is, do we consider time as data? And if yes, would we consider this as an intrinsic good in itself? Seeing as it is one of the most valuable things that every human has and is limited in supply?

Improving the state of the world could be considered both an intrinsic and an extrinsic good. Whichever the case, the importance of improving the state of the world is supported by the UNCTAD (2019) digital economy report which sought to understand value in the digital economy in the context of social and economic inclusion for developing nations (UNCTAD, 2019). There is also not a significant amount of literature on the relationship between the digital economy

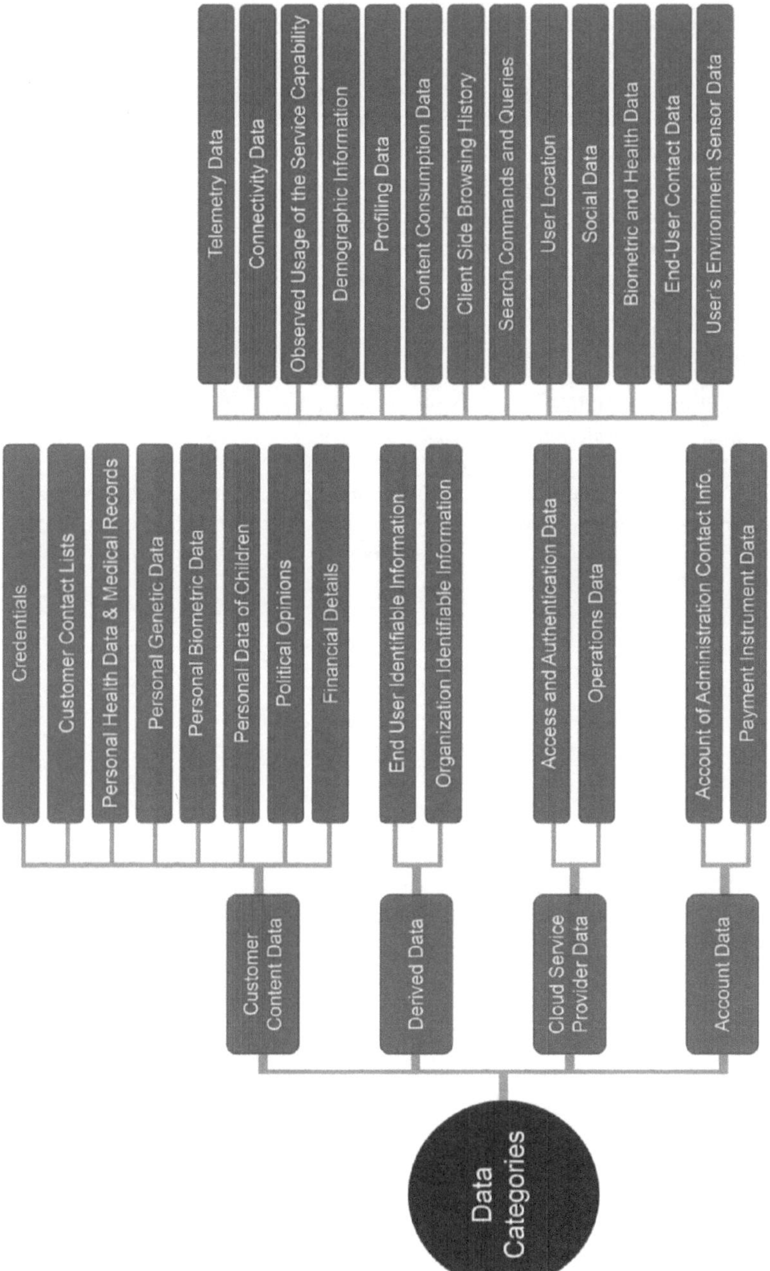

Figure 13.1 Data categories (first produced in ISO/IEC standard 19944) (Nguyen & Paczos, 2020).

and digital currencies. This is a critical gap given that currencies have evolved through history as stores of value with which individuals could use to represent and trade resources. This is an opportunity to rethink how the digital economy can support value creation and value capture for the individual. As has been the case historically, governments have played a role in facilitating the human interaction that takes place in society and is now facilitated by the digital economy. This role is primarily in creating the enabling environment for the digital economy and digital technologies, through policy and investments. Given that a large part of the global approach to value in the digital economy has centred around monetization of data, it is also critical that regulation is in place to protect the individual, who has given up their rights from the state of nature, to participate in civil society; whether through a government or other entity.

Bibliography

Nguyen, D. & Paczos, M. (2020). *Measuring the Economic Value of Data and Cross-Border Data Flows: A Business Perspective*. Paris: OECD.

Savic, V. & Kennedy, A. (2019). *Releasing Trapped Value is Key to Success in the Digital World*. [Online] Available at: https://www.weforum.org/agenda/2019/02/releasing-trapped-value-is-key-to-success-in-the-digital-world/ [Accessed 12 July 2021].

UNCTAD. (2019). *Digital Economy 2019 - Value Creation and Capture: Implications for Developing Countries*, Geneva: UNCTAD.

Part IV

Time

14 The Concept of Time

The three previous parts of this book have established how the state is formed, the central role of economic value in the social contract, as well as various approaches to value in the digital economy. Now, we will explore the concept of time, given that it is the most important component of this theory.

> *Time is what prevents everything from happening at once.*
>
> – Ray Cummings (Cummings, 2007)

The subject of time deserves its own dedicated and extensive review, given the multiplicity of perspectives on the subject. As in the previous discussions on various disciplines, this book does not attempt to present a conclusive summary of all the perspectives on the subject, but rather looks to highlight the various schools of thought on time, as well as the key characteristics of each school of thought. The resulting review on the literature on time should present a sufficient understanding of the subject to understand its application in the broader context of this research. To do this, we look at some perspectives captured in *Time* by Nina Emery, Ned Markosian, and Meghan Sullivan in 2020 (Emery et al., 2020); *Time* by Bradley Dowden (n.d.); and *An Introduction to the Philosophy of Time and Space* by Bas C. van Fraassen (Fraassen, 1970).

According to Emery et al., some of the main topics in the philosophy of time include:

> fatalism, reductionism and platonism, topology of time, McTaggart's argument, A-theory and B-theory, presentism, eternalism, and growing block theory, 3-dimensional/4-dimensional debate about persistence, dynamic and static theory, moving spotlight theory, time travel, physics, and rationality.
>
> (Emery et al., 2020)

Dowden classifies the philosophy of time into three broad schools, namely, presentism, growing block or growing past theory, and eternalism (Dowden, n.d.). According to proponents of presentism, only objects and experiences that are occurring in the current time are a part of reality, while objects and experiences that have occurred in the past or may occur in the future are not considered a part of reality. Proponents of growing block or growing past theory, on the other hand,

DOI: 10.4324/9781003330417-18

believe that both objects and experiences that occurred in the past as well as those occurring in the current moment are considered a part of reality; however, objects and experiences that may occur in the future are not part of reality. The eternalism school of thought differs from the previous two in the sense that it suggests there is no difference between past, present, and future, and that perspectives on what is considered past, present, or future are the result of subjectivity (or are just how the individual sees things). The philosophy of time can also be approached from two broad perspectives on the core nature of time whether as static or as dynamic. According to static theorists, time is similar to a multidimensional space within which objects exist and events occur. Dynamic theorists, on the other hand, believe in the passage of time in a chronological manner. Growing block theorists, for example, may consider themselves as part of the dynamic theory, while eternalists may align better with static theory.

According to Emery et al., there are key highlights of the **static theory** that summarize its position (Emery et al., 2020):

1 This theory suggests that the universe is made up of four similar dimensions which together are referred to as "space-time".
2 Physical objects which are found at different points in time are so because they have different temporal parts for each time where they are located. This means that the object is supposedly made up of multiple temporal parts that exist at the different points in time.
3 A-properties do not exist and instead can be considered in relation to B-relations. B-theory suggests that all forms of change can be considered as being "before" or "after" and occur across different locations on the space-time manifold. On the other hand, A-theory posits that change must happen in relation to the past, present, or future (dynamic).
4 Reality always includes objects from every region of space-time.
5 Truths are unconditional and do not change over time, so there is no need for verbal tenses.
6 Time does not pass.

Emery et al., go on to present a summary of the key elements of **dynamic theory** (Emery et al., 2020):

1 This theory suggests that the universe is made up of three dimensions which are physical spaces.
2 Objects which are located at different times are fully present at those times, instead of having temporal parts of their being present at multiple points in time.
3 A-properties (past, present, future) are real and cannot always be considered with regard to B-relations (before and after).
4 Reality changes over time and only objects in the present time exist.
5 A proposition has a truth at a certain time; however, this truth can change over time and is not unconditional.
6 The passing of time is real.

These perspectives on time so far present another question on the topology or structure of time. If time is considered linear, that is, moving in a direction, from the past, through the present and into future, then one might consider this to be a line. This approach raises further questions on the nature of this line: Is it a straight line? Does the line have a beginning and an end? On the other hand, if time is considered as a space within which events and objects exist, then one might consider time as a randomly uneven surface. The discussion on whether time has a beginning or end has implications from physics to religion, with questions emerging around what caused the beginning of time. Among the historical philosophers that pondered this question was Aristotle. In *Physics*, he wonders whether a thing can come into existence without having a beginning. Despite this contemplation, Aristotle identified time as being infinite and therefore did not consider time to be subject to this dilemma.

> The fallacy of Melissus is obvious. For he supposes that the assumption "what has come into being always has a beginning" justifies the assumption "what has not come into being has no beginning.
>
> (Aristotle, 350 BC)

> But on the other hand, to suppose that the infinite does not exist in any way leads obviously to many impossible consequences: there will be a beginning and an end of time, a magnitude will not be divisible into magnitudes, number will not be infinite.
>
> (Aristotle, 350 BC)

Bradley Dowden presents a further classification of time as physical, psychological, and biological (Dowden, n.d.). According to him, physical time is the time that is common to everyone and is counted by clock. Biological time refers to the body's natural processes while psychological time (also called perceived time) is subjective and refers to the individual's approach to the recognition and passing of physical time. Each of us is most likely familiar with the three last categories of time described here. When you are having fun, time seems to pass quicker. When you are bored, time is perceived to pass slower. When you are younger, your body tends to process things faster. Presentism, growing block or growing past theory, eternalism, dynamic and static theory, A and B theory, topology of time, physical time, psychological time, and biological time are all just pieces of the time puzzle. There are other approaches that look at time and change from the perspectives of relationism and substantivalism. Bradley Dowden summarizes the definition of relationism as "the thesis that space is only a set of relationships among existing physical material, and time is a set of relationships among the events of that physical material". Substantivalism is defined according to him as "the thesis that space and time exist always and everywhere independently of physical material and its events" (Dowden, n.d.). Relationism or "reductionism with respect to time" suggests that time cannot exist without change, that as long as there is time, there is change. This theory was proposed by Aristotle in *Physics*, where he says, "neither does time exist without change" (Aristotle, 350 BC). Aristotle's position on the relationship between time and change can be further summarized by saying that as humans, we do not recognize the passing of time itself, but rather can recognize the changes that happen as time passes. Bas C. Van Fraassen also highlights this position in his book *Introduction to the Philosophy of Time and Space*, where he highlights that "time is neither identical with nor entirely independent of movement, and it remains for us to determine the relation between them" (Fraassen, 1970).

Substantivalism, on the other hand, suggests that time can exist independent of the objects or events that take place within it and, as such, time can exist without change. Substantivalism has also been referred to as absolute theory of time, because of the position it takes saying that time is absolute and exists independent of any and everything. Einstein's 1905 theory of relativity would ultimately lead to physicists abandoning classical substantivalism (Dowden, n.d.). Other approaches to the subject of time include the theory of Fatalism which suggests that every experience or event that can take place in the future is already determined and no agent in the present can alter or prevent these future events from happening. The Moving Spotlight Theory has sometimes been used to describe the Dynamic Theory. This theory suggests that there is a spotlight that is moving through a "temporal dimension", periodically illuminating sections of that dimension that come in its path. The theory suggests that it is only objects or events that are illuminated within the spotlight that exist. This approach further suggests that once an object is no longer within the spotlight, it ceases to exist (Emery et al., 2020). This is an exciting subject when you think about the different perspectives and the implications of each perspective. As promised, there are indeed several schools of thought on the philosophy and theories of time. Most of the schools of thought look at time either as linear or as a space. Philosophers have also debated the independence or dependence of time in relation to movement and change. Time has also been debated in relation to the movements of earth in space. While we have referenced ancient and historic thinkers, this is in fact not an old conversation. According to Ben Turner commenting on a recent article published in the journal *Nature*, astronomers have been able to detect "light coming from behind a black hole for the first time, proving Albert Einstein right" (Turner, 2021) in relation to Einstein's theory of general relativity. The findings were published in the journal *Nature* by D.R. Wilkins, L.C. Gallo, E. Costantini, W.N. Brandt and R.D. Blandford (Wilkins et al., 2021). According to Einstein's general relativity theory, the supermassive black hole, which was being observed, was **warping space-time** around itself and that is how light from behind the black hole was visible to astronomers. Important to note that the gravitational pull of black holes is so strong that light cannot escape them (Lewis, 2021). This finding and the further research that it prompts may have potential implications on how time is perceived, whether as a linear function, as space-time, with multiple planes, etc. For example, it is assumed that the warping process slows down the passing of time. This, however, does not impact the assumptions made in this book, where we focus on the passing of time as linear and dynamic.

Bibliography

Aristotle. (n.d. 350BC). *Physics*. s.l.:s.n.

Cummings, R. K. (2007). *The Girl in the Golden Atom*. s.l.: The Project Gutenberg eBook.

Dowden, B. (n.d.) *Time*. [Online] Available at: https://iep.utm.edu/time/ [Accessed 21 June 2021].

Emery, N., Markosian, N., & Sullivan, M. (2020). *Time*. [Online] Available at: https://plato.stanford.edu/entries/time/ [Accessed 17 June 2021].

Fraassen, B. V. (1970). *An Introduction to the Philosophy of Time and Space*. 1 ed. s.l.:Random House.

Lewis, S. (2021). *Astronomers Spot Light from Behind a Black Hole for the First Time — Proving Einstein Right, Again*. [Online] Available at: https://www.cbsnews.com/news/supermassive-black-hole-light-behind-einstein/ [Accessed 5 August 2021].

Turner, B. (2021). *Light from Behind a Black Hole Spotted for 1st Time, Proving Einstein Right*. [Online] Available at: https://www.livescience.com/einstein-proven-right-black-hole [Accessed 5 August 2021].

Wilkins, D. R. et al. (2021). Light Bending and X-Ray Echoes from Behind a Supermassive Black Hole. *Nature, 595*, 657–660.

Part V

Deep Dives into the Research

15 Deep Dive

Research Insights

Several well-documented challenges and limitations exist to current social and economic models of interaction, as well as current financial systems. These limitations exist in part, as a result of humanity's perceptions and understanding of "value". The book until now has argued that the perception of value must further evolve to allow for new financial models that enable greater social and economic development. As such, the purpose of the research that inspired this book, was to highlight how the concept of "value" has evolved so far and make recommendations for how it should further evolve. The research thus presents a foundation for the adoption of "time as a store of value", and as a tool that can be used as a financial instrument in trade and economic exchange. In addition, the research aimed at demonstrating that consumers in low-resource settings are willing and already effectively positioned to use alternative, non-cash-based forms of payment, which emphasizes that value is indeed evolving in the contemporary state of nature (i.e., outside the reach of governments).

Objectives of the Research

Considering the purpose of the research, a set of objectives were outlined to guide the process. These objectives were to:

a) highlight how the core subjects/disciplines that make up the sum of the research have evolved, as well as establish a clear relationship to link these concepts/disciplines. These core concepts include "State and Political Society", the Concept of "Value" in economics, "Digital Economy/Fourth Industrial Revolution" and "Time";
b) present a logical framework and justification for the adoption of a time-based digital currency as a store of value and means of exchange;
c) understand whether consumers in low-resource settings and informal economies are willing to interact with social and economic value outside of conventional cash (fiat currency) systems;
d) observe how consumers in low-resource settings and informal economies interact with each other when capturing and transferring value without the use of conventional stores of value and means of exchange like cash (fait currency).

DOI: 10.4324/9781003330417-20

Research Questions

This research was built around the core concept of "value" and the impact that contemporary understandings of social and economic "value" have on approaches to social development. To assess this, the research aimed to answer the following questions through a literature review, survey, and critical analysis:

a What factors lead to and influence the formation of the political state or civil society?
b What factors have guided human interaction in society?
c What are the interpretations of "value" in economics and how have these interpretations varied through history?
d What factors drive innovation (process or product) in society?
e How has the concept of economic value been perceived through the various stages of industrialization history and into the current stage of the fourth industrial revolution?
f Are individuals in the informal economy willing to move away from cash-based transactions to non-cash-based forms of economic exchange and trade?
g Can technology (mobile devices, mobile-based software) be leveraged to facilitate non-cash-based economic interaction in low-resource settings?
h Can alternative approaches to capturing and transferring economic value, such as non-cash-based stores of value and mediums of exchange, be leveraged to meets consumer needs and potentially increase access to markets?

Research Methodology

Given the purpose, objectives, and scope of the research, a mixed methodology is applied to ensure a robust and comprehensive study of the subjects.

Data Collection

A mixed data collection methodology was applied for this research. Primary data included data from the surveys. Secondary data included extensive desk reviews.

Primary Data

Surveys

Surveys were used to collect data to answers the question "to what extent are individuals in the informal economy willing to move away from cash-based transactions?" Survey data was also used to understand whether consumers in low-resource settings are willing to interact with social and economic value outside of conventional cash (fiat currency) systems. The surveys will be collected from randomly selected respondents within a low-income community, across industries, jobs, and demographics

Survey Objectives

The objectives of the survey were to:

a) Collect data to understand to what extent individuals willing to move away from cash-based transactions.
b) Understand to what extent mobile devices are used in facilitating non-cash-based transactions.
c) Understand to what extent the mobile networks (internet and mobile bandwidth) facilitate non-cash-based transactions in low-resource settings.

Survey Design

This research employed a **cross-sectional survey design**. Cross-sectional surveys are typically administered to subsets of larger populations and allow for quick and reliable insights to be gained on what the respondents think of a subject (QuestionPro, 2021). These types of surveys tend to be short and are designed so that they are easy for respondents to flow through. In addition, cross-sectional surveys are designed to answer a simple question and present a "snapshot of respondents opinion" (Gingery, 2019).

Observational Study

A simple observational study was designed to test out a key hypothesis of this research which is that consumers consider value in relation to utility and are willing to capture and transfer social and economic value using non-cash-based methods. Observations of a closed group were used to record the behaviour of consumers/participants while they engage in non-cash-based economic interactions. This observational study was designed to record the behaviour of participants as they engaged with each other on non-cash-based economic interactions. To achieve this, the study tested out the concept of time as a store of socio-economic value by basing the trade of goods and services on units of time spent creating social and economic value. The information gained from the observational study provided insights into how low-income households in an underserved community would react to non-cash-based transactions. The study builds on the findings from the survey collected from the same community. Findings from both the survey and observational study laid the ground for future research into economic interactions around value and will influence the design of a final time-based digital currency.

Note that the term "observational study" used here does not refer to the observational study as used in medicine which refers to observing "a risk factor, diagnostic test, treatment or other intervention without trying to change who is or isn't exposed to it" (Institute for Work & Health, 2016).

Objectives of the Observational Study

The objectives of the observational study were to:

a) Identify key behaviours of consumers in low-resource settings when engaging in trade and economic interactions using alternative approaches to value capture and transfer.
b) Identify key factors that enable alternative stores of value and alternative methods of payment to function effectively in low-resource settings.

Observational Study Methodology

The observational study employed a combined methodology of naturalistic observation and controlled observation.

Naturalistic observation observes the study subjects in their natural environment and under normal circumstances. **Controlled or structured observation** occurs under special circumstances and often in a laboratory or controlled environment, where the researcher defines the environment and parameters of observation (Jhangiani et al., 2019).

This research employed a combined approach for the following reasons:

- Participants were to be observed in their natural environment, that is, in their homes and businesses as well as anywhere else where they engaged in non-cash-based economic interaction as part of the study,
- Participants were guided on what to do each time they had a need for a good or service. This support was essential to ensure that participants understood the process; however, it meant that there was a level of structure to the observation, even though it was taking place in the participants' natural environment.

In addition to observing the overall behaviours and interactions of participants engaged in the study, the observational study paid close attention to the following:

- Types of goods requested and offered
- Types of services requested and offered
- Willingness or hesitancy to engage with alternative stores of value and means of exchange
- Verbal cues
- Physical behaviour
- Frequency of interaction among participants
- Frequency of interaction with study coordinator
- Emotional reactions and interactions
- Use of technology in the interaction process

Scope of the Observational Study

a <u>Sample Population</u>

- The behaviours and interactions of 11 individuals were directly observed as part of the study. A further 12 individuals were indirectly observed as part of the study, bringing the total number of observed participants to **23 individuals**.
- This sample population was drawn from the 400 respondents to the survey and represents 5% of that population. The sample population represents:
  - 11 households
  - 7 businesses
- Characteristics of the sample population include:
  - Male and female
  - Individuals, families, and businesses
  - Ages 13–60
  - Basic knowledge of mobile technology (feature phone and smartphone)
  - Ability and willingness to work
  - Possession of at least 1 core skill

b Duration

- The observational study ran for 7 days from the Sunday, 21 February 2021, to Sunday, 28 February 2021.
- This duration allowed for detailed observations of the participants in their natural environments; it also allowed for a wide range of daily activities to be observed.

c Geographical Location

The observational study was conducted in Ajegunle, a community in Lagos, Nigeria. Ajegunle is a neighbourhood/community in the Ajeromi-Ifelodun Local Government Area (LGA) of Lagos State in Nigeria. There is limited official statistics on the population of Ajegunle; however, recent studies from 2013 place the figure between 429,381 (Akinwale et al., 2013) and 550,000 (Asomba, 2013) (Agbola & Agunbiade, 2007). Unofficial estimates, however, place Ajegunle's population between 1.5 and 3 million (Akanle & Adejare, 2017).

The population of Lagos has grown exponentially over time; however, there are disputing figures about the total population size of 2021. World Population Review estimates Lagos population in 2021 at 14,862,111, up from 325,218 in 1950. The Lagos State Government, however, estimates the population at over 17 million inhabitants, while the Nigerian Government estimates the state's population at over 21 million (World Population Review, 2021). Lagos State has an estimated gross domestic product (GDP) of $136bn (Pilling, 2018).

Lagos serves as the economic capital of Nigeria and has a port which opens up into the Gulf of Guinea, making it one of the more prominent trade routes/hubs for the country. The city of Lagos which sits within the broader State of Lagos has a surface of over 1,171.28 square kilometres (452.23 square miles), and a population density of approximately 6,871 residents per square kilometre (17,800 per square mile).

Located in Western Nigeria, the predominant language and culture present in Lagos is Yoruba; however, the city features cultures and traditions from the surrounding states and neighbouring countries and is estimated to host over 250 ethnic groups.

Preparatory Steps

As part of preparation for the study, the team followed the steps outlined below (Table 15.1):

Table 15.1 Preparatory steps for the Observational study

#	*Activity*	*Notes*
1	Onboarding	• Identifying suitable candidates, • registering suitable candidates to collect required information, • conducting a base survey.
2	Needs assessment	• Cataloguing a set of core needs (products and services) for each member of the sample population. For the sake of this study, the set of core needs will focus on basic human requirements.
3	Market study and assessment	• Cataloguing the market prices and demand-supply conditions of the core needs identified for the sample population.
4	Conversion process	• Converting the market price of each identified need to the corresponding units of time (establishing the conversion value of the core needs for the sample population). • Once the core needs have been catalogued and agreed on for the study, these needs will be assigned codes that study participants can use in trading on a day-to-day basis.
5	Training	• Participants will receive basic training on how to interact with the study as well as on communication requirements.
6	Study Launch	

Study Coordination Process

Once the observational study had commenced, the following process described in Table 15.2, was used to coordinate among study participants. Note that this study was carried out manually, with a focus on assessing interactions and perceptions of value. Further studies will be carried out using the proposed technology tools described in earlier chapters.

Table 15.2 Observational study Coordination Process

Step	*Activity*	*Notes and Examples*
1	Each morning, send out an SMS message to all users reminding them to send a request (via SMS) if they need any good or service during the day.	—
2	User-x sends a request for a good or service.	E.g. User-x needs something to eat "food"
3	Coordinator checks the "micro-economy" to see if the requested good or service is available.	Check the micro-economy document to see who has "food"
4	If the request is available in the "micro-economy", check the price and communicate this to User-X	The prices of goods and services have been converted to units of time, so instead of paying with naira (the national currency of Nigeria), User-X will be required to work for a period of time in order to pay for the good or service which was requested.
5	Remind the User-Y who has the requested good or service of the price of this product or service and get their confirmation to proceed with the transaction. The User-Y who has the "food" should also tell the coordinator what product or service they need for that day or the next day.	—
6	If User-X accepts the offer/price, then the coordinator should connect User-X to User-Y to collect the product or service.	E.g. if User-X is a barber and User-Y sells food, User-X should be ready to give a haircut to pay off the price of the food. If User-Y wants to get a haircut, then the transaction is completed. If User-Y does not want to get a haircut, then their alternative request is noted and fulfilled once available.
7	If request cannot be met, the coordinator puts it on hold until it can be met by another transaction.	—
8	The coordinator continues this process with all users throughout the day to complete as many transactions as possible.	User-X needs something from User-Y, User-X has something that User-Z needs, User-Y needs something from User-Z, User-Y has something User-X needs, User-Z needs something from User-X, User-Z has something User-Y needs, and so on.

Secondary Data

Literature Reviews

A literature review of key documents was carried out including but not be limited to policy documents, articles, books, and other related material. The literature review explored in depth the various core concepts of this research which include the political state/civil society, economic value, innovation, and the digital economy.

Data Analysis

Before starting the data analysis, it was important to validate all the data collected and ensure that this was fit for the subsequent analysis. As part of this validation process, the data was checked to ensure that respondents were real individuals and that responses were not fraudulent. To achieve this, survey respondents were asked to leave in contact information so that they could be reached for this verification. In addition, survey collectors were grouped into teams to ensure that the lead survey collector was not coercing respondents into answering or participating in the survey. Data collected was also reviewed to ensure that as much information as needed was consistently available across the responses received.

In analysing the data collected as part of this research, various methods of data analysis were employed. These included:

a **Qualitative analysis** – the qualitative analysis sought to answer a set of questions using narratives as to why elements in the research interact the way that they do.

b **Prescriptive analysis** – a prescriptive approach was taken to provide recommendations for the future based on findings from the past and present.

In addition, case studies were used to compare and analyse between two examples on the origin of the state in the real-world context, as well as the impact that the origin of the state has (if any) on economic value.

Ethical Considerations and Limitations

This section presents the ethical considerations and limitations to the study as a whole, including limitations to the data collection and observational study.

Ethical Considerations

The research considered the challenges faced by low-income communities which include individuals and households. The sensitive nature of the data collected and the potential impact on daily life that the research seeks for its participants required a careful approach to defining the interactions with these population categories. In addition, the research required a careful approach to data privacy, safety, security, and accessibility. Prior to commencing the data collection and observational study, a brief review was conducted to understand areas for ethical consideration, and to ensure that the methodology reflected these points. The general literature reviewed to understand the best approaches to ethical considerations included "Ethical Considerations in Research: Focus on Vulnerable Groups" by Shaké Ketefian. Here, Ketefian highlights the historic atrocities committed on human subjects that subsequently led to the world developing standards for research involving human subjects (Ketefian, 2015). "The Nuremberg Code", developed following the "judgment by the war crimes tribunal", set out a set of guidelines for research on human subjects that was widely accepted and adopted by the international community (Journal, 1996). In addition, the research also considered the ethical considerations of the Helsinki Declaration (World Medical Association, 1964). In addition to reviewing general guidelines for ethical considerations when conducting research with humans as well as with vulnerable populations, this research also conducted a brief review to understand and apply what guidelines exist in the specific context of Nigeria where the data was collected. The literature reviewed on the subject included the "National Code of Health Research Ethics" (2007) and "Ethical Review of Research Involving Human Subjects in Nigeria: Legal and Policy Issues" (Nwabueze, 2003).

While the bulk of the literature on research involving human subjects focuses on medical research, there are indeed still several considerations that apply to other non-medical areas of research involving human subjects. Based on the findings from these reviews, the ethical considerations that were taken into account in developing this research are highlighted below:

a **Informed consent to participate** – the participants to the pilot as well as the survey respondents were fully aware of the subject of the research and its objectives. Given the varying levels of education of participants, an approach was identified to communicate the core elements of the research in a manner that could be appreciated by all participants. The survey questions reflected these core components such as willingness to engage in cashless payments and use of mobile devices for payments. The survey and study process were also designed to collect only relevant information in an accessible manner for participants.

b **Voluntary participation** – no force, deceit, aggression, persuasion, or other such coercion was applied to engage participants in the study or survey. Participants agreed to participate voluntarily, based on their understanding of the study and their understanding of the potential benefits which they stood to gain from participation.

c **No harm to participants** – the study was designed to ensure that no harm came to participants, whether physical, mental, or emotional.

d **Confidentiality** – all information gained directly or indirectly as part of the study remained confidential.

e **Relevant information** – only information that was critical to the study was collected from participants.

In addition to these,

- The observational study was designed such that at no point would it require financial commitments from the participants, and at no point would it result in a financial burden on participants.
- The research was designed with the final objective of improving the state of the community through financial inclusion enabled by alternative measures of economic value.

Limitations to the Study

Several limitations became clear during this research. This section takes a close look at these limitations and the steps that were taken to overcome them. This section would also highlight some issues for future researchers on the subject to take note of, and potentially solve using the same or different approaches.

i **Cost of research coordination** – a potentially limiting factor at this stage of the research is the cost to coordinate an extensive pilot where a much larger sample population is trading goods and services without the introduction of cash.

ii **Limited time frame for data collection** – this meant that in any instance, only a limited amount of data could be collected. In the event that future studies are conducted into this research, a longer time frame is recommended to allow for much more data to be collected.

iii **Limited number of participants to the observational study** – the observational study set out to test the core tenet of the concept which is "time" as a store of value and, as such, did not need a large sample size to assess the interaction of random individuals with the concept. However, future studies will need to assess the concept on a much larger scale to determine micro- and subsequently macro-level implications.

iv **Manual approach to coordination** – the pilot was carried out using a simple manual approach; this meant that the coordination of interaction among participants was done via mobile SMS/text message, as opposed to being coordinated through a dedicated mobile application. Again, while this study looked to test out the core concept in the unique context of a slum and was successful in that regard, future studies will need to leverage the relevant software to improve effectiveness.

v **Unavailability of data bandwidth** – this research proposes leveraging fourth industrial revolution technologies such as digital currencies to bridge the value creation gap towards greater social and economic development. The research suggests using mobile technologies as a key leverage point; however, despite a high mobile phone penetration (over 90% in Nigeria), there is limited cell phone network coverage in certain communities, meaning that interventions may not run as efficiently as they possibly could.

Bibliography

Agbola, T. & Agunbiade, E. M. (2007). *Urbanization, Slum Development and Security of Tenure: The Challenges Of Meeting Millennium Development Goal 7 in Metropolitan Lagos, Nigeria.* [Online] Available at: http://www.ciesin.columbia.edu/repository/pern/papers/urban_pde_agbola_agunbiade.pdf [Accessed 26 July 2021].

Akanle, O. & Adejare, G. S. (2017). Conceptualising Megacities and Megaslums in Lagos, Nigeria. *Africa's Public Service Delivery and Performance Review*, *5*(1), a155.

Akinwale, O. et al. (2013). Living Conditions and Public Health Status in Three Urban Slums of Lagos, Nigeria. *South East Asia Journal Of Public Health*, *3*(1), 36–41.

Asomba, I. (2013). *Horrible link Road: Ajegunle, on Verge of Isolation.* [Online] Available at: https://www.vanguardngr.com/2013/05/horrible-link-road-ajegunle-on-verge-of-isolation/ [Accessed 26 July 2021].

Gingery, T. (2019). *Survey Basics: Types of Survey Designs.* [Online] Available at: https://www.cvent.com/en/blog/events/survey-basics-types-survey-designs [Accessed 26 July 2021].

Institute for Work & Health. (2016). *Observational vs. Experimental Studies.* [Online] Available at: https://www.iwh.on.ca/what-researchers-mean-by/observational-vs-experimental-studies [Accessed 2 August 2021].

Jhangiani, R. S., Chiang, I.-C. A., Cuttler, C., & Leighton, D. C. (2019). *Research Methods in Psychology*. 4 ed. s.l.:Kwantlen Polytechnic University.

Journal, B. M. (1996). *The Nuremberg Code.* [Online] Available at: https://media.tghn.org/medialibrary/2011/04/BMJ_No_7070_Volume_313_The_Nuremberg_Code.pdf

Ketefian, S. (2015). Ethical Consideration in Research: Focus on Vulnerable Groups. *Investigación y Educación en Enfermería*, 33, 164–172.

Nwabueze, R. N. (2003). Ethical Review of Research Involving Human Subjects in Nigeria: Legal and Policy Issues. *Indiana International & Comparative Law Review*, 14, 87–116.

Pilling, D. (2018). *Nigerian Economy: Why Lagos Works.* [Online] Available at: https://www.ft.com/content/ff0595e4-26de-11e8-b27e-cc62a39d57a0

QuestionPro. (2021). *Types of Survey with Examples.* [Online] Available at: https://www.questionpro.com/blog/types-of-survey/ [Accessed 2 August 2021].

World Medical Association. (1964). *WMA Declaration of Helsinki – Ethical Principles for Medical Research Involving Human Subjects.* [Online] Available at: https://www.wma.net/policies-post/wma-declaration-of-helsinki-ethical-principles-for-medical-research-involving-human-subjects/

World Population Review. (2021). *Lagos Population 2021.* [Online] Available at: https://worldpopulationreview.com/world-cities/lagos-population

16 Deep Dive

Research Findings

This section presents the findings of the research, including findings from the surveys collected and findings from the observational study surveys as well as literature review which are represented in the case study. The section also provides various analyses on the findings and observational study, as well analysis of the findings from the literature review. This includes an analysis of key findings from the data collection, through the lens of the various theories discussed earlier.

Survey Findings

Surveys including seven questions were collected from up to 400 participants in Ajegunle in Lagos, Nigeria. The surveys set out to assess the extent to which consumers in an underserved and/or unserved community would be disposed to receiving alternative forms of payment other than "cash" for goods and services.

Important notes about the survey (Table 16.1):

- Every respondent did not answer every question; as such, the total numbers may not all add up to the same tally. This results in a slight discrepancy of less than 2% in the total number of respondents across each question.
- Surveys were collected over a five-week period in the year 2020.

Survey Analysis

Cross-sectionally designed surveys were used to collect data. The survey engaged a balanced number of male and female respondents in order to ensure as much diversity as possible. The survey also engaged a wide age group to understand potential impacts of age on perceptions of value and disposition to digital technology. The survey found that the largest population of respondents was people aged between 20 and 30 years. It is important to note that Nigeria has a high youth population, with over 61.4% aged above 13 years, and over 51.6% of the population is aged between 16 and 64 years (Kemp, 2021) (Figure 16.1 and 16.2).

Respondents also showed daily expenditure above N1000 (one thousand naira) (Figure 16.3).

DOI: 10.4324/9781003330417-21

Table 16.1 Outline of Survey Findings

180	Were female
186	Were male
62	Were less than age 20
172	Were between ages 20 and 30
98	Were between ages 30 and 40
34	Were between ages 40 and 50
10	Above age 50
16	Responded to spending less than N100 per day
150	Responded to spending greater than N500 per day
235	Responded to spending greater than N1000 per day
392	Responded yes to having a phone
5	Responded no to having a phone
312	Responded yes to using the internet on their personal phone
79	Responded no to using the internet on their personal phone
273	Responded yes to receiving money through their personal phone
114	Responded no to receiving money through their personal phone
213	Responded yes to sending money through their personal phone
177	Responded no to sending money through their personal phone
285	Responded yes to being willing to work if the only way they are paid is with money received on their personal phone
99	Responded no to being willing to work if the only way they are paid is with money received on their personal phone
167	Responded yes to using their personal phone to pay for food with their personal phones
218	Responded no to using their personal phone to pay for food with their personal phones

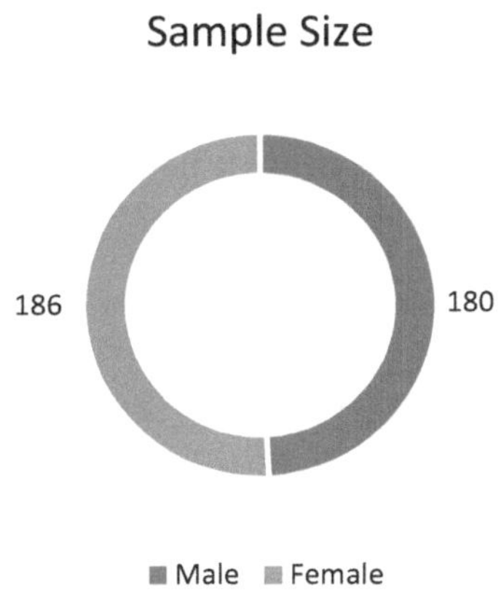

Figure 16.1 Sample Size of Survey.

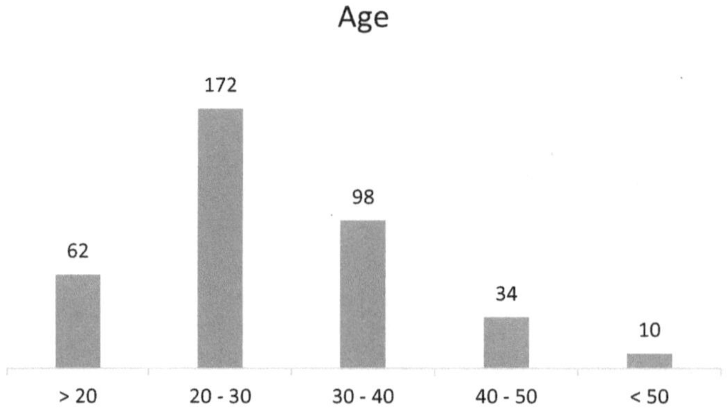

Figure 16.2 Age of Survey Respondents.

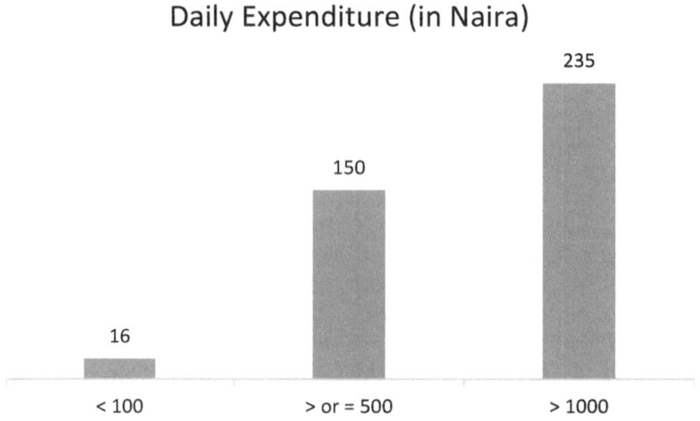

Figure 16.3 Graph of Daily Expenditure from Survey.

Almost everyone in this group had access to mobile phones. For the sake of this survey, mobile phones included every category of mobile device, from analogue phones to feature and smart phones. In addition, 25% of respondents are able to use the internet on their phone. This signalizes a high mobile penetration and a decent level of mobile literacy. These findings are aligned with other studies showing high mobile penetration in Nigeria. To put this in context, the Digital2021 Report highlights that of the total population of 7.83 billion people in the world, there are 5.22 billion mobile phone users (66.6%), of which 4.66 billion (59.5%) are internet users. The same report highlights that 96% of Western Africa has mobile connections, suggesting consistently a high mobile penetration in the countries across the Western Africa region (Kemp, 2021). In Nigeria, of the 208.8 million people, 187.9 million (90%) have mobile connections – up from 50% in 2018 (Oyelola, 2021) – and 104.4 (50%) million are internet users. It is important to note that the report highlights a 10% increase in mobile connections in Nigeria between January 2020 and January 2021, and a 22.1% increase in internet users within the same period (Figure 16.4 and 16.5).

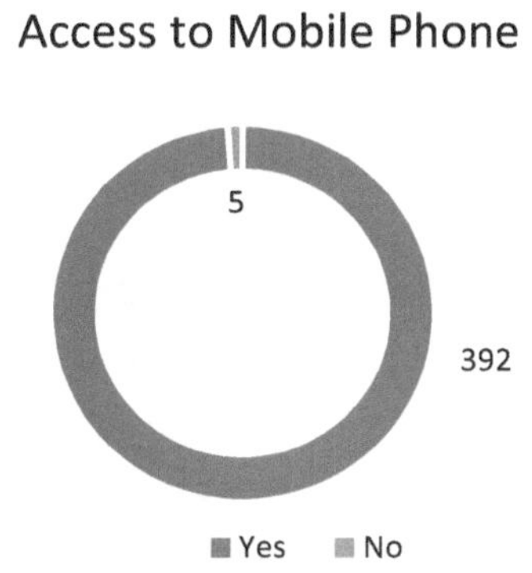

Figure 16.4 Graph of Access to Phone.

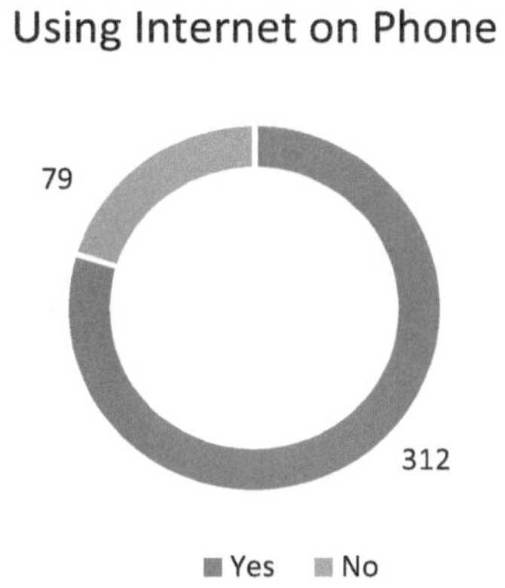

Figure 16.5 Graph of Access to Internet.

A high percentage of respondents also showed willingness to receive and send money via mobile phones. This high level of activity reflects the importance that mobile devices play in improving the lives of people in underserved communities. With limited social infrastructure, mobile devices have become a key tool in connecting previously unconnected communities to formal society. According to the Digital 2021 Report, 97.8% of internet users in Nigeria aged between 16 and 64 years of age use social networking apps, 51.5% use shopping apps, and 47.9% use banking and financial services apps (Kemp, 2021). In addition, the report highlights that of the population aged above 15 years, 5.6% have mobile money accounts and 6.3% make online purchases or pay their bills online. This highlights the potential opportunity for growth in connecting consumers to markets through mobile devices and is reflected in the survey findings (Figure 16.6).

Despite the fact that not a large percentage of the sample population (as is the case with Nigeria's overall population) has mobile money accounts, the survey shows a high interest in receiving remuneration for work done via mobile phones (Figure 16.7 and 16.8).

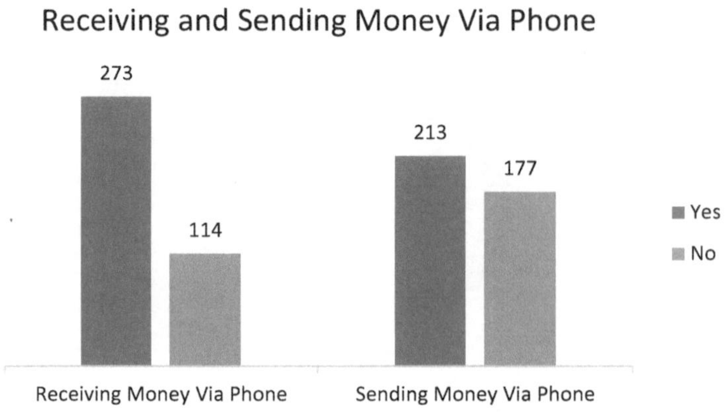

Figure 16.6 Graph of Receiving and Sending Money via Phone.

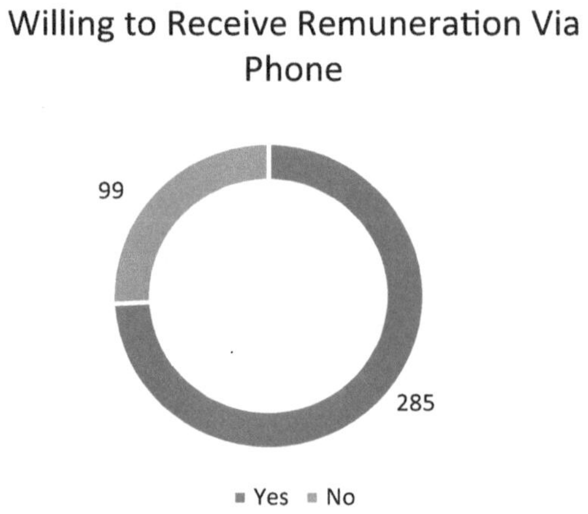

Figure 16.7 Graph of Willing to Receive Remuneration via Phone.

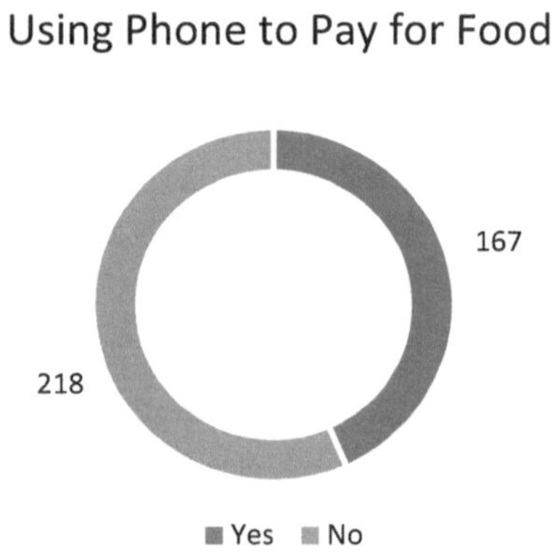

Figure 16.8 Graph of Using Phone for Payments.

Observational Study Findings

An observational study was conducted to test out cashless transactions where participants traded goods and services for other goods and services. The observational study adopted a barter approach, augmented by the use of "time" as an additional measure of the exchange value. Key findings from the observational study include the following:

a **Willingness to receive cashless remuneration** – participants in the study demonstrated a willingness to work without receiving cash as their remuneration. Instead, participants were willing to receive a pre-specified good or service which they needed, and which they would have normally had to use cash to buy.

b **Interchangeability** – throughout the study, participants traded goods and services from different categories. This interchangeability meant that participants could have a higher variety of their needs met.

c **Non-direct or non-connected trade** – participants of the study showed a willingness to work and have their needs met. This finding stayed true even when participants were not going to receive their requested good or service from the particular participant whom they were offering a good or service to, or whose needs they were themselves meeting.

d **Honest declaration of needs** – as expected, participants were honest about their needs.

e **Honest declaration of work** – participants made honest declarations about the work they did. This was the case for all goods or services provided in direct relation to the participant having their need met.

f **Variety of needs** – This observational study showed that participant needs range from tangible to non-material. Participant requests ranged from food and data bandwidth to services like cleaning or non-tangible requests like job fulfilment.

g **Trust as a factor** – trust plays a key role in trade and commerce. This study found that trust plays an even more significant role in cashless trading.

h **Centralization as a requirement for trust in the informal economy** – given the limited nature of services, infrastructure, etc., centralization plays a critical role in ensuring trust as it offers individuals a more tangible point of reference. This study found that participant trust increased with the presence of a central entity coordinating cashless transactions and cashless transfers of value.

i **Multiple approaches to centralization** – this observational study found that centralization can be achieved either through a digital platform or through human coordination. In the observational study, the level of trust did not vary significantly between the use of a rudimentary digital platform and the engagement of a human entity for coordination.

j **Social infrastructure as a key element for cashless transactions** – the lack of electricity in underserved and unserved communities is a significant barrier to radical and disruptive change in these communities.

Observational Study Analysis

The observational study of this research was conducted against the backdrop of social and economic development. This research takes the key position that humanity needs to redefine value in a way that works to improve the lives of people around the world. The research further suggests that in order to improve the lives of individuals/consumers living in low-income settings, novel tools must be applied to enhance the process of interaction.

The observational study findings suggest that the core understanding of value has broadened over time. The findings corroborate the core assumption of this research that "time" plays a key role in defining value. The findings also highlight how a vast number of factors influence how the consumer perceives the value of a commodity at any given time. This is an important point given that far more inputs influence consumer behaviour than were possible when the initial tools to measure value were developed. These findings are in line with the research position which states that the definition and approach to measuring and transferring value must change. In addition to time playing a key role in defining value, utility, which has also historically been referred to as "happiness" or "usefulness", remains a central element in defining the value of a good or service to a consumer. The analysis attempts to shed light on the findings in the context of value theory, to understand how these theories are reflected in the real-world context.

a Willingness to accept non-cash remuneration:
Participants in the study demonstrated a willingness to work without receiving cash as their remuneration. Instead, participants were willing to receive a pre-specified good or service which they needed, and which they would have normally had to use cash to buy. This emerged as a utilitarian approach in the sense that participants were concerned primarily with the good or "utility" they stood to gain. Participants in the study ranked the non-cash remuneration based on their core needs, which was in line with William Stanley Jevons' proposition that utility seeks to satisfy man's basic needs. Consumer willingness to receive non-cash remuneration also delinks the concept of value from the concept of money. In this example, all the goods and/or services requested as forms of remuneration were requested for the value that they possessed in themselves, and not for their ability to attain something else.

b Interchangeability:
Throughout the study, participants traded goods and services from different categories. This interchangeability meant that participants could have a higher variety of their needs met. This aligns with Taussig's theory which emphasized the value of a commodity based on its exchangeability with other commodities (Clark, 1915). For many participants, the ability to store value in a good or service that could later be redeemed for another good or service was critical. In comparing value and measuring up interchangeability, it was not necessary for both goods and services to have the same common attributes, which

goes against the approach suggested by General F.A. Walker (Clark, 1915). According to Irving Fisher, a clearly mathematical calculation would make it possible to measure the utilities offered by commodities to each consumer, and in this instance could have supported calculations on the interchangeability of the commodities in trade. This research, however, chose to calculate value based on time and the associated inputs.

c Non-direct trade:
The willingness of participants to receive non-cash remuneration stayed true even when participants were not going to receive the non-cash-based remuneration immediately or from the consumer to whom they were offering a good or service. This factor on non-direct trade suggests that these consumers' behaviour is aligned with the Carver theory which says that in order to measure the value of two goods, both goods have to have common attributes. In this instance, this means that the consumers believe that there is a common attribute across the goods and services offered, which allows them to compare the value of each. This study used "time" as the underlying common attribute to measure the value of each commodity or service on offer. Carver goes on to note that the goods or services must have a common quality present in definite quantitative degree. This quality is "value", and the exchange ratio will vary with the extent to which the common quality is present in each of the goods (Clark, 1915). This approach further buttresses the proposition that time is the ultimate store of value and is the common quality present in all goods and services.

d Honest declaration of needs:
As expected, participants were honest about their needs. Again, building on the work of William Stanley Jevons, this finding suggests that consumers were looking at utility from the perspective of satisfying their basic needs such as feeding and transportation. It was not possible in this study, however, to ascertain whether participants would have responded differently under alternate conditions.

e Honest declaration of work:
Participants made honest declarations about the work they did. This feature is interesting when you consider the arguments on utility by the early political economists on the subject. Early arguments positioned that "the morally right action is the action that produces good" and that people would naturally tend towards these actions because it was also in their best interest if everyone acted morally right (Driver, 2014). This approach suggests that the individual is doing the "right thing" not just because they have a personal conviction to do so, but also because they believe others to be doing the right thing. John Gay highlights the obligations that motivate consumers to act towards promoting happiness, which could be applied in the case of this study. Following Gay's propositions, participants of the observational study could have felt an

obligation to be honest about the work they did for the following reasons (Driver, 2014):

- Based on what the participant felt would be the natural consequences or outcomes of their actions.
- From civil obligations and laws, that in this case would have included theft or lying about a commitment. While these were not written commitments, the tacit understanding is understood to be binding in informal economy contexts.
- From the need to be "virtuous" and based on the individuals value system.
- From the authority of God and the religious requirements to be honest.

All of these obligations are likely to have played a significant role in influencing the participants' declaration of work. In the context of the fourth industrial revolution, technology allows us to take trust out of the hands of the individual and into the digital realm.

f Variety of needs:
This observational study showed that participant needs ranged from tangible to non-material. Participants listed a wide variety of items to receive as remuneration, ranging from food items and mobile data bandwidth to services like cleaning and teaching for other members of their respective households. Participant requests also included non-material requests like "job fulfilment" and "sense of recognition".

g Trust as a factor:
Trust plays a key role in trade and commerce. This study found that trust plays an even more significant role in cashless trading. As part of the observational study, a "Study Coordinator" was employed to support communication with the participants as well as to serve as a Project Manager and Facilitator. This coordinator was selected as a "trusted individual" from within the community. It is highly likely that this coordinator's presence contributed to the consumers' decision-making process with regard to honest declarations of work.

h Centralization as a requirement for trust in the informal economy:
Given the limited nature of government services in informal economy contexts and the limited social infrastructure such as consistent electricity, centralization plays a critical role in ensuring trust, as it offers individuals a more tangible point of reference in their interactions. This study found that participant trust increased with the presence of a central entity coordinating cashless transactions and cashless transfers of value. This finding suggests that there is a role for a central authority to play in transferring value. Even in relatively decentralized settings, a degree of centralized coordination is important, possibly in the form of nodes in a network.

i Multiple approaches to centralization:
This observational study found that centralization can be achieved either through a digital platform or through human coordination. In the observational study, the level of trust did not vary significantly between the use of a rudimentary digital platform (mobile phone) and the engagement of a Project Manager for coordination.

j Social infrastructure as a key element for cashless transactions:
The lack of electricity in underserved and unserved communities is a significant barrier to radical and disruptive change in these communities as it limits the effectiveness of digital solutions. This study found that offline solutions, or digital solutions that accommodated offline data collection, would play a key role in improving digitalization of the value capture process.

Proof of Concept (Wireframes)

A proof of concept designed as wireframes shows the flow of the proposed currency from the user perspective, from when the user is onboarded onto the digital platform housing the currency, to when the user is able to start using the currency to pay for goods and services. Wireframes are also referred to as screen blueprints or page schematics that attempt to show a realistic user journey through a software or application.

The proof of concept is an initial technical proof that the proposition of this research to have a time-based digital currency deployable on mobile devices is technologically viable using fourth industrial revolution technologies. As described by Mary K. Pratt, a proof of concept is not meant to show the market demand or production process for a product, but rather meant to demonstrate the feasibility of the core idea (Pratt, 2020).

Designing the Proof of Concept

As mentioned earlier, a digital currency backed by time is one of the propositions of this research. Given the evolving nature of social interactions and the increasing reach/influence of non-state actors like the private sector, the proposed currency would be issued and managed by a private entity, with the aim of supporting how humanity measures and captures value. The possibility to combine fourth industrial revolution technologies (which in this case include blockchain, big data and analytics, cloud storage, and advanced algorithms) aligns with the findings of this research that social and economic value has historically been redefined during periods of industrial revolutions.

Designing this proof of concept followed the following process:

a) Understanding the process for value creation in the real-world context – this first step required the concept of value creation to be contextualized in the realities of underserved, low-income, and low-infrastructure communities.

This step included critically thinking through what it means for a consumer and/or producer in various contexts to create value.

b) Defining the parameters for the proposed digital currency as a store of value – the next stage was to define the parameters of a time-based digital currency by answering questions including:

- How would value be measured and how would each unit of currency capture the true value of and productivity in each unit of time?
- How would the currency be introduced into micro and macro economies, and how will this be managed?
- How would this be deployed for use in daily trade? What factors will influence scalability, security, and back-end consensus?

c) Developing use case examples to understand the user experience with the proposed digital currency as a store of value – this step was required to outline various use cases on how the currency could be used.

d) Defining a critical path for the user from value creation to value measurement, storage, and transfer – defining a critical path was important to understand the flow of activities and expectations from production through to trade and subsequently to consumption. The critical path was also important in highlighting the expected interaction of the currency with the various factors of production.

e) Identifying the essential technologies needed to realize each stage of the critical path – once the initial parameters of the currency had been outlined, it became necessary to identify the most effective and efficient technologies to satisfy each parameter and enable each function of the currency.

f) Introducing the digital currency design to the case studies and stress testing these case studies to understand how well the digital currency applies – the next stage was to take the essential elements of the newly designed currency and to introduce these elements into the various use cases to see how well these elements would hold against the requirements in each use case.

g) Refining the currency design and back-end technology to ensure the appropriate fit for each stage of the use experience.

h) Developing wireframes to show the clear journey from user onboarding to currency use in real-world examples – the wireframes developed as the proof of concept show what the journey of a user would be from the moment they register on the platform (using the example of a mobile application). This journey allows users to be both producers and consumers, based on the understanding that each individual can use their skills to produce services that are of utility to others in society.

Figures 16.9–16.11 highlight various stages in the design of the user journey. These stages were critical to understanding how users in low-resource settings would interact in an economic exchange. These stages also ensured that the final design could be simple and easy to use, while leveraging mobile devices/mobile phone technology as a platform. It is important to remember that mobile phones

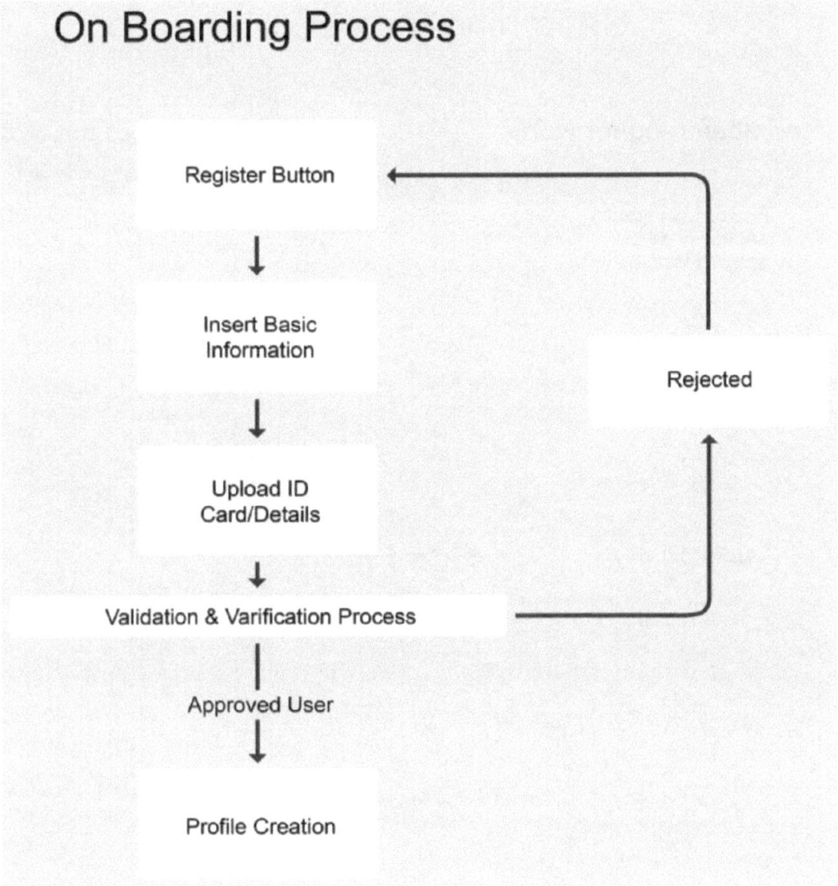

Figure 16.9 Digital onboarding.

and mobile technology were identified through the data collection process as key levers for non-cash-based trade.

Once the various stages of the user journey had been identified, and the process for generating each unit of currency had been mapped out, it was important to design a full user journey workflow. The user journeys derived from this process are indications that consumers with access to a mobile device and relevant software are able to generate, store, and transfer an alternative store of value – time-based digital currency – in their day-to-day activities.

The proof of concept should not be taken as the final example/design of what a mobile or web application could look like, but, rather, pieces in a larger puzzle that paint a picture of how consumers interact with an alternative store of value: a digital currency that is generated at the point of value creation.

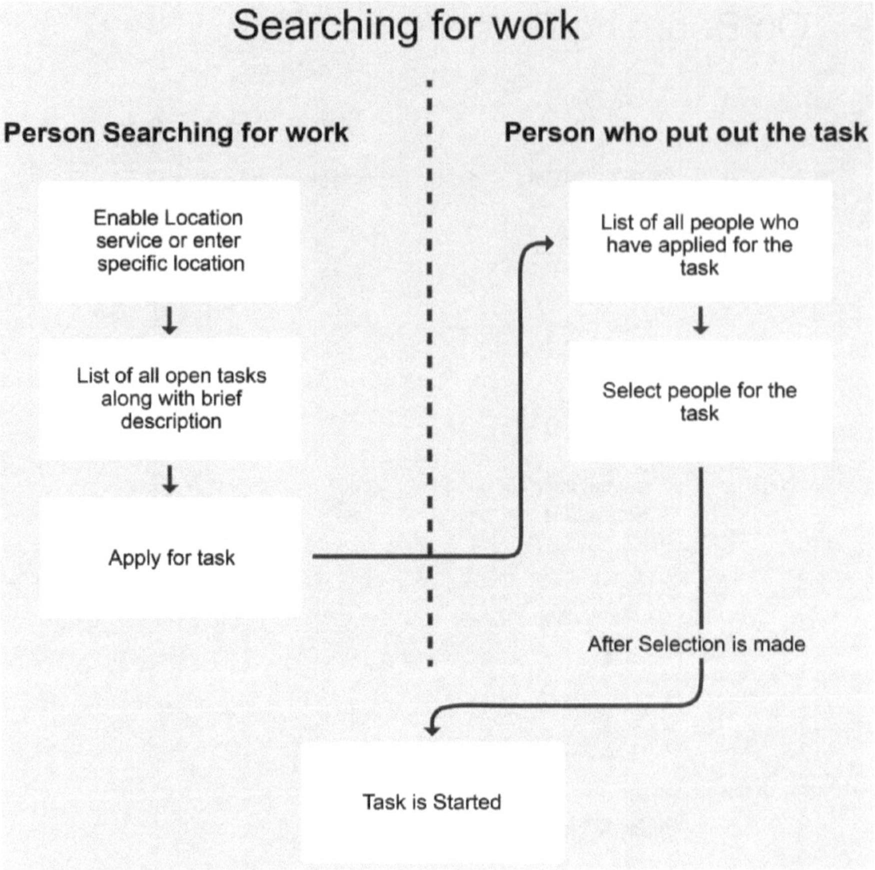

Figure 16.10 User journey using digital platform to search for work which is paid for using the proposed currency.

Analysis of the Proof of Concept

The proof of concept, as the name implies, sought to establish the technological viability of the proposed time-based digital currency. This also sought to highlight the user experience with the technology in a real-world context.

This research started out by exploring the origin of the state before moving on to the other concepts of value, time, and the digital economy. The research found that examples exist where states (represented by governments) are unable to meet their obligations as stated in the social contract. Because of these unmet obligations, citizens are left without social infrastructure, access to resources, or security. This form of existence for the citizen is akin to the state of nature where according to Hobbes there is insecurity and harm, and according to Locke and Rousseau there is no safeguard of (or even access to) property. Given the reach of businesses

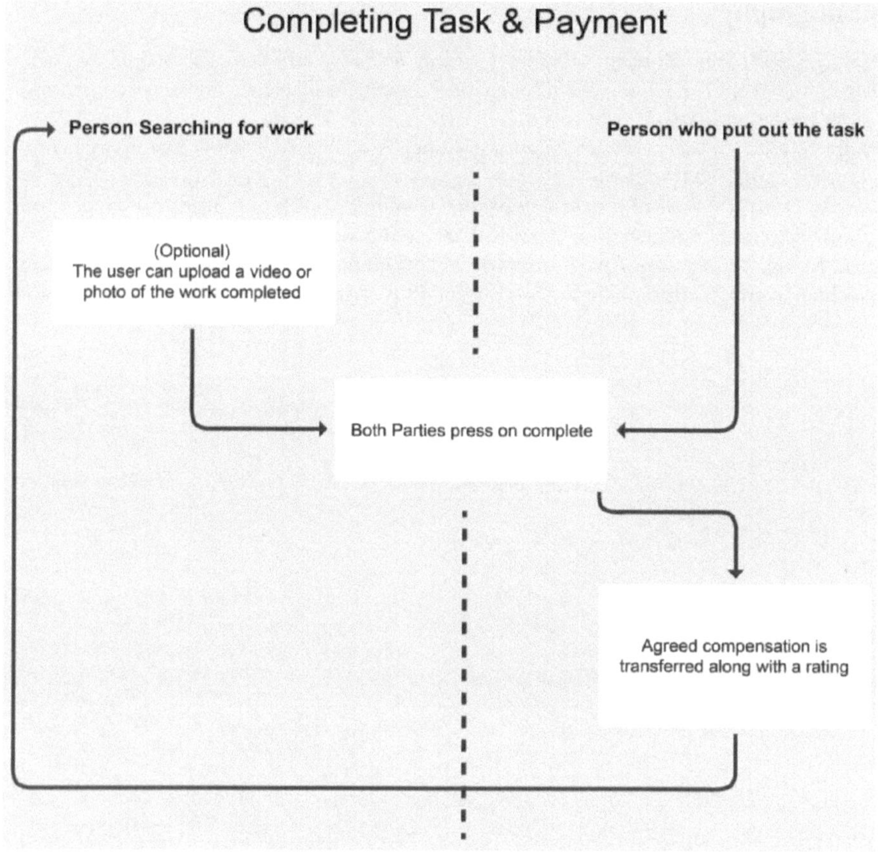

Figure 16.11 User journey showing task completion and payment process using the proposed currency.

and their ability to meet consumers in the most remote settings, the research proposes a role for the private sector in bringing individuals out of the state of nature. This role is proposed in how value is measured, captured, stored, and transferred, with digital currencies emerging as the ideal solution for this.

The proof of concept shows that this is technologically possible and that a business can develop a mobile application that is easy to deploy and use, and that from a technological perspective will support financial inclusion for the marginalized communities that it targets. Countless examples already exist of business-run mobile applications reaching remote communities. This research emphasizes the need to channel these mechanisms towards financial inclusion and ultimately social development. Furthermore, this proof of concept is just one of various models through which a time-based digital currency (or digital token in this example) could be delivered through a mobile device.

Bibliography

Clark, J. (1915). The Concept of Value. *Quarterly Journal of Economics*, 29, 663–673.

Driver, J. (2014). *The History of Utilitarianism.* [Online] Available at: https://plato.stanford.edu/entries/utilitarianism-history/

Kemp, S. (2021). *Digital 2021: Nigeria.* [Online] Available at: https://datareportal.com/reports/digital-2021-nigeria

Oyelola, F. (2021). *Mobile Penetration in Nigeria.* [Online] Available at: https://www.geopoll.com/blog/mobile-penetration-nigeria/ [Accessed 5 August 2021].

Pratt, M. K. (2020). *Proof of Concept (POC).* [Online] Available at: https://searchcio.techtarget.com/definition/proof-of-concept-POC [Accessed 2 August 2021].

Part VI

Industry and Innovation

17 (Industrial) Revolution = Opportunity (for Humanity)

The previous chapters have examined the political state and economic value. Furthermore, these chapters have attempted to situate the concept of economic value within the context of civil society, and the fundamental need for citizens to collectively manage scarce resources. Building on these notions, the following chapter examines the various perspectives on value and productivity during the major periods of social and economic acceleration in human history: the industrial revolutions. The industrial revolutions were periods in history characterized by exponential advancements in technology. These advancements in technology happened at a pace and scale that disrupted human activity and understandings of productivity in society. These historical periods brought about changes in the tools and processes used to create and capture value whether at the state, organizational, community, or individual level (Vries, 1994). David Landes, in his book *The Unbound Prometheus*, provides a few perspectives on how to approach defining the term "industrial revolution". According to him, the term "industrial revolution" referred to the technologies that made it possible to substitute human labour for machine work. The term also referred to any instances where there were rapid and exponential improvements to technology. Finally, Landes highlights a third perspective on the term "Industrial Revolution",[1] which refers to that very first instance where humanity moved away from the labour-intensive agrarian society to a society supported by machine-enabled productivity (Landes, 1969).

The Pre-Industrial World

Before going further into the industrial revolutions whether as periods in history, or as events in history, it is important to understand the political and economic contexts of the world before this time. Prior to the first industrial revolution, the limited population of the world approached economic productivity from labour-intensive and craft-based perspectives, and even while there was economic growth and wealth creation, all of this would seem limited when compared against even limited industrial (machine enabled) economic activity. Peter N. Stearns, in the book *Debating the Industrial Revolution*, notes that the switch from an agrarian society to an industrial one was so significant in that it could only possibly be compared to the switch from hunter-gathering to agriculture (Stearns, 2015).

DOI: 10.4324/9781003330417-23

Productivity being based on human and animal strength (and therefore availability) meant that the world could only take a limited approach to production, in terms of scope, capacity, and diversity. In the pre-industrial world, production was centred around family units, with parents and children working side by side to produce the goods and services which they consumed and ultimately sold. This had a direct impact on roles and responsibilities within the family, as well as on the nature of the family structure itself, with larger families standing a greater chance at success due to the more hands they could dedicate towards productivity.

The First Industrial Revolution and Economic Value

It was during the first industrial revolution that social and economic structures really experienced their initially significant changes. The first industrial revolution, which is widely agreed to have begun in Britain with the introduction of the steam engine in the 1770s or 1780s (Stearns, 2015), saw a period of mechanization established as the foundation of economic development. During this period, the development of technology as one of the primary drivers of economic activity would impact every aspect of human life and interaction. It is noteworthy that some of the fundamental technological advancements that contributed to the success and longevity of the industrial revolution had already started to take place many years prior, such as the invention of the "flying shuttle" in the 1730s (Stearns, 2015). Some of the landmark changes that occurred during this period of the industrial revolution include:

1 The use of new materials like iron and steel in the production process.
2 The introduction of new sources of energy to power the economic process. This included coal and the steam engine.
3 New machines were invented to replace human labour, especially in the textile industry for example which saw major changes.
4 The introduction of non-human-powered machines led to the creation of factories, but also opened new possibilities for transportation, communication, and science.

While many historians highlight Britain as the birthplace of the industrial revolution; there is a school of thought that argues otherwise. Gregory Clark, among others, is part of this school of thought. He suggests that several more significant technological advancements had taken place in other parts of the world prior to the period of industrialization in Britain. His paper "The Secret History of the Industrial Revolutions" presents ten key points on why this period in England was not more special than any other period. Among these points, Clark highlights some of the following as justifications (Clark, 2001): First, that per capita output was slower during the industrial revolution and England was considered wealthier in the pre-industrial days than during industrialization. William J. Ashworth also agrees with Clarke that England was wealthier pre-industrialization (Ashworth, 2017). Clarke goes on to suggest that growth during the industrial revolution centred around the textile industry alone, and this growth was also not widespread across Britain as well as that labour wages fell, and labour conditions deteriorated in the industrial revolution compared to pre-industrial conditions. Clarke also points out that other parts of Europe saw similar periods of increased productivity similar to what Britain experienced between 1760 and 1860. Despite the arguments on the exact birthplace of the industrial revolution, the focus here is on the technological advancements and the associated socio-economic changes that these advancements inspired.

Concerning value theory during the first industrial revolution, the focus on new production methods and new approaches to manufacturing suggests that economic value was defined by the factors of production. This assessment of economic value theory in the context of the first industrial revolution is aligned with the objective classical theory of value which focuses on the same: i.e., production. Stearns highlights this focus on production in his description of the working conditions around factories, including the focus on minimizing costs, maximizing labour outputs as well as the labour conditions that factory workers faced (Stearns, 2018). Contextualizing this economic value requires an understanding of the political context surrounding the industrial revolutions. According to William J. Ashworth Britain would not have been able to industrialize at the time and in the manner that it did without state intervention in the form of protectionist policies, labour exploitation, and colonization, among other factors (Ashworth, 2017). Here, we see the roles that both the public and private sectors had to play in the value creation process: with the public sector driving policy and the private sector managing the factors of production.

The Second Industrial Revolution and Economic Value

With the start of the industrial revolution, the world had been propelled into a new phase of its growth. This phase would be characterized by new ways of working and interacting, and new ways of managing scarce resources within the context of the state or civilized society. Building on the foundations established during the first wave of industrialization, the second industrial revolution between the years 1870 and 1914 was greatly influenced by the application of electric power in the mass production process. According to Stearns in the book *The Industrial Revolution in World History*, in addition to the technological advancements that would be built on, three important factors characterized the second phase of the industrial revolution which were "industrialisation outside the west, redefinition of the West's industrial economy and growing involvement of non-industrial parts of the world" (Stearns, 2018).

The subjective approach to value theory, led by proponents like William Stanley Jevons, Leon Walras, and Carl Menger, started to emerge at around the same time as the second industrial revolution after 1870. The subjective approach to value theory focused on elements like marginal utility, marginal productivity, and product distribution. This suggests links between perceptions of value and the advancements in mass production that were starting to take place at the time, facilitated by advancements in energy and machine manufacturing.

The Third Industrial Revolution and Economic Value

As in the case of the previous two phases of the industrial revolution, the third phase builds on the technologies, systems, and processes established earlier. Like in the case of the first industrial revolution, there were social, political, and economic factors that necessitated the shift away from the status quo and facilitated the adoption of the new way of doing things. Jeremy Rifkin sets the scene for these factors in *The Third Industrial Revolution: How the Internet, Green Electricity, and 3-D Printing Are Ushering in a Sustainable Era of Distributed Capitalism*. According to Rifkin, the overdependence on fossil fuels as the driving force for production, rising unemployment, rising debt, and overall economic downturn had forced the world to reconsider its approach to growth and productivity (Rifkin, 2012).

The third industrial revolution, often referred to as the "Digital Revolution", saw a shift from mechanical processes and tools to digital alternatives, as well as unprecedented changes in production relationships due to newly available computing power. In particular, the internet as a central element in the productive process highlights the fundamental shift between phases of the industrial revolution. According to Brian H. Roberts, the foundation of the internet was built in 1969 in the form of the Advanced Research Projects Agency Network (ARPANET). This system would go on to be the first network to use protocol suite TCP/IP and would ultimately lead to the development of the internet (Roberts, 2015). In addition to the benefits of the internet, the third industrial revolution or third phase of the global industrial revolution would see a rise in electronics, communication, and computing power, all of which build on factors from earlier phases like electricity and manufacturing capacity. According to Rifkin, the third industrial revolution must be built on five pillars (Rifkin, 2012):

1. Adoption of renewable energy sources
2. Integration of renewable energy in infrastructure and networked capabilities
3. Advancements in renewable energy storage technologies
4. Internet-enabled energy management systems
5. Renewable energy–enhanced transport systems

In the case of the third industrial revolution, the decline in economic activity, increase in competition, and rise in consumerism enhanced the subjective approach to value theory because it aligned with an increase in utility. By the third industrial revolution, the world was thinking critically about how to meet consumer needs amidst increasingly scarce resources like fossil fuels. At the same time, the increasing focus on the factors of production as part of a drive to improve the conditions of production also enhanced the objective approach to value theory. The third industrial revolution could therefore be said to have been a period of complementarity between both schools of thought.

During each stage of these revolutions, modern societies were able to advance themselves by taking advantage of the available technologies in the resource management and value creation processes. At the same time, human living conditions have greatly improved with an ability to meet more needs and solve/prevent more problems.

The Fourth Industrial Revolution and Economic Value

The current industrial revolution (the fourth industrial revolution) is unique because it is the harmonious integration of exponential technologies. These technologies include automated devices, additive manufacturing or 3D printing, nanotechnology, biotechnology, materials science, energy storage, and quantum computing (Schwab, 2016). On their own, these technologies are on exponential growth curves, while together they present an opportunity for integrated approaches to social and economic development. Beyond just development, the combination and application of fourth industrial revolution technologies has the potential to fundamentally enhance our existence from a centrally "human experience" to a holistic **vivos experientia** or "life experience" that recognizes humanity as part of a larger fabric of living beings, including the earth and all living organisms both on and potentially off the planet, that must co-exist responsibly.

Klaus Schwab highlights the technological drivers of the fourth industrial revolution under three broad categories: physical, digital, and biological (Schwab, 2016). The World Economic Forum report titled "Technological Tipping Points" highlights six "megatrends" that will shape the fourth industrial revolution (Espinel, 2015). By 2022, these megatrends have already started to shape a new wave of solutions and business models:

1. **People and the internet** – highlighting the increased role that the internet will play in human interaction.
2. **Computing, communications, and storage everywhere** – the democratization of computing power will make greater computing power available to more people.
3. **The Internet of Things** – more and more objects connected to the internet and interacting with each other.
4. **Artificial intelligence (AI) and big data** – data-driven decision-making more than ever.
5. **The sharing economy and distributed trust** – a shift from conventional perspectives on ownership and utility.
6. **The digitization of matter** – the manufacturing process transformed by 3D printing/additive manufacturing.

The report highlights how these technologies, while unique individually, are more interesting when taken from a holistic perspective on their potential impact on society. Both Schwab (2016) and Espinel (2015) agree that the point where these technologies enter the mainstream will be a critical moment that alters the human experience, potentially even more than in previous industrial revolutions.

Note

1 David Landes suggests that the definition of the term changes slightly between when the words are capitalised and not, i.e. "industrial revolution" versus "Industrial Revolution".

Bibliography

Ashworth, W. J. (2017). *The Industrial Revolution : The State, Knowledge and Global Trade.* London: Bloomsbury Academic.

Clark, G. (2001). *The Secret History of the Industrial Revolution.* [Online] Available at: http://faculty.econ.ucdavis.edu/faculty/gclark/papers/secret2001.pdf [Accessed 13 June 2021].

Espinel, V. (2015). *Technological Tipping Points.* Geneva: World Economic Forum.

Landes, D. S. (1969). *The Unbound Prometheus.* Cambridge: Cambridge University Press.

Rifkin, J. (2012). *The Third Industrial Revolution: How the Internet, Green Electricity, and 3-D Printing are Ushering in a Sustainable Era of Distributed Capitalism.* [Online] Available at: https://www.siaf.ch/files/130410-rifkin-1.pdf [Accessed 14 June 2021].

Roberts, B. H. (2015). *The Third Industrial Revolution: Implications for Planning Cities and Regions.* [Online] Available at: https://www.researchgate.net/publication/278671121_The_Third_Industrial_Revolution_Implications_for_Planning_Cities_and_Regions [Accessed 14 June 2021].

Schwab, K. (2016). *The Fourth Industrial Revolution; What it Means and How to Respond.* Geneva: World Economic Forum.

Stearns, P. N. (2015). *Debating the Industrial Revolution.* London: Bloomsbury Academic (Debates in World History).

Stearns, P. N. (2018). *The Industrial Revolution in World History.* 4th ed. New York: Routledge.

Vries, J. D. (1994). The Industrial Revolution and the Industrious Revolution. *Journal of Economic History, 54*(2), 249–270.

18 Innovation

The Holy Grail of Private Sector Competition

Innovation and the private sector have been synonymous for a while, but should they be? Or are they two distinct concepts with specific areas that link the two concepts? Exploring this question is important if we will remodel the structure of our societies to better reflect the new relationships and responsibilities of non-state actors. This is all the more important if some of these responsibilities will be predicated by our ability to innovate. Previous chapters explored the evolving social relationships and lines of interaction in contemporary society. These chapters also highlighted the evolving nature of value, as well as how this concept has evolved through the various periods of the industrial revolution. One finding that stays consistent through all of those discussions is the role that non-state actors have historically played in driving value. Let us now explore in some detail the role that the private sector plays in driving innovation for social development. Here, we will look at innovation both as a process and as a product/outcome.

An important assumption behind this need to understand the private sector is the understanding that in many states (countries), the private sector has more influence on the citizen than the government. The governments in these states may face certain challenges that limit their abilities to meet the needs of their citizens, as defined by the conventional social contract. Instead, these private businesses, with their extensive market access and brand loyalty, are able to reach citizens with products and services. This assumption suggests that the private sector's influence in a new social contract should be recognized (or at least space created to debate what this role should look like). This is particularly important because if a government wants to cater to the needs of its population without having to take on greater risks than each individual would be comfortable taking on their own, then the state in question would need to engage the private sector in a new social contract. This allows the state and government to benefit from a dedicated and skilled vehicle in designing and integrating innovations that ultimately improve the lives of citizens worldwide. This approach also means that the associated costs of developing and integrating innovations do not rest with any one institution or entity.

So what is the private sector? A definition of the private sector is that "organisation or enterprising entity engaged in commercial, industrial or professional activities, towards the production of a good, offering of a service or retailing of an

DOI: 10.4324/9781003330417-24

already manufactured good for profit" (Investopedia, n.d.). In addition to this, the private sector is every and any "part of the economy that encompasses all for-profit business that is not owned by the state" (Investopedia, n.d.). Note, however, that this definition of the private sector might evolve slightly depending on where you are in the world and how much the Royals in your location have invested in the country's businesses. The private sector is private-owned and private-run businesses, which are meant to satisfy private interests. Despite being led by private interests, businesses continue to operate within the political, economic, and social boundaries of the state. This is the case either with regard to the location of the founder (or management/headquarters), or with regard to the location of its business activities/customers. Whatever the case, it holds that in order for private businesses to create value, they must use natural resources owned/located within any given state. As resources are generally scarce from an economic perspective, it makes sense that both the public and private sectors have to compete for access to these resources, whether directly or indirectly. This competition, which is fuelled on by private interests and varying risk dispositions, ultimately leads to the public and private sectors developing capabilities and capacities at different speeds. Despite being driven by private interests, businesses are still bound (to a large extent) by the regulations of the state and must still exist in the context of the state. This competition is an important factor in any society because it creates options for citizens in terms of products and services. At the same time, the private sector is often the largest employer of labour, when you consider everything from small corner stores to large multinationals.

Now equipped with this understanding of the private sector, and some of the questions that warrant its exploration, let us further explore this entity within the context of the state. It was important to start the broad discussion of this book with a review of the state because association is the first experience for humans. At birth, the individual starts to associate with a family, which in turn must associate with other families to form a community. This was highlighted by Johannes Althusius, who noted that the interaction within families is the first stage of interaction in the state structure (Althusius, 1614). It was also important to start by looking at the origin of the state because it is in this context that contemporary human interactions are still largely defined, in relation to resource management. Once the origin of the state and conditions for the emergence of civilized society had been outlined, the logical next step was to take a critical look at a core concept behind resource management: the theory of value. The theory of value is identified here as a core concept in resource management because "resource management" and "resource use" are driven by utility which in turn determines value to an individual. In other words, a natural resource, for example wood, will be harnessed from a forest, because it is useful to an individual who needs to build a house. According to this example, wood is valuable to the individual. Consider this example in the context of a community that is made up of many more individuals looking to get wood from the same forest to build their individual houses. This creates a situation of high demand and low supply and drives up the relative value of wood. This principle of demand and supply is an important foundational principle in economics but is not the subject of this discussion. This example highlights interactions between individuals in relation to a resource. Now imagine the example of these individuals all needing wood and imagine that these individuals lived in a sort of free community without a leader or government. According to Hobbes, individuals would be at liberty to fight each other for the wood, while according to Locke and Rousseau, even though the individuals did not resort to violence to settle their disputes on access to the resource, they would still need some form of protection of property. This example highlights the fundamental connection that politics and economics have at their core and that is why the underlying research for this book has taken this approach to understanding and building on both concepts.

The next component of this chapter that deserves some attention is the topic on innovation. Defining this buzzword is important for many reasons, including the fact that your chosen definition impacts potential outcomes. According to Yale Information Technology Services, innovation is "the process of implementing new ideas to create value for an organisation" (Yale ITS, n.d.). Another definition of innovation refers to it as "the creation of value from ideas" (Rahim, 2017) and "the process of translating an idea or invention into a good or service that creates value or for which customers will pay". The nuances in defining the subject continue. According to Victor A. Thompson in the 1965 article "Bureaucracy and Innovation", innovation is "the generation, acceptance and implementation of new ideas, processes products or services" (Thompson, 1965). Anahita Baregheh, Jennifer Rowley, and Sally Sambrook also offer a definition of innovation that is worth considering, which is that innovation is "the multi-stage process whereby organizations transform ideas into new/improved products, service or processes, in order to advance, compete and differentiate themselves successfully in their marketplace" (Baregheh et al., 2009). According to the *Webster Dictionary*, innovation is "a new idea, method, or device" (Merriam-Webster, n.d.). If these definitions are not enough, here are a few more definitions, compiled by Nick Skillicorn in the article "What Is innovation?" (Skillicorn, 2016):

- Nick Skillicorn – "Innovation is turning an idea into a solution that adds value from a customer's perspective".
- David Burkus – "The application of ideas that are novel and useful. Creativity, the ability to generate novel and useful ideas, is the seed of innovation but unless it's applied and scaled it's still just an idea".
- Robert Brands – "Innovation needs to be defined and agreed upon in each organization, making sure it is strategically and everybody is aligned. Without it, misalignment results in less than optimal focus and results. As long as it includes "new" and it addresses customer needs and wants, any variation goes".
- Stefan Lindegaard – "I try not to define "innovation" as we should tone down our use of the word and term".
- Jorge Barba – "something new or different that delivers value to the world, with the key criteria that I'm not innovating if I'm not bettering people's lives. Put simply, it is the future delivered".

- Rita McGrath – "a new product, of course, which is what people usually think of. But it can also be a new process, a new combination, a new workflow – really across the board changing the existing order of things, but in such a way that new value is created".

Despite having multiple definitions, three important themes emerge as common features to define innovation: creativity as a process, the application of creativity as an action, and value creation. These themes highlight that innovations as ideas need to be different from what exists and need to create value in relation to organizations providing goods and services for consumption. The industrial revolutions were historic periods of innovation that altered how humanity approached value creation, value capture, and value transfer. An important feature in each stage of the industrial revolution was the role that businesses played in the industrialization process; from the creation of the steam engine to advancements in digital technology, businesses led the process of value creation. This value was captured and turned into new goods and services for the consumer, such as the automobile and personal computer. These new products and services were furthermore turned into packages and services, signalling a further shift from away from just products to the more holistic satisfaction of needs. Each stage of the industrial revolution saw advancements in technology, and this has no doubt continued into the fourth industrial revolution (McGinnis, 2020). The fourth industrial revolution is a unique combination of these innovative technologies that have the capability to interact with each other to create hybrid systems and solutions (Lavopa & Delera, 2021).

Keeping in mind the definitions of "private sector" and "innovation", the next question is, "has the private sector driven innovation in society? If yes, how has this worked?" Businesses operating within the context of scarce resources have had to seek maximum efficiencies in order to compete effectively. This has meant minimizing inputs, maximizing outputs, increasing profits, and at the same time maintaining or increasing quality where possible. This competition and need for efficiency has driven the private sector to innovate in their search for value. In seeking greater efficiencies, businesses are ultimately creating a social good because they are developing solutions in their respective industries that are creative, more resource-efficient, and more valuable for the consumer. Consider the example of the automobile. As more companies strive to make cars, they compete against each other to produce the most energy-efficient, comfortable, safe, and reliable cars possible that meet consumer demands at a given time. This process means that each automobile company will reasonably invest in creating the best possible products. In this same train of thought, one could conclude that business innovation, which is driven by private interests, ultimately drives sustainable development by creating efficiencies in resources management, creating tools for improved social and economic interaction as well as improving humanity's understanding of the world and environment.

With the understanding that value has historically been approached in the context of the political state or civil society, the discussions until now went on to present a brief case for innovation and how this is driven by the private sector.

Competition among businesses has historically forced them to seek efficiencies in the production process. This drive for efficiency means that businesses look for ways to create more outputs (products and services) with less inputs (natural resources). This process of seeking greater efficiency is what results in innovation and is one important way that the private sector creates socio-economic value. The value here is not the innovation in itself (which is an extrinsic good), but rather the value is in what the innovation helps humanity to achieve. Here, improving humanity is the intrinsic good. Take the example of the community of individuals looking to build houses with wood from a limited forest. Introducing private sector innovation to this equation could, for example, see local businesses use a fraction of the natural wood used in constructing the house, to make an artificial wood that could easily be multiplied. Private sector innovation in this example could also come in the form of building that requires less material.

As humanity has expanded, the approach to private interests being engaged in resource management within the state has evolved, and, as expected, different types of states have taken different positions on the extent of freedom of private interests. Monarchies, for example, where the Sovereign is absolute, preferred to limit private interests, especially since all resources in the territory belonged to the Sovereign. Throughout history, economic value was defined in relation to this relationship (individual and state) in the context of scare resources. At the same time, the private sector was nothing more than family-based production which was often agriculture-oriented or focused on artisanal crafts. While there were businesses that existed prior to the first industrial revolution, such as traders and ship farers, it was during the first industrial revolution that the private sector truly started to emerge as a full-fledged, independent, non-state entity. The opportunities created by mechanization and the use of new materials in the production process would change production methods. The creation of factories would also change the relationship between the worker and the resources they interacted with, as well as with the owners of the factors of production. With the turn of the industrial revolution, value was largely objective in approach. This is because at the time, value theory could only have focused on the factors and conditions of production, since after all that was the major and most significant shift which the world had experienced until then. In the second and third industrial revolutions, the subjective approach to value theory began to emerge. Advancements in technology, production methods, and consumers' demand had started to bring about a focus on the consumers" needs and were re-emphasizing the role of utility in defining what was valuable to the consumer. By the fourth industrial revolution – which is currently ongoing – it is possible to argue that value theory is in its most hybrid form yet. Human interaction is no longer defined solely in the context of the state, but also in the context of the environment, and in the context of consumerism spurred by private interest (private sector). At the same time, technology is supercharging the human experience to the point where interaction is happening on more levels than previously possible.

Given that the concepts of the political state and economic value have evolved through history to reflect the current realities of the time, the approach to measuring and capturing economic value should also change. Importantly, technologies of the fourth revolution make it possible to measure economic value in the most truly holistic and inclusive ways yet. Furthermore, private sector innovation and efficiencies are making it easier for humanity to improve living conditions for the marginalized.

If we agree that:

- The social contract should evolve because states no longer hold the monopoly on bringing individuals out of the state of nature;
- The private sector and other non-state actors have influence and the capabilities to bring people out of the state of nature;
- The private sector drives innovation in search of efficiencies, value creation and amidst scarce resources;
- PPPs allow governments to leverage private sector expertise and resources to access and deploy innovations,

then in principle, we should also agree that the private sector can be enlisted as a new party to the social contract to formally handle public administration, which would include bringing people out of the state of nature.

If social interaction is evolving and social contract has evolved, should the private sector be allowed to manage public administration? If the world is tending towards decentralization, should the private sector serve as complimentary nodes that bring people out of the state of nature and into society through a new digital social contract?

Bibliography

Adhikari, S. (2018). *18 Challenges of MDG and 16 Positive Scopes of SDG*. [Online] Available at: https://www.publichealthnotes.com/18-challenges-mdg-16-positive-scopes-sdg/ [Accessed 6 July 2021].

AFDB. (n.d.) *Millennium Development Goals (MDGs)*. [Online] Available at: https://www.afdb.org/en/topics-and-sectors/topics/millennium-development-goals-mdgs [Accessed 5 August 2021].

Althusius, J. (1614). *Politica*. 1995 ed. Indianapolis: Liberty Fund.

Baregheh, A., Rowley, J., & Sambrook, S. (2009). Towards a Multidisciplinary Definition of Innovation. *Management Decision 47*(8), 1323–1339.

David, W. P., Edward, B., & Markandya, A. (1990). *Sustainable Development: Economics and Environment in the Third World*. London: Edward Elgar Publishing Limited.

Delmon, J. (n.d.) *4 Steps to Improving Public-Private Partnerships*. [Online] Available at: https://www.weforum.org/agenda/2015/06/4-steps-to-improving-public-private-partnerships/ [Accessed 3 May 2018].

Gavi the Vaccine Alliance. (2016). *Rwanda Launches World's First National Drone Delivery Service Powered by Zipline*. [Online] Available at: https://www.gavi.org/library/news/gavi-features/2016/rwanda-launches-world-s-first-national-drone-delivery-service-powered-by-zipline/ [Accessed 3 May 2018].

Investopedia. (2021). *Public-Private Partnerships*. [Online] Available at: https://www.investopedia.com/terms/p/public-private-partnerships.asp [Accessed 2 July 2021].

Investopedia. (n.d.-a) *Business*. [Online] Available at: https://www.investopedia.com/terms/b/business.asp [Accessed 15 April 2018].

Investopedia. (n.d.-b) *Private Sector.* [Online] Available at: https://www.investopedia.com/terms/p/private-sector.asp [Accessed 15 April 2018].

Lavopa, A. & Delera, M. (2021). *What is the Fourth Industrial Revolution?.* [Online] Available at: https://iap.unido.org/articles/what-fourth-industrial-revolution [Accessed 2 July 2021].

McGinnis, D. (2020). *What Is the Fourth Industrial Revolution?.* [Online] Available at: https://www.salesforce.com/blog/what-is-the-fourth-industrial-revolution-4ir/ [Accessed 5 August 2021].

Merriam-Webster. (n.d.) *Innovation.* [Online] Available at: https://www.merriam-webster.com/dictionary/innovation [Accessed 5 August 2021].

Rahim, H. (2017). *What is Innovation and how can Businesses Foster it?.* [Online] Available at: https://www.telegraph.co.uk/connect/better-business/innovation/what-is-innovation-and-how-can-businesses-foster-it/ [Accessed 25 April 2018].

Skillicorn, N. (2016). *What is Innovation? 26 Experts Share Their Innovation Definition.* [Online] Available at: https://www.ideatovalue.com/inno/nickskillicorn/2016/03/innovation-15-experts-share-innovation-definition/ [Accessed 17 January 2021].

Thompson, V. A. (1965). Bureaucracy and Innovation. *Science Quarterly, 10*(1), 1–20.

UNDP & WBG. (2015). *Transitioning from the MDGs to the SDGs.* s. l.: UNDP & WBG.

UNESCO Institute of Statistics. (2021). *Out of School Children and Youth.* [Online] Available at: http://uis.unesco.org/en/topic/out-school-children-and-youth#slideoutmenu

United Nations. (2015a). *The Millennium Development Goals Report 2015.* s.l.: United Nations.

United Nations. (2015b). *Transforming Our World; the 2030 Agenda for Sustainable Development.* New York: United Nations.

WHO. (2018). *Millennium Development Goals (MDGs).* [Online] Available at: https://www.who.int/news-room/fact-sheets/detail/millennium-development-goals-(mdgs) [Accessed 5 August 2021].

World Bank Group. (2018). *What are Public-Private Partnerships.* [Online] Available at: http://ppp.worldbank.org/public-private-partnership/overview/what-are-public-private-partnerships [Accessed 3 May 2018].

World Bank. (n.d.) *The 8 Millenium Development Goals.* [Online] Available at: https://www5.worldbank.org/mdgs/ [Accessed 20 July 2021].

Yale ITS. (n.d.) *What is Innovation.* [Online] Available at: https://its.yale.edu/about/innovation-its/what-innovation [Accessed 20 April 2018].

Part VII

What Future?

19 New Networks and Applications

Web 3.0?

Blockchain has been identified as a technology that will revolutionize the finance industry, if applied properly, with the right design and consumer protections in place. Beyond its applications in finance, blockchain is also allowing us to rethink the very structure of the internet. This chapter will explore one of the key propositions for the new version of the internet, including what it has evolved from, what it is built on, and what opportunities this new version presents for *vivos experientia*.

Consider the status of the world from where you currently exist. Across regions, industries, and ideologies, there is a consensus that this is a period of change. This change is captured in terms like the Fourth Industrial Revolution which looks at technology change; the great resignation and future of work (Chugh, 2021), which look at the seismic upheavals in the way that we approach work and productivity; the push for decentralization and greater citizen autonomy; and the push for a new type of internet, among others. The momentum behind these movements reflects the appetite for change in the way that our societies are structured, as well as the *need* for change to keep up with the evolving nature of social and economic interactions. This momentum is likely to grow as we get a better grip on the exponential technologies available today, and as our knowledge of these tools enables our creativity.

One group of technologies that are at the heart of this, of course, is the internet (network) and the web (pages and platforms on the internet). Most people would agree that compared to humans even just a 100 years ago, our applications of technology give us near-superhuman capabilities, like controlling objects with gestures, predicting the weather, and preventing/curing/treating some of the vilest diseases. Most people would also agree that at the current pace of change, it is difficult to predict exactly what the future might look like, although it is a fun exercise to try. Considering this, we can, with a degree of confidence say that we do not really know what the world would look like in 50 years or say that we know what the internet would look like even in 25 years. What we can also do is take incremental steps each day to build the best possible version of the internet and web, with the knowledge that we already have. Before getting to that next iteration of the web, let us start with the initial version: Web 1.0, or Web1 as it is also called. This version of the internet allowed users to primarily read data on static pages that offered

DOI: 10.4324/9781003330417-26

primarily one-way traffic for information. This version of the web, also called the Read-Only web by many, is estimated to have run from the 1990s to approximately 2004. At the time, this was sufficient for much of our social and economic interactions, but as soon as our societies started to evolve, so did the web. Cue in Web 2.0 or Web2, a notion coined by Tim O'Reilly, who described this as an "internet where you could read and write data". It is believed that Web2 started around 2004 and has continued until present day. In this current phase of the web's evolution, information is no longer running on a one-way street (digital street), but, rather, in multiple directions, as users now can create content, generate data, and share information in multiple directions. One characteristic of this read-write Web2 is that user data is commodified and serves as a major source of revenue for the traditional custodians of value that have, over time, dominated the internet. This is closely related to the earlier discussion on value in the digital economy which has until now focused on the monetization of data. Considering all the changes discussed so far, and reflecting on the status of our world, one might see how the calls for a new system make sense. Cue in Web 3.0 or Web3. Already gaining much popularity in the years since Gavin Wood first mentioned the term, Web3 is being presented by many as an ace in humanity's arsenal against redundancy. One definition refers to Web3 as the "internet where you could read, write, and own data" (Stackpole, 2022). A similar definition according to Juan Benet refers to Web3 as the internet where you can "read, write and trust" (Benet, 2018). Robert Stevens says that Web3 "represents the next generation of the internet, one that focuses on shifting power from big tech companies to individual users" (Stevens, 2022). Stevens also captures some of the challenges with Web3 when he talks about "decentralization theater, where blockchain projects are decentralized in name but not in substance", but these challenges will be discussed later. While several definitions of the term already exist, and there are more to come, let us focus on Web3 as a catch-all phrase for the next iteration of the internet and web. From these definitions, a few ideals start to emerge, two of which are a call for decentralization, and a call for greater user empowerment. At the heart of these changes is the application of blockchain technology to the flow of data on the internet and across the web. Ethereum defines some ideas which are believed to be foundational to Web3 (Ethereum, 2022). These include the idea that Web3 is decentralized, and the influence of large co-operations is minimized. Another idea central to Web3 according to Ethereum is that it is or will be permissionless, meaning in principle that anyone and everyone could participate in the value creation and value exchange process. A third important notion is the role that cryptocurrencies will play on Web3, and finally the fourth notion that Web3 is trustless. This idea on the trustless nature of the future web is one that is foundational to Web3. Rikus Bruwer and Riaan Rudman also present similar perspectives on what the key elements of Web3 are (Bruer & Rudman, 2015). Both authors argue that Web3 will see the introduction of new programming languages that improve how machines can understand, interact with, and process data. This will be complemented by the ability for software to obtain, store, and retrieve information in new ways, as well as the ability to carry out these tasks from multiple sources, and at larger sizes. Rounding off their arguments, Bruer and Rudman (2015) note that

Web3 will feature a level of unprecedented connectivity where data travels seamlessly across networks and devices. This is particularly interesting when contextualized with the growth of the Internet of Things (IoT), connected devices that make up our daily lives.

Being built on blockchain means that data in Web3 is not lost when a user switches from one platform to another. One example that comes up frequently is the gaming industry. Perks bought on a game are lost if the user stops playing, or if the game company closes a user's account for example. In a Web3 world, since data is stored on a blockchain, even if they left the platform, they would have immutable ownership of that data and could use it on another platform or sell it to other users. This is a powerful concept when applied in the context of evolving social interactions and economic value. Value in an economy is circular; Web3 improves how this circular flow is captured and transferred across platforms and people. Another critical feature of Web3 and blockchains is identity management. Current models mean that we all have multiple ID documents, both physical and digital. Web3 and blockchains (in particular, the application of distributed ledgers) mean that one ID document could be used across multiple platforms. This feature is referred to as portability and is an important aspect of ID systems going forward. There are many other ways to think about Web3. According to Usman W. Chohan, you could consider Web3 from the perspectives of social, economic, and cultural. The social perspective suggests that Web3 can empower the sense of community that many seek from their digital interactions. The economic perspective suggests that Web3 could serve as the "domain of economic value creation". The cultural perspective sees Web3 in the context of "the creative production of cultural artifacts and content" (Chohan, 2022).

A lot of the discussion around Web3 and new forms of the internet is driven by a consensus that value lies with the individual, and that new tools are needed to truly enable the vast amounts and varieties of value that come with interaction, both physical and digital. Realizing this value and enabling these new interactions in society will be made possible by a broad stack of technologies. One of the key features that will contribute to Web3's capabilities to meet the demands that we now have of it is "Intelligent Agents". In this seamless, digital future that we have discussed so far, data must flow unhindered across platforms, sets, services, etc. This is particularly important when you think of digital currencies that process ultra-large data sets from numerous sources, to determine the true value of each currency as it is generated in real time. Intelligent agents will make this possible. When combined with ultra-large data sets that are stored on distributed ledgers and easily verifiable, this creates a reliable and immutable network of trusted data that feeds into the economic process. While the notion of a new internet holds some benefits and is an important discussion, it should not be seen as perfect. We will not dwell on these imperfections here as they are covered in detail by other experts.

Web2 has seen several types of inequality emerge, as well as oligopolies in the form of a tech status quo. Our current understanding of Web3 does not give any conclusive evidence to suggest that it will do away with these inequalities. Our current approaches to Web3, while nascent, have not yet started to overcome the mechanisms that entrench inequality in the system. This can be said of cryptocurrencies which have mainly empowered those with the wealth to invest, but we will discuss this more in later chapters. Chohan (2022) also notes that there could be multiple versions of Web3 just as there are multiple versions of Web2. To put this in context, compare the different versions of the internet that exist today. There are countries with closed versions of the web that do not allow foreign content in, and this varies significantly depending on where you are in the world. There is also the dark web, which, to a large extent, functions in line with the structures of Web2, albeit with some tweaks that are not as readily available to regular users.

Web3 represents a larger movement for the evolution of society to better reflect the nature of what it means to be alive, and what it means to conduct social and economic interactions. This push for a new internet, in whatever form it comes, will enable individuals to capture, store, and transfer value in new ways, as underpinned in this theory. Importantly, with our lives being increasingly digital, Web3 will require a digital social contract that also strengthens the link between the physical user and their digital data, among other things.

Bibliography

Benet, J. (2018). *What Exactly is Web 3.0?*. [Online] Available at: https://web3.foundation/about/

Bruer, R. & Rudman, R. (2015). Web 3.0: Governance, Risks And Safeguards. *The Journal of Applied Business Research*, *31*, 1037–1056.

Chohan, U. W. (2022). *Web 3.0: The Future Architecture of the Internet?*. [Online] Available at: https://papers.ssrn.com/sol3/papers.cfm?abstract_id=4037693

Chugh, A. (2021). *What is 'The Great Resignation'? An Expert Explains*. [Online] Available at: https://www.weforum.org/agenda/2021/11/what-is-the-great-resignation-and-what-can-we-learn-from-it/

Ethereum. (2022). *Introduction to Web3*. [Online] Available at: https://ethereum.org/en/web3/

Stackpole, T. (2022). *What is Web3?*. [Online] Available at: https://hbr.org/2022/05/what-is-web3#:~:text=Put%20very%20simply%2C%20Web3%20is,a%20decentralized%20app%20(dApp)

Stevens, R. (2022). *What Is Web 3 and Why Is Everyone Talking About It?*. [Online] Available at: https://www.coindesk.com/learn/what-is-web-3-and-why-is-everyone-talking-about-it/

20 The Present-Future of Interaction

(De)Centralization?

Social and economic interactions are evolving. Value can be captured through multiple mechanisms, and we need technology to facilitate these mechanisms. Peer-to-peer and/or community-based transactions and ecosystems can be trustless and permissionless. So, just how decentralized do our societies need to get, to enable these new interactions and new tools for value? Is decentralized finance really the answer to world poverty and hunger? The answer to this last question could be yes, but this decentralized system would need to be built around a new type of finance (Figure 20.1).

The calls for decentralization come from a good place and have several benefits worth seriously considering. A level of decentralization could mean that technology tools can be more freely applied at the grassroots level to solve problems without the delays and bureaucracy that come with multiple layers of intermediaries. That said, any approach to empowering communities and driving social and economic inclusion would need to balance out the benefits of decentralization with the structure and reliability of centralization (even if structure and reliability can be encoded into our systems). This assertion is based on the notion that some level of coordination will be needed to effectively reach, onboard, empower, and protect the vulnerable populations that are still in the "state of nature" and depend on these combined advancements in societal structures and technology to bring them into civil society. Beyond decentralization in how financial services are provided, there could also be decentralization from a regulatory perspective and of course from a service provider perspective, all of which must be considered carefully so as to not "erode traditional forms of accountability and the effectiveness of traditional financial regulation and enforcement" (Zetzsche et al., 2020). Furthermore, a large portion of contemporary society is driven by consumerism; producing because we need to buy, buying so that we can consume, and because we consume, we produce more.

Rethinking the social and economic value system will allow humanity to refocus productivity and consumption in a way that potentially increases how we recognize an individual's contributions in society. This approach of digitally monetizing time allows users to take ownership of the value that they create, while also allowing a level of coordination at the community level that ensures cohesion.

DOI: 10.4324/9781003330417-27

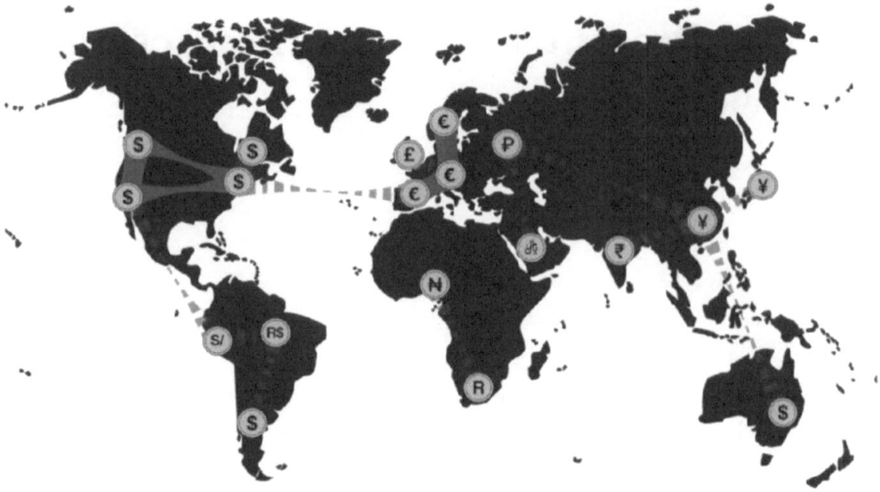

Figure 20.1 The global financial system is predominantly driven by centralized hubs that operate in silos, with limited mechanisms for peer-to-peer transactions. Design by Margaryta Pugach.

A core tenet of decentralized finance (DeFi), is that it leverages blockchain technology to encode trust (Ojog, 2021), thereby removing unnecessary intermediaries. Trust has historically been a facilitator of all kinds of interactions. People traded with those they trusted, and this concept has survived very much until the time of writing this book. Consumers build brand loyalty based on a combination of factors, with trust taking a large percentage. Transparency has also been an important factor. Take this definition of transparency for example and apply it to any transaction that you have completed in the past. "The transparency of a process, situation, or statement is its quality of being easily understood or recognized". So if two people had to engage in a transaction and they did not know each other, in opposite ends of the world, or even in the same community, how could they ensure trust and transparency? In more recent history, the proliferation of social media and communication tools has made it easier to verify claims and identity, allowing our societies to trust more and have more transparent processes. This trend is set to increase out of necessity. Let us scale up this example. If multiple people need to engage in transactions and agree on decisions, how would they each ensure trust among strangers and transparency of processes? This is where technology comes in, and this is the objective of decentralized finance. To contextualize what it really means to encode trust, imagine that any technology attempting to do this must meet certain criteria. David Horsager has proposed Eight Pillars of Trust which are clarity, compassion, character, competency, commitment, connection, contribution, and consistency.

Technology allows us to encode all of these features in direct response to evolving social and economic interactions. The characteristics of this new interaction model are mainly:

- Greater empowerment for **peer-to-peer transactions**, balanced by a seamless network of coordinating entities that ultimately create a global ecosystem. At first read, this might seem like a trend towards homogeneity, which could be a good thing. This approach would allow humanity to standardize the underlying foundations of what a currency are, while allowing this currency to adjust in real time based on the economic nuances of where it is being generated. In addition, by standardizing the underlying foundations, communities gain more flexibility in how the top layers of the instrument are applied.
- Greater **security and privacy** for users. Advancements in cryptography, among others, are improving the reliability and protection offered by digital tools. While these tools still have some improving to do, the technology at our disposal, and the improvements that are coming with Web3, are giving greater autonomy and control back to the individual. As the line between physical and digital continues to blur further, security and privacy will increase in relevance. This is also true as even more data is harnessed from society.
- Greater **accountability** of stakeholders and actions. Conventional intermediaries in the way that they have existed offered a unique benefit for their clients. They offered a sense of accountability, since they stood behind any financial instruments being offered. These intermediaries made it possible for entities to interact across geographies and ideologies without necessarily knowing each other. Without these intermediaries, transactions until now may have been difficult and less transparent. For this, we must thank the institutions and players that upheld these layers. Today, this notion of an indispensable intermediary has already started to change, and our systems can have accountability encoded in, such that each individual is accountable to themselves and to the whole in a transparent manner. Much like the Leviathan of Thomas Hobbes.

In addition, a decentralized approach built on technology encoded with trust and transparency will facilitate other components of the financial and economic ecosystem beyond just financial inclusion. For example, technology-enabled decentralization could benefit from quicker post-trade settlements. Typically, buyers and sellers compare trade details either before or after a transaction. By combining distributed ledgers and smart contracts, the trade settlement process could be automated and digitalized to improve operational efficiency. In their paper on decentralized finance, Zetzsche et al. (2020) argue that traditional finance is built around a hub model that presents redundancies for the consumer (Zetzsche et al., 2020). This is true given that traditional finance is built on siloed currencies that require a significant amount of physical, digital, and policy infrastructure to connect these silos. Decentralized digital currencies, on the other hand, are not necessarily pinned by the same challenges. Taking the blockchain as an analogy, think of hubs in a digital world as nodes on a blockchain, facilitating a unique global currency that does away with the silos (multiple currency systems) of the past.

For this decentralized reality, with the features described above, to exist, there are certain things that need to be in place. Zetzsche et al. (2020) argue that DeFi is based on three points. The first of these points is Moore's law which states that data processing power will continue to grow exponentially. The second point is Kryder's law which states that data storage capacity will grow exponentially. The third factor refers to the "growth in communications bandwidth combined with decreasing costs" (Zetzsche et al., 2020). When taken together, these factors will make it possible for digitally enabled societies to leverage even more data in value creation.

Calls for decentralization in society are not new. In fact, calls for decentralization in finance are not new. According to Friederich Hayek in 1976, "the government monopoly on money must be abolished to stop the recurring bouts of acute inflation and deflation" (Hayek, 1976). Already over 40 years ago, Hayek's arguments were laying the foundation for the decentralized, private sector–led digital currencies needed to enable the future. Hayek's thoughts on this are captured in the following statement:

> So long as money is managed by government, a gold standard, despite its imperfections, is the only tolerably safe system; but it is better to take money completely out of the control of government.
>
> (Hayek, 1976)

Hayek goes on to make certain suggestions on competition in private currency; however, the effect and impact of this are up for debate. Hayek's work is an important contribution to the discussion on decentralization for many reasons. Hayek believed that inflation was a terrible problem, but one that was easy to solve, nonetheless. He believed that inflation was caused by centrally controlled government money and sought a reliable alternative to this. Earlier chapters of this book talked about the evolving role of the state in society and the evolving nature of social interactions. These chapters align well with Hayek's thinking, and further buttress the central notion that social interaction and the role of the state can never be the same again. Given his perspectives on the need for private competing money, one could argue that Hayek would be impressed by the range of decentralized, community-supported digital currencies like Bitcoin and Ether, among others. According to Hayek, the main benefit of his decentralized money idea is that it would make it difficult for government to hide depreciation, and that governments would be disincentivized from continuing bad policies if these were having a negative effect on the currency. This point on government policy in defining general direction is important, given the policy landscape currently surrounding the few digital currencies at humanity's disposal.

Centralized societies existed to serve a purpose. How well these structures have served humanity's needs is up for debate but is not the subject of this discussion. As humanity's needs have continued to evolve towards a greater level of peer-to-peer value transfer, the calls for decentralization will no doubt ring a familiar bell to economists and political philosophers alike. Finding the right balance will mean leveraging technology, understanding history, and listening to the end user, as we design the societies and financial systems of the future. Decentralization also does not have to mean that humanity completely does away with coordinating structures. Instead, we can focus on this to mean a greater focus on building the systems, policies, and tools that empower peer-to-peer transactions everywhere and enable value transfer at every level of society (Figure 20.2).

Figure 20.2 Decentralized finance based on our most universal and valuable resource: time. Design by Margaryta Pugach.

Bibliography

Hayek, F. (1976). *The Denationalisation of Money*. London: Institute of Economic Affairs.

Ojog, S. (2021). The Emerging World of Decentralized Finance. *Informatica Economica, 25*, 43–53.

Zetzsche, D., Arner, D., & Buckley, R. (2020). Decentralized Finance. *Journal of Financial Regulation, 6*, 172–203.

21 Financial Technology and the New Value

Previous chapters discussed the technologies defining the digital economy, as well as the approaches to creating and measuring value in the digital economy. An underlying assertion in this book is that a digital currency should be leveraged to improve social and economic development. This underlying assertion will be discussed further in the next chapter on the philosophy of digital currencies. Digital currencies are financial instruments, and so before diving into this philosophy, it is important to start by understanding the historical evolution of financial systems, including the key technologies that have underscored these systems. This knowledge, complemented by a review of the technologies that will underscore the future of finance, set the backdrop for any attempt at designing the digital currencies of a financially inclusive future.

The digital economy and technologies of the fourth industrial revolution are bringing about exponential changes to every industry sector, from improving efficiencies to increasing the use cases and applications of technology tools (Winarsky, 2019) (theatlantic, n.d.). According to Gordon E. Moore's law, the "number of transistors on integrated circuits doubles approximately every two years" (Roser & Ritchie, 2013). The finance industry is not left out of this change and has been identified by many as one of the sectors most influenced by technological advancements (Code Institute, 2021). Like every other industry, banking and finance have had to evolve to meet growing consumer demands, not to mention the need to stay competitive in an ever-increasing landscape of stakeholders. The evolution of the finance sector has happened at the personal and business levels, but also at the economic and structural levels. Banking, for example, has had to evolve to meet up with diversified consumer needs and a larger volume of trade. According to Ricardo Barradas (2015), the evolution of the finance sector has happened through three phases of financial repression, financial development, and financialization (Barradas, 2015). In this first phase, Barradas (2015) notes that the financial sector was heavily regulated, from interest rates to the types of products that were available to consumers. The second phase of evolution in the finance sector, according to Barradas, took place from the 1980s and was spurred on by a significant deregulatory effort. This process of loosening regulation resulted in a focus on investments and savings in the global financial system, but also paved the way for more active engagements in instruments and platforms like "loans and stock markets, … derivatives,

DOI: 10.4324/9781003330417-28

securitization" (Barradas, 2015). This process would lead to what Barradas (2015) refers to as the third phase of the finance sector's evolution: financialization which is characterized by a disconnect between the finance sector and the real economy. Barradas (2015) highlights the widely accepted view that the finance sector contributes to economic growth and notes that the finance sector acts as a "motor to economic growth" (Barradas, 2015). These arguments are laid out to highlight the need for a new phase in the evolution of the finance sector, one that is characterized by de-financialization and refocuses the finance sector on serving as the motor to economic growth. This statement is in line with the assumptions and assertions made in this book, which seeks to leverage financial instruments, i.e. digital currencies, in improving financial inclusion towards social and economic development. Beyond the phases of evolution defined by Barradas, there is a much more historical context for the evolution of financial systems that is closely linked to the evolution of money. This evolution dates to pre-industrial times when exchange happened on a smaller scale and was largely barter-based. As the need for trade increased, so did the need for mediums of exchange, along with systems to manage these new mediums of exchange. The growth of early financial systems was also spurred on by the need for loans and credit (World Bank, n.d.).

Impact of Technology on the Evolution of the Finance Industry

The finance industry is a key driver of the economy because it is through financial instruments that individuals and institutions can interact around value creation and value transfer (resource management, trade, etc.). According to Kimberly Amadeo, banking is concerned with managing "cash, credit, and other financial transactions for individual and businesses alike" (Amadeo, 2021). Adam Barone defines banks as "financial institutions (that are) licensed to receive deposits and make loans … (as well as) provide financial (like) wealth management, currency exchange" (Barone, 2021). To achieve these tasks, banks and financial institutions have had to leverage certain technologies throughout history. According to Gartner, a core banking technology is (Gartner, 2021):

> a back-end system that processes daily banking transactions and posts updates to accounts and other financial records. Core banking systems typically include deposit, loan, and credit processing capabilities, with interfaces to general ledger systems and reporting tools.

Elizabeth Judd presents a history of banking technology which has been summarized here (Judd, 2018), starting with **pneumatic capsule transportation in 1836**. This technology, invented by William Murdoch, was used to facilitate deposits and withdrawals by early American banks. According to Judd, the technology allowed bank customers to make withdrawals and deposits without leaving their cars. In **1950**, the **credit card** was developed by the Diners Club. The credit card uniquely allowed customers for the first time to spend in stores against a line of credit (MX, 2019). In **1967**, the first **Automated Teller Machine** (ATM) was installed by Barclays bank in London. According to Judd (2018), the ATM combined several emerging technologies at the time which included digital displays, algorithms that linked banks with ATMs, and magnetic stripe cards (Judd, 2018). In **1973**, the **File Transfer Protocol (FTP)** was set up to facilitate the transfer of files over computer networks. In the same year of **1973**, the **SWIFT** payment network was established (MX, 2019). In **1980**, **electronic cash counters** were introduced into bank branches in Britain, allowing banks to automate cash processes and reduce the need for vaults. By 1989, tablet computers were improving the customer experience and interactions with banks. **PayPal**'s introduction in **1998** facilitated wireless payments (MX, 2019). In 2004, the Check Clearing for the 21st Century Act of 2004 (Check 21) made it possible to process cheques electronically. Coming into more recent times, the introduction of **Bitcoin** in **2009** would spark advancements in crypto and digital currencies. This would be followed closely by the introduction of **mobile point-of-sale devices** in **2010**. Based on this summary on the evolution of financial technologies, a few key points can be identified as below:

- The growth of **digital tools** allowed the financial system to increase the level of interaction with customers but also allowed financial institutions to digitize previously manual processes.
- **Data storage and transfer** technology has greatly improved the ability of financial institutions to offer real-time services and real-time transaction validation. These technologies have also improved the ability of financial institutions to provide identity management and continuity for their customers across regions.
- **Payment platforms, networks, and channels** are facilitating new types of transactions over networks and across use cases.
- **Security systems** are allowing financial institutions to comfortably offer a wider range of services of products outside of the conventional physical bank structure, meaning that financial institutions can meet consumers at their points of need.
- An increasing integration of new technologies is facilitating decentralization in the banking system.

Jesse Mcwaters notes that technology is impacting the finance industry in ways that past innovators had not considered (McWaters, 2015). Some of these include automation and commoditizing high-margin processes as well as taking a platform approach to value creation and value capture.

Applying Technology in the Finance Industry and New Value

As the fourth industrial revolution picks up, financial institutions will be able to apply technologies in new ways to meet consumer needs (Greenwood, n.d.). Lipi Bharadwaj presents a list of ten technologies that will change banking. These technologies are Augmented Reality, Blockchain, Robotic Process Automation, Quantum Computing, Artificial Intelligence, API Platforms, Prescriptive Security,

Hybrid Cloud, Instant Payments, and Smart Machines (Bharadwaj, 2020). These technologies, many of which have been identified as part of the fourth industrial revolution and are key drivers of the digital economy, have unique forward-looking applications for the finance sector.

1 **Augmented reality** – augmented reality offers financial institutions the opportunity to improve the customer experience and enhance the modes of interaction between consumers as well as with the institution (CGS, 2020). According to Bram Nawijn, augmented and virtual reality technologies can be applied in data visualization, virtual trading, virtual reality payments, and security, among others (Nawijn, 2018), all of which hold significant potential for decentralized peer-to-peer transactions.
2 **Blockchain** – blockchain technology refers to distributed ledgers that allow various parties to access the same information at the same time (Bharadwaj, 2020). Blockchain can be applied in security, increasing trust in interactions, facilitating transparency to a certain degree, ensuring privacy as well as high performance and programmability (CommPro, n.d.). In addition, blockchain technology can be applied to cross-border transactions, trade finance platforms, clearing and settlements, identity verification and reporting (Hydrogen, 2019).
3 **Robotic process automation (RPA)** – according to Bharadwaj (2020), banks have to process increasingly large data sets that go beyond conventional banking data and include consumer behaviour and environments. To process these data sets, banks are looking to technologies like machine learning, natural language processing, chatbots, and robotic process automation that, when combined, can replicate and enhance previously human tasks for greater efficiency. RPA use cases range from maintaining data for accuracy, to removing errors from accounting and streamlining reporting between institutions (CiGen, 2020).
4 **Quantum computing (QC)** – according to Bharadwaj (2020), QC unlocks exponential computing power that financial institutions and even other industries are yet to fully maximize. Because QC is able to process immensely large and complex data sets, as well as combinations of these, it has applications such as targeting and prediction, trading optimization, and risk profiling, among others (Yndurain et al., 2019).
5 **Artificial intelligence (AI)** – increasing management of data is a factor that will continue to impact every industry, and this is the case with AI technology and the banking sector. Applications of A I technology include but are not limited to risk management, since data can be analysed for risks, fraud detection, trading, and advisory (Maruti Techlabs, n.d.) (Phaneuf, 2020). AI applications in finance will empower decentralized transactions in a way where each party can leverage complex data sets in their navigation of markets and decision-making.
6 **Application programming interface (API) platforms** – APIs are "programming code that enables data transmission between one software…and another" (Altexsoft, 2021). API platforms are "software intermediary that

allows two applications to talk to each other" (MuleSoft, 2021) and are common across numerous technologies and use cases. In the banking sector, because APIs allow communication and connectivity between software, this technology is facilitating interaction between banking institutions and third parties. According to Samantha Barnes, there are types of API currently being deployed in the finance industry which are: private APIs which function within the institution; partner APIs which connect with trusted third-party partners of the institution; and open or public APIs which, although rare, are open to broader third parties (Barnes, 2020). Because APIs are allowing banks and fintech institutions to connect with other applications, this technology is being applied in areas like payments, transfers, fraud detection, regulatory compliance, and identity verification (Morales, 2020). APIs are also playing a critical role in restructuring financial services as part of the implementation of open banking.

7 **Prescriptive security** – prescriptive security attempts to proactively identify security threats within an institutions network. This technology uses big data analytics and the automation of processes to try and pinpoint security issues as accurately as possible and in a timely fashion (Badstubner, 2019).

8 **Hybrid cloud** – According to Sai Vennam, a hybrid cloud "combines and unifies public cloud, private cloud and on-premises infrastructure to create a single, flexible, cost-optimal IT infrastructure" (Vennam, 2021). These types of cloud systems are uniquely able to manage both public and private clouds, as well as able to integrate workloads on physical premises and traditional networks (IntellectSoft, 2021). Hybrid cloud is being applied in several ways in the banking sector, including in improving storage capabilities; enhancing security since institutions can now safely store backups and worry less on infrastructure failing; improving the management of workloads and data assets across sections within the institution; or accessing this across jurisdictions where the institution operates, among other applications (Korkishko, 2021). With financial institutions in general needing to manage and interact with an increasing amount of data, technologies that facilitate this process are crucial to success. This is particularly important for institutions that are looking to leverage a combination of any of the technologies presented in this list; hybrid cloud lays the foundation for this innovation (Lima, 2020).

9 **Instant payments** – instant payments open up multiple opportunities for financial institutions but also for the customers they serve, whether corporate or individual (Montgomery, 2021). From new business models to improving market interactions, instant payments are considered a key aspect of future economic activity (Sinha, 2019). According to the European Central Bank (ECB), instant payments are not only a means of improving business and commercial relationships, but they are also a tool for financial inclusion since they make it easier to send and receive money on multiple platforms (ECB, 2016).

10 **Smart machines** – According to Konstantin Didur (2018), machine learning "uses statistical models to draw insights and make predictions" (Didur, 2018). Didur (2018) notes that like several other technologies that leverage

data as an input, machine learning, and smart machines can be applied towards automating processes like aspects of customer interaction, improving security, facilitating algorithmic trading, etc.

The ways that these are being applied today are contributing to an ongoing "fintech revolution" as described in the article "Maximising the FinTech Revolution for Sustainable Societies" (2021). In that article, the authors describe a need for this financial revolution to be channelled towards improving the state of society (Albasha et al., 2021). The next iterations of global financial systems will be built on these technologies just described, and the exciting opportunity here is that we have not yet started to scratch the surface of what is possible when you begin to combine these technologies with creativity, policy, and capital.

★★★

Beyond just the technologies, there is still the question on new approaches to value creation that will define societies going forward. Earlier chapters started to explore these new approaches, including in the deep-dive review on the origin of the state and impact on economic value. The reflections in that deep dive offered some insights into the nuances across two different types of societies, and how these nuances have influenced socio-economic interaction. In that review, both states have gone through somewhat unique processes to get to their social contracts. In both instances, and despite the differences in their paths, both states have seen their fintech ecosystems evolve into equally unique environments. In one instance, a stable economy, reliable policy, and strong capital flows have created a world-renowned financial centre. In another instance, a large economy, evolving social infrastructure, and strong capital flows have created a bustling fintech hub. Can you guess which one is which?

The cases of Nigeria and Switzerland offer insights into two distinct worlds. Beyond that, the cases offer insights into what factors influence fintech ecosystems and how these factors influence the outputs of these ecosystems. This understanding is important because as we attempt to design the fintech ecosystems of the future, we must take learnings that ultimately drive financial inclusion and empower communities to harness value. To understand the nuances across both ecosystems, it is important to start by understanding what makes up the fintech ecosystem in a given country. Financial technology or "FinTech" refers to all the technologies that make financial transactions work. This can be quite broad when you consider all the areas, platforms, and services needed to enable the variety of financial transactions that our societies enjoy today. So what makes up this ecosystem? Just as you would with innovation ecosystems, you could break down fintech ecosystems into technologies, infrastructure, policy and regulation, and stakeholders. An interesting fifth category is "demand" (SPDLoad, 2022). Of course, other authors have presented different definitions of fintech ecosystems, but we will not focus on those definitions here.

A myriad of **technologies** come together to enable the final services and products that facilitate daily transactions. This is everything from big data analytics, identity management and cryptography, to APIs and cloud computing. On the **infrastructure** front, you would include everything from telecommunication masts, satellites, servers, and ATM machines. All of these technologies and infrastructure must exist on solid **policies** if they will be scaled successfully and adopted widely. A stable, proactive, and risk-balanced regulatory environment is an important part of any ecosystem. Technology, infrastructure, and policies are made by people, for people; and this is where the stakeholders come in. The **stakeholders** that make up the fintech ecosystem include all the service and product providers like traditional financial institutions, start-ups, investors, and end users, among others. These stakeholders represent the demand and supply landscape of the ecosystem, which ties into the "**demand**" category described by SPDLoad (2022).

Now let us take this understanding of what makes up a fintech ecosystem and apply it to the earlier discussion on socio-economic interactions. For the sake of this phase of the discussion, let us focus on Nigeria, which of the two has more people in dire need of financial inclusion. A struggling economy (African Development Bank, 2020), weak public infrastructure, and a highly competitive society have created a unique environment with a high degree of entrepreneurial ingenuity in Nigeria. Keeping in mind the current social contract environment, social interactions in Nigeria are highly decentralized. From a social contract perspective, no single entity has been able to substantively and consistently claim legitimate control over public administration. Instead, what you have is a fragmented network that exists not necessarily in writing, but certainly in practice. The limited economic infrastructure has meant that social interactions are largely informal. This informality takes place everywhere from the sprawling urban slums and rural communities to the peripheries of the country's megacities. These informal social interactions happen in a peer-to-peer manner, without the intervention of a government. The necessity created by this highly decentralized and informal setting is the mother of invention for Nigeria's fast-growing fintech sector. The fact that the country has such a high population (206 million people) (Credolab, 2022), high mobile phone penetration (90% in 2022) (Credolab, 2022), limited social infrastructure, high number of financially excluded citizens (40% of total population) (Kola-Oyeneyin et al., 2020), and high levels of informality has meant that any financial solutions that want to be successful must be cognizant of this situation and cater to this decentralization. Other factors have also contributed to defining the types of financial instruments that are created, and the nature of the fintech ecosystem, like the high number of remittances. The nature of social interactions and the state of infrastructure in the country have also impacted financial technologies in Nigeria. Instant payments have grown to accommodate the limited availability of point-of-sale machines for traders. Instead, you can often find payments for goods and services done through bank transfers. In 2021 alone, Nigeria recorded 3.7 billion real-time payments, and this is meant to increase to 8.8 billion by 2026 (ACI Worldwide, 2022). This chapter has highlighted the role that technology is playing in reshaping the finance sector, as well as the vast capabilities that these technologies present for finance, from the perspective of value creation and capture through digital currencies. Although the chapter did not go into a great amount of detail, the example of Nigeria offers a glimpse into this world of possibilities, despite the challenges of infrastructure, among other things.

Bibliography

ACI Worldwide. (2022). *Global Payments Report Nigeria*. [Online] Available at: https://go.aciworldwide.com/Global-Payments-Report-Nigeria.html [Accessed 17 July 2022].

African Development Bank. (2020). *Nigeria Economic Outlook*. [Online] Available at: https://www.afdb.org/en/countries-west-africa-nigeria/nigeria-economic-outlook

Albasha, A., Idiong, O., Hohne-Sparborth, T., & Ikpeazu, U. (2021). *Maximising the Fintech Revolution for Sustainable Societies*. [Online] Available at: https://onresearch.ch/wp-content/uploads/2021/03/Maximising-the-Fintech-Revolution-for-Sustainable-Societies_ON-Research-Insight.pdf [Accessed 19 June 2022].

Altexsoft. (2021). *What is API: Definition, Types, Specifications, Documentation*. [Online] Available at: https://www.altexsoft.com/blog/engineering/what-is-api-definition-types-specifications-documentation/ [Accessed 4 August 2021].

Amadeo, K. (2021). *What is Banking*. [Online] Available at: https://www.thebalance.com/what-is-banking-3305812 [Accessed 3 August 2021].

Badstubner, O. (2019). *Prescriptive Security: Vital for Handling the Increased Security Complexity at Financial Institutions in the Digital Age*. [Online] Available at: https://atos.net/en/blog/prescriptive-security-vital-handling-increased-security-complexity-financial-institutions-digital-age [Accessed 4 August 2021].

Barnes, S. (2020). *The Growing Importance of APIs to Banking*. [Online] Available at: https://internationalbanker.com/banking/the-growing-importance-of-apis-to-banking/ [Accessed 4 August 2021].

Barone, A. (2021). *Bank*. [Online] Available at: https://www.investopedia.com/terms/b/bank.asp [Accessed 3 August 2021].

Barradas, R. (2015). *Evolution of the Financial Sector – Three Different Stages: Repression, Development and Financialisation*. [Online] Available at: https://core.ac.uk/download/pdf/153419296.pdf [Accessed 3 August 2021].

Bharadwaj, L. (2020). *Technology in Banking: 10 Innovations That Will Impact Future of Banking*. [Online] Available at: https://www.wowso.me/blog/technology-in-banking [Accessed 3 August 2021].

CGS. (2020). *5 Augmented Reality Use Cases in the Workplace for Financial Services*. [Online] Available at: https://www.cgsinc.com/blog/5-augmented-reality-use-cases-workplace-financial-services [Accessed 3 August 2021].

CiGen (2020). *8 Real World Use Cases for Robotic Process Automation in Finance*. [Online] Available at: https://www.cigen.com.au/cigenblog/8-real-world-use-cases-robotic-process-automation-finance [Accessed 3 August 2021].

Code Institute. (2021). *4 Traditional Industries Changed by Technology*. [Online] Available at: https://codeinstitute.net/blog/4-traditional-industries-changed-by-technology/ [Accessed 3 August 2021].

CommPro. (n.d.) *Role of Blockchain Technology in the Finance Industry*. [Online] Available at: https://www.commpro.biz/role-of-blockchain-technology-in-the-finance-industry/ [Accessed 3 August 2021].

Credolab. (2022). *The Growth of the Nigerian Fintech Ecosystem*. [Online] Available at: https://www.credolab.com/blog/the-growth-of-the-nigerian-fintech-ecosystem-infographic#:~:text=The%20industry%20presents%20a%20diverse,online%20lending%2C%20and%20business%20solutions

Didur, K. (2018). *Machine Learning in Finance: Why, What & How*. [Online] Available at: https://towardsdatascience.com/machine-learning-in-finance-why-what-how-d524a2357b56 [Accessed 4 August 2021].

ECB. (2016). *What are Instant Payments?*. [Online] Available at: https://www.ecb.europa.eu/explainers/tell-me-more/html/instant_payments.en.html [Accessed 4 August 2021].

Gartner. (2021). *Core Banking Systems*. [Online] Available at: https://www.gartner.com/en/information-technology/glossary/core-banking-systems [Accessed 3 August 2021].

Greenwood, A. (n.d.) *The Fourth Industrial Revolution & the Impact on Banking & Finance (Challenges & Opportunities)*. [Online] Available at: https://www.globalbankingandfinance.com/the-fourth-industrial-revolution-the-impact-on-banking-finance-challenges-opportunities/ [Accessed 1 August 2021].

Hydrogen. (2019). *5 Common Blockchain Applications in Financial Services*. [Online] Available at: https://www.hydrogenplatform.com/blog/5-common-blockchain-applications-in-financial-services [Accessed 3 August 2021].

IntellectSoft. (2021). *How Hybrid Cloud Technology Can Help The Banks Deal with Data Management*. [Online] Available at: https://www.intellectsoft.net/blog/hybrid-cloud-solutions-in-banking/ [Accessed 4 August 2021].

Judd, E. (2018). *Timeline: 180 Years of Banking Technology*. [Online] Available at: https://independentbanker.org/2017/10/timeline-180-years-of-banking-technology/ [Accessed 3 August 2021].

Kola-Oyeneyin, T., Kuyoro, M., & Olanrewaju, T. (2020). *Harnessing Nigeria's Fintech Potential*. s.l.: McKinsey & Company.

Korkishko, M. (2021). *Hybrid Cloud: How to Make it Work for Banks*. [Online] Available at: https://www.n-ix.com/hybrid-cloud-banks/ [Accessed 4 August 2021].

Lima, R. K. (2020). *Why Financial Services Providers Are Turning to Hybrid Cloud*. [Online] Available at: https://www.ibm.com/blogs/think/2020/01/why-financial-services-providers-are-turning-to-hybrid-cloud/ [Accessed 4 August 2021].

Maruti Techlabs. (n.d.) *5 Ways AI is Transforming the Finance Industry*. [Online] Available at: https://marutitech.com/ways-ai-transforming-finance/#5_ways_how_AI_has_transformed_the_finance_industry_are [Accessed 4 August 2021].

McWaters, J. (2015). *5 ways technology is transforming finance*. [Online] Available at: https://www.weforum.org/agenda/2015/06/5-ways-technology-transforming-finance/ [Accessed 3 August 2021].

Montgomery, K. (2021). *The Future of Payments is Instant*. [Online] Available at: https://progressivegrocer.com/future-payments-instant [Accessed 4 August 2021].

Morales, W. U. (2020). *FinTech Focus: APIs in Financial Services*. [Online] Available at: https://medium.com/fintechtris/fintech-focus-apis-in-financial-services-cf735150da4e [Accessed 4 August 2021].

MuleSoft. (2021). *What is an API? (Application Programming Interface)*. [Online] Available at: https://www.mulesoft.com/resources/api/what-is-an-api [Accessed 4 August 2021].

MX. (2019). *50 Years of Technology in Banking*. [Online] Available at: https://www.mx.com/thought-leadership/50-years-since-we-landed-on-the-moon/ [Accessed 3 August 2021].

Nawijn, B. (2018). *9 Applications of AR & VR in the Financial Industry*. [Online] Available at: https://www.tjip.com/en/publications/9-applications-of-ar-vr-in-the-financial-industry [Accessed 3 August 2021].

Phaneuf, A. (2020). *Artificial Intelligence in Financial Services: Applications and Benefits of AI in Finance*. [Online] Available at: https://www.businessinsider.com/ai-in-finance?r=US&IR=T [Accessed 4 August 2021].

Roser, M. & Ritchie, H. (2013). *Technology Progress*. [Online] Available at: https://ourworldindata.org/technological-progress [Accessed 3 August 2021].

Sinha, A. (2019). *The Need for Speed: Get Ready for Instant Payments.* [Online] Available at: https://www.citibank.com/tts/insights/articles/article92.html?linkId=76512058 [Accessed 4 August 2021].

SPDLoad. (2022). *Fintech Ecosystem Overview: What It Is and Why You Should Care.* [Online] Available at: https://spdload.com/blog/fintech-ecosystem/

theatlantic. (n.d.) *How Fast Is Technology Accelerating?.* [Online] Available at: https://www.theatlantic.com/sponsored/prudential-great-expectations/how-fast-is-technology-accelerating/360/ [Accessed 3 August 2021].

Vennam, S.. (2021). *Hybrid Cloud.* [Online] Available at: https://www.ibm.com/cloud/learn/hybrid-cloud [Accessed 4 August 2021].

Winarsky, N. (2019). *Exponential Tech Advances Will Change the World Faster Than We Think.* [Online] Available at: https://venturebeat.com/2019/11/17/exponential-tech-advances-will-change-the-world-faster-than-we-think/ [Accessed 3 August 2021].

World Bank. (n.d.) *The Evolution of Financial Systems.* [Online] Available at: https://openknowledge.worldbank.org/bitstream/handle/10986/5972/9780195207880_ch03.pdf [Accessed 3 August 2021].

Yndurain, E. et al. (2019). *Exploring Quantum Computing Use Cases for Financial Services.* [Online] Available at: https://www.ibm.com/thought-leadership/institute-business-value/report/exploring-quantum-financial [Accessed 4 August 2021].

22 Philosophy of Digital Currencies

Social and economic interactions are evolving. Value can be captured through multiple mechanisms, and we need technology to facilitate these mechanisms. Mobile phone penetration continues to grow; as more devices are created across more price points, the cost of mobile services decreases and disruption in technology is increasing the accessibility of complex technologies and solutions to more people. This reality, where data can travel at light speed, to even remote corners of the world, represents the biggest opportunity yet for deploying tools around value creation and transfer. Cue in the digital currency.

Digital currencies can be deployed any and everywhere, in a decentralized manner, allowing populations to access a store of value and means of exchange that results in financial inclusion. This is what digital currencies should do, and this is what they should represent, but before diving further into these two pieces, it is important to understand exactly what is meant by digital currency when the term is used here. In earlier chapters, we saw the evolution of money through history, from livestock in 9000 BC to cowrie shells in 1200 BC and the gold standard in 1816. Through each of these historical periods, the nature of human interaction evolved and influenced the type of money that humanity needed. In these earlier chapters, we also discussed the three primary functions of money around exchange, accounting and storing value. As Hayek advocated for, through history there have been ecosystems of public and private money co-existing together. Sweden is one such example from history. Through a clear regulatory framework that required the convertibility of public and private bank notes, Sweden was able to build a stable ecosystem of diverse money (Bolt et al., 2021).

A simple and straightforward definition offered by Jake Frankenfield says that digital currencies are a "form of currency that are available only in digital or electronic form" (Frankenfield, 2022). Digital currencies are money in the sense that they serve as a means of exchange, accounting, and value storage, all of which take place over digital platforms. Cryptocurrencies are a form of digital currency, but not all digital currencies are cryptocurrencies. While both terms are often used interchangeably, it is important to understand the distinction between them, as this helps in truly appreciating the breadth of possibilities, limitations, and applications. While digital currencies are simply available in electronic format, cryptocurrencies

DOI: 10.4324/9781003330417-29

must have the quality of being cryptographically encoded, to ensure anonymity. Chris Rose (2015) attempts to shed some light on the differences between a virtual currency, digital currency, and cryptocurrency. In the article "The Evolution of Digital Currencies: Bitcoin, A Cryptocurrency Causing a Monetary Revolution", the three terms are defined accordingly. First virtual currencies are "a type of unregulated, digital money, which are issued and usually controlled by the developers, and used and accepted among the members of a specific virtual community". Rose (2015) goes on to define digital currencies as forms of virtual currencies that are electronically created and stored (as seen earlier). Finally, Rose defines cryptocurrencies as a subset of digital currencies that use cryptography to ensure security (Rose, 2015). Going forward, the term "digital currency" will be used to refer to all currencies that exist primarily in electronic format and are generated electronically. Just like you have with money, the more people use a currency, the more valuable it becomes. This is referred to as the network effect (Stobierski, 2020).

Digital currencies are not a new idea. As early as 1983, David Chaum had published the article "Blind Signatures for Untraceable Payments" which outlined the structure of an anonymous digital currency which he would go on to develop in 1989 and call "DigiCash" (Chaum, 1983). At this time, there were already calls not only for digital currencies, but for also for decentralization in finance, a trend that has continued until today. Chaum's approach, inspired by a movement for privacy and control of one's own data, reflected the early seeds of an evolving system of social and economic interaction. The years following Chaum's DigiCash would see creations including Eric Hughes Cypherpunk manifesto and B-Money, HashCash, and Bitcoin which is in fact a cryptocurrency (Kenny, 2019). Cryptocurrencies have received some backlash since they came into the mainstream. In addition to issues around impact on the environment, cryptos have exhibited trends that support inequity, given that the more fiat currency a consumer has access to, the more influence and access they are likely to have to cryptocurrencies (Chohan, 2022). There is a place for anonymous transactions; however, this may not be a priority for those portion of society that is focused on accessing even basic financial instruments. Furthermore, the anonymous, fully decentralized nature of certain currencies may provide difficulties for these categories of society that have no fall-back protection and are more harshly impacted by changes in society and the economy.

Other types of digital currencies exist that each deserves an extensive discussion; however, we will only touch briefly on these to present some background. As the world explores new approaches to social interaction and as we move towards the true realization of Web3 or the new version of the internet, there will be even more attempts at designing digital currencies that meet our needs. The whole of this discussion is in that line. Each of these digital currencies will be designed with new functionalities and populations in mind, and each one will be the source of much argument, until humanity finds the right mix of features and technologies. Among these digital currency options are altcoins, stable coins, and central bank digital currencies.

Given Bitcoin's success as the most widely traded cryptocurrency, and given its early applications of blockchain technology, Bitcoin has taken on something of a core identity within the cryptocurrency space. So much so that all other cryptocurrencies that are not Bitcoin have been conveniently termed altcoins, or alternative coins. Estimates for the total number of cryptocurrencies currently in existence are between 12,000 and 18,000. This wide gap reflects a couple of things: First, it shows again the appetite for decentralized finance tools. Second, it shows the difficulty inherent in managing, tracking, and administering multiple decentralized financial instruments. Note here that difficulty does not automatically mean bad (or good). In fact, this situation, where multiple currencies are developed and administered by the public sector, private sector, and decentralized communities, is exactly what Friederich Hayek described in the "denationalization of money". A common characteristic of these cryptocurrencies has been the fluctuations in their value. Bitcoin alone has had its price fluctuate from $6,000 in March 2020, to $63,000 in April 2021, $35,000 in June 2021 and $19,000 in June 2022 (Coinmarketcap, 2022). Given that the currency is decentralized and therefore community-run, it is difficult (or even impossible) to establish any checks and balances that manage the impact of the fluctuations on those that chose to hold the currency. While these coins have served as a good store of value (despite the fluctuations), many of them have not seen a life as a means of exchange. Isolated use cases exist, but widespread adoption of these cryptocurrencies may still be far off.

This is where stable coins come in. Alyssa Hertig describes stable coins as "cryptocurrencies whose value are pegged to another asset class, such as a fiat currency or gold, to stabilize their price" (Hertig, 2022). Stable coins have attempted to solve the problem of volatility and, even more recently, have attempted to peg value to other cryptocurrencies. All of the digital currencies that have been discussed here so far have seen turbulent times since their inception. On one hand, there is the price volatility that these coins have had to stomach. On the other hand, there are the numerous regulatory hurdles that digital currencies have had to get past. As of 2021, the United States Library of Congress lists over 40 countries with implicit bans and 9 countries with absolute bans on cryptocurrencies (Law Library of Congress, 2021). Major investment firms and governments have been sceptical about the impact of cryptocurrencies, especially given their use in illicit trade, but the truth is that this is not the only use case for them.

One response to the digital currency boom, other than outright bans, has been the development of central bank digital currencies. According to the United States Federal Reserve, a "CBDC is a digital form of central bank money that is widely available to the general public" (Federal Reserve, 2022). CBDCs attempt to address some of the perceived problems of cryptocurrencies, like volatility in price fluctuations, accessibility for populations, and scalability. In addition, CBDCs which do not have the same anonymized characteristics as cryptos are supposedly less susceptible to illicit activity. One issue that regulators and technologists alike will need to look out for is in the design of CBDCs. Fiat currencies were supposedly meant to solve many of the problems that CBDCs seek to solve, but an inherent flaw was hidden in their design; we could just keep printing more bills. While some might argue against this flaw, it is important that CBDCs, and any other attempts at digital currencies, avoid this trap. Bitcoin's design attempts to avoid this problem by limiting the amount of Bitcoin that can be mined. This theory attempts to do the same; there is only so much time in the day for everyone.

Digital currencies bring together multiple concepts discussed in this book. Consider social interaction which also includes the discussions on Web3 and decentralization. We see that the nature of social and economic interaction is evolving. We also see that technology is enabling new levels of decentralized interactions and value exchange. In addition, we see that mobile device penetration and mobile bandwidth reach are at an all-time high. Together, these represent opportunities for how we design and deploy digital currencies (Figure 22.1).

Figure 22.1 Mobile device penetration is high, meaning that technology solutions deployed through mobile devices could be designed to reach and empower people every time, everywhere, and seamlessly. Design by Margaryta Pugach.

Bibliography

Bolt, W., Lubbersen, V., & Wierts, P. (2021). Getting the Balance Right: Crypto, Stablecoin and Central Bank Digital Currency. *Journal of Payments Strategy & Systems*, *16*, 39–51.

Chaum, D. (1983). *Blind Signatures for Untraceable Payments*. [Online] Available at: https://sceweb.sce.uhcl.edu/yang/teaching/csci5234WebSecurityFall2011/Chaum-blind-signatures.PDF

Chohan, U. W. (2022). *Web 3.0: The Future Architecture of the Internet?*. [Online] Available at: https://papers.ssrn.com/sol3/papers.cfm?abstract_id=4037693

Coinmarketcap. (2022). *Bitcoin*. [Online] Available at: https://coinmarketcap.com/currencies/bitcoin/

Federal Reserve. (2022). *What is a Central Bank Digital Currency?*. [Online] Available at: https://www.federalreserve.gov/faqs/what-is-a-central-bank-digital-currency.htm

Frankenfield, J. (2022). *Digital Currency*. [Online] Available at: https://www.investopedia.com/terms/d/digital-currency.asp

Hertig, A. (2022). *What Is a Stablecoin?*. [Online] Available at: https://www.coindesk.com/learn/what-is-a-stablecoin/

Kenny, J. (2019). *Digital Currency: A Brief History*. [Online] Available at: https://medium.com/block-journal/digital-currency-a-brief-history-98be6f6f0f10

Law Library of Congress. (2021). *Regulation of Cryptocurrency around the World*. [Online] Available at: https://tile.loc.gov/storage-services/service/ll/llglrd/2021687419/2021687419.pdf

Rose, C. (2015). The Evolution Of Digital Currencies: Bitcoin, A Cryptocurrency Causing a Monetary Revolution. *International Business & Economics Research Journal*, *14*, 617–622.

Stobierski, T. (2020). *What are Network Effects?*. [Online] Available at: https://online.hbs.edu/blog/post/what-are-network-effects [Accessed 22 June 2022].

Part VIII

A Theory of Monetizing Time

23 Theory Statement and Logical Framework

This book's underlying research set out to identify time as an ideal store of economic value and lays out a framework for approaching and understanding this claim. In earlier chapters, the term "store of value" was defined as "asset, currency, or commodity that maintains its value over a long period" (Corporate Finance Institute, 2021). The framework presented here is meant to serve as an outline in thinking through and linking the various concepts presented and should, however, not be taken as exhaustive.

The position is that a time-based digital currency as a store of social and economic value has the potential to truly unlock the benefits of the fourth industrial revolution, since it could significantly unlock access and mobilization of a critical factor of production: labour. This logical framework for a time-backed digital currency, or a digital currency pegged to time, also considers the evolution of the finance sector, as well as the technologies that are currently reshaping traditional approaches to finance, as part of the digital economy. The logical framework is presented as a geometric proof, meaning that each subsequent statement builds on the previous statements.

Theory Statement

New and alternative methods of measuring, capturing, and transferring social and economic value are necessary to reflect the evolution of social and economic structures in society, as well as to reflect the evolution of interactions among stakeholders, resources, and the environment. A proposed alternative mechanism for measuring, capturing, and transferring social and economic value is the digital monetization of time as a digital currency. This is based on a set of key assumptions:

- *Social interaction is driven by resource management with utility at its centre,*
- *the ability to measure utility in society has improved thanks to new methods and tools,*
- *the ability to measure labour input in relation to outputs has improved,*
- *the structure of labour inputs has changed and is no longer limited to conventional working relationships,*
- *technology has improved how well humanity can capture the circular flow of value in the economy,*

DOI: 10.4324/9781003330417-31

- *improving the living experience or vivos experientia is an intrinsic good,*
- *the private sector should be a party to the social contract.*

Building on these assumptions, this proposed value mechanism is based on the assertion that time is the primary common denominator to all productivity capable individuals, resources, and processes. In the context of the fourth industrial revolution, exponential technological advancements mean that each unit of currency is deployable at the point of value creation, and holistically reflects the range of data points that would influence perceptions of value in an economy. Furthermore, a time-pegged digital currency issued and managed by a private entity on behalf of a government would serve as the basis for a new digital social contract, reflective of contemporary social interactions.

Monetizing Time: A Logical Framework

1 **The ability to measure utility has improved significantly** – while different philosophers may have referred to utility as happiness/good/benefit, this theory will stay with the definition of utility as the "good that a consumer receives from consuming x units of a good or service", based on the definitions offered in earlier chapters. Happiness is not adopted in this definition because it is subjective. Measuring the "good" that a consumer receives from a product or service, on the other hand, is possible using mathematical calculations. This assumption holds when utility is considered in terms of the price that a consumer is willing to pay for a good or service at any given point in time. This price could be considered a representation of the utility which the consumer receives from consuming the good or service. In contemporary society, this would mean leveraging a vast array of data points to understand the nature of the product or service, the needs of the consumer, and the surrounding factors influencing the availability of the product or service to the consumer. In addition, employing big data analytics, artificial intelligence, and cloud computing technologies makes it possible to compute all of these data points in real time and specific to each individual consumer.

   In the book *Measuring Utility: From the Marginal Revolution to Behavioural Economics*, Ivan Moscati presents a good overview of the historical challenges that have affected attempts to measure utility. According to Moscati and as summarized by Lukas Beck and Anna Alexandrova, the difficulties in measuring utility ranged from issues in assigning utility ratios, to the role of preference in utility as well as "expected utility theory" (Beck & Alexandrova, 2019). This research, however, posits that measuring utility is possible when utility is considered as the value that a consumer gains, and when that value is measured in terms of the price or other value coefficient. The key point here is that the price or value coefficient would be measured using data points across ultra large data sets in real time, in a decentralized manner.

2 **The ability to measure labour input in relation to outputs has improved** – the production process has also equally evolved throughout history. The National Statistics Office of Italy (ISTAT) notes that measuring

labour input considers the number of hours spent working as well as the total number of persons that have been employed (on a full-time basis, converting a part-time work to full-time terms) (Baldassarini & Veroli, 2009). The International Labour Organization defines labour productivity as the total amount of output (as gross domestic product) that is produced by per unit of labour (ILO, 2020). Bruce W. Chew, in the *Harvard Business Review* article titled "No-Nonsense Guide to Measuring Productivity", presents a simple calculation for labour productivity as shown below (Chew, 1998):

$$\text{Productivity} = \frac{\text{Units of Output}}{\text{Units of Input}}$$

Various factors influence the quality of labour such as training/education, health, physical disposition, emotional disposition, and psychological disposition (Brown, 1998). This theory posits that it is now more possible than ever to leverage technology in measuring how much of a unit of labour input would result in an output. This would be achieved by factoring in historical and current trends. It is also possible to collect data over a period of time to draw up precise averages, as well as monitor fluctuations to any of the elements influencing the labour inputs in real time.

3 **The structure of labour inputs has changed and is no longer limited to conventional working relationships** – workers are no longer limited to factory floors or office cubicles where time spent creating value in relation to outputs was so strictly defined. Possibly spurred on by consumerism and the ever-increasing demand for new goods and services, there has also been a seismic shift in the nature of work, with new jobs emerging to meet new needs. At the same time, advancements in technology and humanity's own evolutionary process are contributing to the changes in labour structures and relationships.

4 **Technology has improved how well that humanity can capture the circular flow of value in the economy** – this means that it is easier to capture value that was deferred or residual value that is only unlocked at a later stage following a sequence of other productivity actions. By this perspective, the potential value that an action can create will not be ignored or lost simply because the value is not realized immediately. If there is a chance that this action can concretely contribute to unlocking value at a later stage, the individual in question should be able to benefit from it since they have contributed to the overall creation of value within that ecosystem.

5 **Improving the human experience as an intrinsic good** – given the increasing focus on sustainable social and economic development, as well as the understanding that we must protect the environment, this theory takes the position that improving the "life experience" or "vivos experientia" is an intrinsic good and that all other activities are extrinsic because they build up to this final goal. Based on this position, if the objective is to improve the "life experience" or "vivos experientia", then value creation should be anything

that contributes to improving the lives of people. In the context of the state, this would mean any action that contributes to improving the overall welfare of the community which the individual is a citizen of. At the same time, since the individual is no longer directly related to just the state and there is now comparable influence from the private sector and other NSAs on the life of the individual, this new role for private sector interests should be identified and properly integrated in the social contract.

6 **The private sector as a party to the social contract** – this theory asserts that the private sector should have a more defined role in the social contract and in the process of bringing individuals out of the state of nature. This assertion is made based on the understanding that the private sector takes resources out of society and uses these resources to create products and services which may sometimes be used by individuals or groups who could be considered to still be in the state of nature (e.g. citizens in slums and informal economy contexts that are out of the reach of the government and are not benefitting from any of the ramifications of the social contract of the country whose land they are on). This proposed role is in key areas of public administration, for example, the management and deployment of digital currencies.

7 **A common denominator** – in defining a new digital social contract, it is important to identify a common denominator that is considered valuable to all individuals, whether they are within the state (consciously party to the social contract) or whether they are in the state of nature (willingly or unwillingly). It is also important that this common denominator is limited, measurable, capturable, and transferrable. A common denominator is important because it forms the basis for creating and transferring value.

8 **"Time" as the common denominator** – this theory identifies "time" as that common denominator that satisfies all of these qualities. Time is also limited to each individual, but can be measured, captured, and transferred. This digitalization process would allow units of time to be measured in relation to the value creation process, ensuring that all forms of value creation can be captured and transferred with limited barriers.

9 **Time as a key factor in the value creation process** – the combination of inputs and resources does not equal an output unless time is added to the equation. Given this crucial role, digitally monetized time should be used to directly measure value creation.

10 **Fourth industrial revolution technologies to leverage time as a store of value** – the digital economy, big data analytics, artificial intelligence, and blockchain systems (distributed ledgers, smart contracts, cryptography) can be combined into software that is used to measure how much time is worth a unit of value. Big data analytics, as well as artificial intelligence (AI) can play a role in measuring in real time the true value of a unit of time in relation to a value-creating action, as well as in relation to the factors of supply and demand relative to other consumers in the ecosystem. The combination of these technologies makes it possible to capture value in a new way and allows for greater inclusion since value that was previously lost can now be captured. All of these technologies can be combined into digital currency that is easily

accessible and deployable on mobile devices, both on- and offline. Mobile phone penetration is at an all-time high around the world. This would make the currency available to anyone who has a mobile device, which is more effective and efficient in reach than current financial systems and policies have been able to achieve. This is particularly important because not only does it make the currency available to anyone with a phone, it makes the process of generating the currency easier as well.

11 **A time-backed digital and new social contract** – this currency could be managed by a private entity on behalf of the government(s). By signing on to use this digital currency, the user signs on to a new social contract to contribute to improve the overall state of the society by creating social and economic value. In this approach, the government retains its responsibility of defining the political ideology and direction of the state, while the private entity takes on the responsibility of administering the technology behind this hybrid-decentralized instrument of value.

Bibliography

Baldassarini, A. & Veroli, N. D. (2009). Labour Input Productivity: Comparative Measures and Quality Issues. In: *Productivity Measurement and Analysis*. Paris: OECD and Federal Statistics Office, 239–258.

Beck, L. & Alexandrova, A. (2019). Measuring Utility: From the Marginal Revolution to Behaviourial Economics. *Journal of Economic Methodology*, *26*(4), 380–384.

Brown, E. H. P. (1998). *Labour Economics*. [Online] Available at: https://www.britannica.com/topic/labour-economics#ref66904 [Accessed 2 August 2021].

Chew, W. B. (1998). No-Nonsense Guide to Measuring Productivity. *Harvard Business Review*, *66*, 110–118.

Corporate Finance Institute. (2021). *Store of Value*. [Online] Available at: https://corporatefinanceinstitute.com/resources/knowledge/valuation/store-of-value/ [Accessed 25 June 2021].

ILO. (2020). *Indicator Description: Labour Productivity*. [Online] Available at: https://ilostat.ilo.org/resources/concepts-and-definitions/description-labour-productivity/ [Accessed 2 August 2021].

24 Time Is Money

Earlier on, we explored multiple perspectives and theoretical approaches to the concept of time. In those chapters, we saw that time could be viewed as either linear or spatial, independent of or dependent on change. Questions around the origin and topology of time also reflect on time beyond what humans count with clocks, to contemplate the concept from a metaphysical perspective.

Considering all of these perspectives on the nature of time, this theory approaches time from a combination of the growing block and dynamic theory. In addition, at this stage, given the information available and considering humanity's current approach to interacting with time, this theory assumes that the passing of time is linear. Bradley Dowden provides a consumable summary of the growing block theory which says that objects and experiences in both the past and present are part of reality (Dowden, n.d.). Dynamic theory, on the other hand, also goes on to include the "future" as an important part of reality, and this addition is central to this analysis. Emery et al. highlight characteristics of dynamic theory which are further analysed below:

- Dynamic theory suggests that the universe is made up of three dimensions which are physical spaces.
- Objects which are located at different times are fully present at those times, instead of having temporal parts of their being present at multiple points in time. This characteristic might raise a slight contradiction from an economic perspective. The question here might be, what then happens in the case where a consumer has an asset which receives utility for the consumer at different points in time without the consumer being there physically, would this be considered a temporal part? The answer is no, because the asset is considered a representation of the consumer and as such, the consumer is fully present in that moment when the utility is received.
- A-properties (past, present, future) are real and cannot always be considered with regard to B-relations (before and after). From an economic value perspective, this is an important characteristic of dynamic theory that enables a consumer to take actions today that can potentially create value in the future, and to have that potential future value recognized today.
- Reality changes over time and only objects in the present time exist. This statement holds true to the extent of reality changing over time. However as

DOI: 10.4324/9781003330417-32

mentioned earlier, this research also posits that objects and experiences in the past are real. Furthermore, the research posits that it is possible to calculate the probability of future events occurring.

- A proposition has a truth at a certain time; however, this truth can change over time and is not unconditional. This characteristic builds on the characteristic above with regard to future events which are subject to change. Past and present events, however, are held as undeniable truths. These past and present events may be recorded immutably.
- The passing of time is real. In accordance with the movement of the earth around the sun, this research holds that the passing of time is a real phenomenon regardless of whether humans can recognize change or not. This is because the earth and planets continue to experience this movement of time in space. Furthermore, it is important to consider that the impact of these changes may vary from planetary surface to planetary surface, and as such, the calculation of time in the numerical form adopted on earth may vary under different conditions. This theory, however, does not attempt to explore this broader context on the calculation of time outside of humanity's context. Note that while anomalies in space, such as time dilation, may affect the passage of time, they do not mean that it does not exist.

As highlighted earlier, time is a unique concept that offers up opportunities in redefining value. While the concept has several philosophical connotations and representations, this theory does not concern itself extensively with these, but rather focuses on the passage or flow of time in its widely understood form as described above.

Based on the characteristics of the theories identified and combined here, "digitally monetized time" has been identified as an ideal (but not the only) store of economic value. Justifications on time as a store of value focus not only on the concept itself, but on some of the supporting elements that make this concept a viable option towards redefining value. In particular, the justifications provided here look at capturing time through a digital currency enabled by a combination of fourth industrial revolution technologies.

Justifications identified as part of this research include those listed below; however, it is important to note that further justifications exist for digital currencies as a store of value, as well as for time-based digital currencies. This list is therefore not exhaustive but meant to serve as a foundation for further research:

a) **A common denominator** – time is a common denominator to all humans; it is considered valuable to both those within the civil state and in the state of nature being limited, measurable, capturable, and transferrable. Time is considered limited to each individual in the sense that the time each individual has counts from birth to death. It is also measurable in relation to the earth's revolutions around the sun. This also makes it possible to capture time; more importantly, as seen in the literature review, it is possible to capture (record) the changes that take place during each unit of time. This means it is possible to capture the value created within each unit of time. The transferability of time refers to the possibility of not only capturing time and the value created within each unit of time, but also transferring that value that has been recorded as created within each unit of time. A simple example of this would be spending time on an activity today instead of sleeping and making up for the lost sleep time later. As highlighted here, the passage of time is standardized and follows a widely accepted formula that therefore makes it easy to record. Time is also a common denominator to the factors of production (land, labour, entrepreneurship, and capital).

b) **The building block factor** – this theory approached time from a growing block perspective meaning that events in the present build on events in the past. Blockchain technology not only allows for peer-to-peer verification of actions and claims to value creation; in addition, the very nature of blockchains means that the truths held in each block are based on the truths held in previous blocks. In other words, each block in the chain builds on previous blocks. In the context of this research, this would mean that value captured in each unit of digital currency (time) is based on previous units of time spent creating value. This point is particularly important in relation to utility and the community. If a community comes together out of the state of nature to facilitate better resource management among the citizens, then in principle, every action within the community should bring utility either to the individual or to another individual or group of individuals. In other words, every unit of time spent should create value (utility) for the individual or for others within the community. The building block approach makes it possible to capture this point.

c) **The calculability/computation implication** – digital currencies make it possible for each unit of currency to reflect as much data on the true nature of the market and the true nature of the currency at any given time. This is possible since digital currencies, which are ultimately software applications, can receive and process larger portions of data from more sources than currencies controlled through policy instruments. In the context of the fourth industrial revolution, the specific technologies that enable this justification are algorithms, cloud computing and cloud storage, big data analytics, artificial intelligence, and blockchains. These technologies, although not essentially new[1], have advanced significantly over the years. In their current forms, the combination of these technologies has the capacity to effectively compute previously impossible real-time calculations of value in the context of demand and supply as well as accounting for various other metrics that could previously not be computed by standard financial systems/instruments. This would make the value of each unit of time adjust automatically to the real-world circumstances.

d) **The deployability factor** – a time-based digital currency can be deployed on mobile devices through an on-/offline mobile application. Already, mobile money solutions exist around the world as an alternative payment platform. At the same time, mobile phone penetration as of 2020 was estimated at over 78% (S O'Dea, 2021). This high level of mobile penetration and the ease of deploying software and applications onto mobile devices mean that a time-based digital currency can be rolled out effectively to large populations. It is important to note that deployability is also impacted by the nature and combination of technologies; for example, there are challenges with deploying certain types of blockchain solutions because of the processing power or storage capacity required. This example, however, does not take away from the key point that a digital currency, specifically a time-based digital currency, can be deployed easily to reach populations.

In addition to the features identified above an additional justification of a time-based digital currency is in the fact that this type of currency can be weighted against something that is widely accepted as valuable: time. Current "cryptocurrencies" are not conventionally pegged to any commodities, and as such, their values tend to fluctuate significantly (Etoro, n.d.) (Powell, 2021). "Time is Money" is an old phrase that most people are familiar with; however, the concept of time as a digital currency is first widely recorded in 1980 by the late Professor Edgar Cahn. According to Professor Cahn, the Time Bank was invented as a "medium of exchange that would act as a way to encourage and reward the work needed to build strong, resilient communities" (timebanks.org, n.d.). Professor Cahn's approach to monetizing time allows users within a community to exchange units of time for services, enabling a level of reciprocity that he believed was not possible with conventional volunteering. Another approach that also tries to capture the value of time as a store of value is the Time Bank as implemented in Switzerland, and while that approach was not discussed in this text, it further reflects the potential of time as an alternative store of value. Note that the approach adopted in the observational study aligns with the general approach adopted in Professor Cahn's approach as well as with versions of the Time Bank as implemented in Switzerland. This underlying belief that time can be monetized as a means of exchange holds true across all iterations of time banks and time-based digital currencies. What this book attempts is to situate this concept within the evolution of social and economic processes in society. In addition, this book attempts to highlight the role that specific technologies can play in mainstreaming a global time-based digital currency, with the objective of facilitating a new wave of financial inclusion and value creation for the fourth industrial revolution.

Implication of This Approach on Contemporary Society and Sustainable Development

The proposed redefinition of value has potentially significant implications for contemporary society beyond the proposal for a time-based digital currency. Redefining how value is measured and captured will affect humanity as did the same exercise during previous industrial revolutions. The implications of this research and the suggested approach therein are twofold. First, the research has implications on sociopolitical interaction in the context of the state or political society. Second, the research has economic implications in the context of financial inclusion for marginalized communities.

"Markets; Push or Pull" by Ugochukwu Chigoziem Ikpeazu, Ganvie, Benin Republic (2016).

As of July 2021, progress on the Sustainable Development Goals is stunted. In January 2021, the United Nations Economic and Social Council produced a report where it noted that the "COVID-19 pandemic has had an impact on all 17 Sustainable Development Goals, showing that what began as a health crisis has quickly become a human and socioeconomic crisis" (U.N, 2021). The impact of the pandemic and measurements on progress towards the 17 goals are captured in the Sustainable Development Goals Report 2020:

1 **No poverty** – according to the United Nations (2020) report, over 71 million were forced into acute poverty during the pandemic in 2020 (U.N, 2020). According to the World Bank, up to 150 million people would be pushed into poverty in 2021 as a result of the pandemic (World Bank, 2020). The IISD notes that at the current rate, global poverty levels will be 7% in 2030, higher than the targeted 3% (IISD, 2021).
2 **Zero hunger** – according to the United Nations (2020) report, the percentage of the global population that was affected by food insecurity rose from 22.4% in 2014, to 25.9% in 2019 (U.N, 2020). A recent report by Oxfam International notes that conflict, COVID-19, and climate change are the biggest contributors to increasing global hunger (Oxfam International, 2021). The report further notes that a staggering 11 people are likely dying every minute of hunger, reflecting the slow pace made by the international community towards addressing global hunger.
3 **Good health and well-being** – according to Reid et al, "COVID-19 has served as a 'stress test' for health systems" (Reid, et al., 2021). Health

interventions around the world suffered as a result of the pandemic. Over 60 immunization campaigns in 50 countries had to be postponed as a result of the pandemic, putting over 228 million people at risk, according to Gavi the Vaccine Alliance (Gavi, 2021).

4 **Quality education** – according to the United Nations (2020) report, more than 200 million children around the world will not be in school by 2030 (U.N, 2020). In addition, UNESCO estimates that over 100 million children will lack the minimum reading proficiency in 2021 (UNESCO, 2021).
5 **Gender equality** – according to the World Economic Forums Global Gender Gap Report 2021, it will take over 135 years to close the global gender gap following the current path (WEF, 2021).
6 **Clean water and sanitation** – according to the United Nations (2020) report, over 3 billion people do not have access to handwashing facilities at home, while up to 700 million people could be displaced by water scarcity by 2030. According to Water Aid, 4 million people are currently living in areas that are considered water-scare, and this number is expected to rise to 5 billion by 2050 (Oboko & Callister, 2021).
7 **Affordable and clean energy** – according to McKinsey's Global Energy Perspective 2021, energy demand will need between one and four years to rebound to 2019 levels (McKinsey & Company, 2021).
8 **Decent work and economic growth** – according to the United Nations (2020) report, up to 1.6 billion workers in the informal sectors around the world are at risk of losing their jobs.
9 **Industry, innovation, and infrastructure** – the United Nations (2020) report highlights a need for increasing investments in industry and sustainable infrastructure.
10 **Reduced inequalities** – according to the World Economic Forum, it could take the world's poorest people up to a decade to recover from the economic losses sustained between 2020 and 2021, while the 1,000 richest people in the world were able to cover their loses in the space of nine months (Bucher, 2021).
11 **Sustainable cities and communities** – according to the United Nations (2020) report, over 4 million deaths were caused by air pollution in 2016.
12 **Responsible consumption and production** – according to the United Nations (2020) report, the world continues to misuse natural resources; for example, electronic waste has grown by approximately 38% by 2019.
13 **Climate action** – according to the United Nations (2020) report, global commitments remain low towards combating the effects of climate change. UN Secretary General notes that 2021 is the "make it or break it year", emphasizing the need for urgent action in order to reach the SDGs (WMO, 2021).
14 **Life below water** – according to the United Nations (2020) report, the sudden and significant reduction of human activity around the world meant that the planet could recuperate briefly. Unfortunately, as human activity starts to pick up again around the world, more will need to be done to protect the ocean, its resources and biodiversity.

15 **Life on land** – according to the United Nations (2020) report, over 2 billion hectares of land have gotten to the point where they are completely or almost completely unusable, affecting over 3 billion people.
16 **Peace, justice, and strong institutions** – according to the United Nations (2020) report, despite protection from international laws, over 100 persons are killed on a daily basis in armed conflicts around the world. In addition, the Global Peace Index for 2021 notes that the economic impact of violence around the world in 2020 was over US$14 trillion in terms of purchasing power parity (IEP, 2021).
17 **Partnerships for the goals** – according to the United Nations (2020) report, foreign direct investment was expected to decline by 40% around the world. While this was largely due to the COVID-19 pandemic, the UN report highlights that even net overseas development assistance was already plateauing pre-pandemic.

Progress on the Sustainable Development Goals has varied across each goal and influenced by a range of factors. While these are not exclusively related to financial and currency systems, the availability of financial resources and financial instruments for economic activity is a central factor across the goals.

The Social Contract as proposed by Jean Jacques Rousseau, Thomas Hobbes, and John Locke described political society as predominantly made up of individuals and states. This social contract described a situation where individuals left the state of nature and entered into civil society to create the state and government. This book's research also highlighted a key element across all social contract theories as being the need for resource management (value creation) in the newly created state. The research also highlighted the role that the private sector has historically played in first facilitating resource management (value creation) and subsequently in leading value creation through competition-driven innovation. This is the first expected implication of this research on contemporary society, the notion that the private sector should have a better-defined role in a new social contract. The private sector plays a significant role in managing natural resources, and in many societies, citizens interact more with businesses and brands than they do with their respective governments. In addition, in many societies, especially in low-income and lower-middle income economies where social/government services and infrastructure are limited, it is more likely that citizens get their basic services from businesses. In these settings, it is possible to conclude that it is the private sector that is bringing individuals out of the state of nature and into political society since it is through the private sector that the individual participates in some form of civil society. The report "Doing Business in Special Contexts: Under-Served Communities - A Brief Case Study from Ajegunle, Lagos, Nigeria", by Ugo Ikpeazu and Godwin Abaimun, highlights just how important commerce and trade are in informal economy contexts, but most importantly, the report highlights how far the reach of private entities is (Ikpeazu & Abaimun, 2020). Despite the limited infrastructure in the subject community of the case study, telecom operators still functioned effectively, offering a range of solutions to citizens, and ultimately facilitating social inclusion, although limited.

The second expected implication of this research on contemporary society is with regard to the opportunities in financial inclusion offered by the adoption of digital currencies. Adopting digital currencies has significant potential to improve financial inclusion for marginalized populations and underserved communities. According to the World Economic Forum, the mass use of digital finance tools has "boosted the annual GDP of all emerging economies by $3.7 trillion" (Moy & Carlson, 2021). Large-scale financial inclusion would mean an expansion of the workforce that is available to contribute to macro-economic productivity. The availability of this workforce would in principle allow faster industrialization for poor economies since the newly unlocked workforce can be engaged to support large-scale industrial projects. One of the current limitations to industrialization is the lack of resources to pay for large workforces, despite the availability of this workforce, the existence of skills and competences within this workforce, and the existence of raw material resources. In line with the systemic labour re-organizations that took place during previous industrial revolutions, use of the proposed digital currency could be tied or closely linked to large-scale industrial projects that improve the overall state of the community. This would particularly be beneficial for poorer economies who would be better positioned to channel labour resources into maximizing raw materials in their surroundings.

In addition to these, the implications of reviewing how society measures and captures value include but are not limited to the following:

a) **Informal economy integration** – informal economies can be better integrated with the micro and macro economies since value created within the informal sector can easily be measured and reflected in micro/macro-economic planning. Integrating informal economies opens up opportunities for marginalized populations including increasing access to formal markets and job opportunities, in line with the SDGs. The impact of digital currencies (whether fiat, crypto, or other) on the informal economy is widely recognized for its potential in financial inclusion (Said, 2019) (ATKearny; Visa, n.d.).
b) **More skills recognized** – more skills and competencies can be recognized for their contributions to society and ability to create social and economic value. This would remove situations where an individual has a skill, but no consumer is able to pay for the use of this skill since the consumers lack the cash to do so. As the future of work continues to evolve, new financial instruments will play a critical role in enabling new working relationships for a digital world (WEF, 2020). Nonetheless, a nuanced approach is required to apply technology in this new labour landscape (Anner, et al., 2019).
c) **Expanding demand** – building on the previous point, this will also reflect on an increase in the demand for goods and services as well as an increase in the type and variety of goods and services demanded. According to the European Commission, over 5 billion people will be considered as middle class by 2030, meaning a significant increase in global purchasing power, and an increase in demand for product and services (European Commission, n.d.). Africa's population is expected to reach 1.7 billion by 2030, with consumer expenditure hitting $2.1 trillion by 2025 (Signé & Johnson, 2018).

Consumption is also expected to double in ASEAN economies (Jurgens & Ingilizian, 2020).

d) **Eradication of poverty** – poverty in its current form (i.e. characterized by a lack of access to the basic needs such as food, shelter, and clothing) could be eradicated, since it will become easier for individuals to meet their basic needs. The added implication of this is that humanity moves into another stage in its evolutionary process including but not limited to further investments in science and technology that ultimately make extra planetary exploration possible. The potential for digital currencies to improve financial inclusion and reduce poverty is not new, as this is already being debated for central bank digital currencies (CBDC) (Pantuliano & Tyson, 2021) (Foster, et al., 2021).

e) **Greater gender equality and female inclusion in commerce** – with access to financial instruments, more women are able to participate in the economy, ultimately reducing their dependence on a spouse (or other such figure) for sustenance. In addition, this reduces the burden on families to employ child labour since it is easier for both parents to engage in gainful activity. The impact of digital currencies on improving gender equality is already being felt in society today (Hammond & Young, 2018) (Anon., 2020).

This theory aimed to lay the groundwork for a new approach to the social contract and the concept of value. It is important that further studies into a time-based digital currency continue to hold financial inclusion and the eradication of poverty in its current form as their core driving factor. This is because a shift from these objectives might result in the development of stores of value similar to cryptocurrencies like Bitcoin and Ethereum, which, while innovative and novel in their approach to value, are limited in their ability to bridge the financial gap for the billions of people around the world who need a new financial system to support their livelihoods.

Note

1 As at June 5, 2022.

Bibliography

Anner, M. S., Pons-Vignon, N. & Rani, U., 2019. For a Future of Work with Dignity: A Critique of the World Bank Development Report, The Changing Nature of Work. *Global Labour Journal*, 10(1), pp. 2–19.

Anon., 2020. *Advancing Women's Digital Financial Inclusion.* [Online] Available at: https://www.gpfi.org/sites/gpfi/files/sites/default/files/saudig20_women.pdf [Accessed 5 August 2021].

ATKearny; Visa, n.d. *Digital Payments and the Global Informal Economy.* [Online] Available at: https://navigate.visa.com/$/v/2/m/x/Digital_payments_and_the_global-informal-economy-report.pdf [Accessed 5 August 2021].

Bucher, G., 2021. *COVID-19 Has Shown us the True Extent of Global Inequality. In 2021, Let's Commit to Ending It.* [Online] Available at: https://www.weforum.org/agenda/2021/01/covid19-inequality-virus-report-oxfam/ [Accessed 27 July 2021].

Dowden, B., n.d. *Time.* [Online] Available at: https://iep.utm.edu/time/ [Accessed 21 June 2021].

Etoro, n.d. *Why Does Bitcoin's Price Fluctuate So Much?.* [Online] Available at: https://www.etoro.com/crypto/why-bitcoin-fluctuates/ [Accessed 27 July 2021].

European Commission, n.d. *Growing consumption.* [Online] Available at: https://knowledge4policy.ec.europa.eu/growing-consumerism_en [Accessed 5 August 2021].

Foster, K., Blakstad, S., Gazi, S. & Bos, M., 2021. *Digital currencies and CBDC Impacts on Least Developed Countries (LDCs)*, s.l.: UNDP; UNCDF.

Gavi, 2021. *Immunization Services Begin Slow Recovery from COVID-19 Disruptions, Though Millions of Children Remain at Risk from Deadly Diseases.* [Online] Available at: https://www.gavi.org/news/media-room/immunization-services-begin-slow-recovery-covid-19-disruptions-though-millions [Accessed 27 July 2021].

Hammond, A. & Young, D., 2018. *Can Blockchain Disrupt Gender Inequality?.* [Online] Available at: https://blogs.worldbank.org/psd/can-blockchain-disrupt-gender-inequality [Accessed 5 August 2021].

IEP, 2021. *Global Peace Index 2021*, Sydney: Institute for Economics & Peace.

IISD, 2021. *HLPF Reviews Progress Towards Nine SDGs.* [Online] Available at: https://sdg.iisd.org/news/hlpf-reviews-progress-towards-nine-sdgs/ [Accessed 28 July 2021].

Ikpeazu, U. & Abaimun, G., 2020. *Doing Business in Special Contexts: Under-Served Communities - A Brief Case Study from Ajegunle, Lagos, Nigeria*, Geneva: Ark Hudson.

Jurgens, J. & Ingilizian, Z., 2020. *Future of Consumption in Fast-Growth Consumer Markets: ASEAN*, Geneva: World Economic Forum.

McKinsey & Company, 2021. *Global Energy Perspective 2021.* [Online] Available at: https://www.mckinsey.com/industries/oil-and-gas/our-insights/global-energy-perspective-2021# [Accessed 27 July 2021].

Moy, C. & Carlson, J., 2021. *Cryptocurrencies can enable financial inclusion. Will you participate?.* [Online] Available at: https://www.weforum.org/global_future_councils/gfc-on-cryptocurrencies/articles/cryptocurrencies-financial-inclusion-help-shape-it

Oboko, E. & Callister, F., 2021. *Turn the Tide: the State of the Worlds Water 2021*, s.l.: Water Aid.

O'Dea, S., 2021. *Global smartphone penetration rate as share of population from 2016 to 2020.* [Online] Available at: https://www.statista.com/statistics/203734/global-smartphone-penetration-per-capita-since-2005/ [Accessed 25 June 2021].

Oxfam International, 2021. *World in the Midst of a 'Hunger Pandemic': Conflict, Coronavirus and Climate Crisis Threaten to Push Millions into Starvation.* [Online] Available at: https://www.oxfam.org/en/world-midst-hunger-pandemic-conflict-coronavirus-and-climate-crisis-threaten-push-millions [Accessed 27 July 2021].

Pantuliano, S. & Tyson, J., 2021. *Can Central Banks Digital Currencies deliver for people in poverty?.* [Online] Available at: https://odi.org/en/insights/can-central-banks-digital-currencies-deliver-for-people-in-poverty/ [Accessed 5 August 2021].

Powell, A., 2021. *Taking the crypto out of digital currency.* [Online] Available at: https://news.harvard.edu/gazette/story/2021/06/cryptocurrency-expert-discusses-recent-fluctuations/ [Accessed 27 July 2021].

Reid, M., Abdool-Karim, Q., Geng, E. & Goosby, E., 2021. *How will COVID-19 Transform Global Health Post-Pandemic? Defining Research and Investment Opportunities and Priorities.* [Online] Available at: https://journals.plos.org/plosmedicine/article?id=10.1371/journal.pmed.1003564 [Accessed 27 July 2021].

Said, A., 2019. *The Economic Impact of Digital Fiat Currency (DFC): Opportunities and Challenges.* Aswan, International Telecommunications Society.

Signé, L. & Johnson, C., 2018. *Africa's Consumer Market Potential Trends, Drivers, Opportunities, and Strategies*, s.l.: Brookings Institute.

U.N, 2020. *The Sustainable Development Goals Report 2020*, New York: United Nations.

U.N, 2021. *Progress report on the Sustainable Development Goals in*, Bangkok: Economic and Social Commission for Asia and the Pacific.

UNESCO, 2021. *Education: From Disruption to Recovery*. [Online] Available at: https://en.unesco.org/covid19/educationresponse [Accessed 27 July 2021].

WEF, 2020. *The Future of Jobs Report 2020*, Geneva: World Economic Forum.

WEF, 2021. *Global Gender Gap Report 2021*, Geneva: World Economic Forum.

WMO, 2021. *2021 is "make or break year" for Climate Action*. [Online] Available at: https://public.wmo.int/en/media/news/2021-%E2%80%9Cmake-or-break-year%E2%80%9D-climate-action [Accessed 27 July 2021].

World Bank, 2020. *COVID-19 to Add as Many as 150 Million Extreme Poor by 2021*. [Online] Available at: https://www.worldbank.org/en/news/press-release/2020/10/07/covid-19-to-add-as-many-as-150-million-extreme-poor-by-2021 [Accessed 27 July 2021].

25 Getting There

A Cashless Future

Imagine a world where you could engage in a value-creating activity, anywhere, anyhow. Imagine that it was possible to automatically record that value that you had created, as currency on a virtual wallet, without you having to take any specific action. Imagine in that world, you could go anywhere in your immediate community, or even travel across continents, and spend that value (those digital currencies) without having to open a new account, or convert currencies, with transaction settling and universal wallet updates happening in real-time.

– Ugochukwu Chigoziem Ikpeazu

The above statement describes a cashless society, and the discussions leading up to this point have explored the basis for this cashless society as the next phase in social interaction, as well as the technologies that would make it possible. Going cashless is not just an opportunity to enhance social and economic interaction. It is importantly the opportunity to improve living conditions for countless numbers of citizens around the world. Fully cashless societies mean that transactions can happen anywhere a network can go. This possibility will unlock new levels of creativity that we are not yet aware of. Combining fully digital currencies with innovative and new approaches to capturing social and economic value will enable us to solve problems that we have not yet started to consider. And this does not even start to cover the types of new products and services that we could have access to. An important caveat here is that the drive for a cashless society does not mean that paper money should be abolished, or that paper money is inherently bad. The reality is that paper money will have to stick around for a bit because there is still some time before we get to the scenario described above. Because there are still millions of people who do not have access to inexpensive and reliable internet connections, there will still be people who do not have access to digital currencies. Even if these currencies are designed to work in offline mode with the best interoperability designed in, it is important that no one is left out of this future that we co-design. And so while effort is made to get to that inter-galactic, cashless, society, by building the right infrastructure and enacting relevant policies, it is also important that we push current systems to do what they can in helping people.

From an implementation perspective, there are clear challenges that humanity will need to overcome if it will get to this future. Specifically, while this theory of monetizing time attempts to offer an innovative approach to measuring and capturing economic value, the approach is not without its limitations.

DOI: 10.4324/9781003330417-33

There are limitations to digital currencies, as well as limitations to deploying digital currencies at scale. Among these limitations are:

a) **Scalability** – in their current forms, many cryptocurrencies have issues with scalability. Bitcoin, for example, has consensus mechanisms that make it difficult to deploy at scale for large percentages of the population to use in daily transactions (Makarenko, 2018) (Kenny, 2019). Future digital currencies, or modifications to existing digital, virtual, or cryptocurrencies, must be able to solve the problem of scalability, especially as a medium of exchange at scale. This will mean designs that are accessible, with limited impact on the environment and the capacity to handle innumerable transactions at light speed and in real time. This brings back the topic of the scalability trilemma[1] (Seba Bank, 2020) and having to choose among security, decentralization, and scalability.
b) **Limited regulation** – regulation for digital currencies varies significantly around the world (Perkinscoie, 2021). While some governments and regulatory institutions are attempting to understand and regulate this new class of financial asset, others are banning, restricting, or prohibiting their use. The regulatory environment will need to evolve rapidly and exponentially to accommodate the opportunities created by digital currencies today and into the future (UKTN, 2021). The IMF, among others, has listed out various regulatory and legal issues affecting digital currencies (especially CBDCs), including the need for central bank and monetary law reforms, as well as issues around interest-bearing tokens (Ledger Insights, 2020). It has taken humanity many years to develop the regulations that have made fiat currencies what they are, and so it only makes sense that we will need some time to figure out the nuances of these new stores of value. Needing time, however, is not an excuse for complacency or filibustering.
c) **Adoption** – while adoption of digital currencies is not a significant limitation for consumers, as highlighted by the adoption of mobile money for example, wide-scale adoption may experience initial delays as large percentages of the population familiarize themselves with a cashless society. According to a PWC report, over 60 central banks around the world are researching CBDCs and 14% of global central banks are in the development or steering phase for their own digital currencies (PWC, n.d.). This last statement was true when this initial research was carried out. Fast-forward a year later and this figure has gone up to "105 countries, representing over 95 percent of global GDP, are exploring a CBDC" (Atlantic Council, 2022). Adoption will also be driven by mass integration efforts, which see services and social infrastructure enabled for digital transactions. In comes the network effect.
d) **Trust** – trust is an important factor in cashless transactions. It is also a critical factor in the consensus mechanisms behind digital currencies. The ITU sees trust as a critical factor in digital currencies and sees standardization as the avenue to achieving trust across stakeholder categories (Lee, 2020). Trust is multidimensional in the sense that it can be rather subjective. Despite the ability for future financial systems to encode trust into their design, a lot of

attention will need to be paid to creating the right ecosystem for this trust to flourish.

e) **Exchangeability** – digital currencies are as effective as the users trust in them as a store of value and medium of exchange. A potential limitation to the wide-scale adoption of digital currencies is how well they can be exchanged for existing fiat currencies or commodities. While this theory suggests a (gradual) shift away from fiat currencies in general, it is impossible to ignore the appeal that fiat currencies will continue to have to segments of society in the years to come. Exchangeability might be even more challenging if society tends towards Hayek's ideals where numerous private currencies exist. The current system, which is already starting to resemble Hayek's reality, sees thousands of digital currencies convertible to fiat currencies like the dollar. Maintaining exchangeability if and when fiat currencies are phased out will be important.

f) **Volatility** – existing digital currencies which are not backed by any commodity or regulated by any authority are volatile since their value is influenced solely by investor perceptions. This is a particularly significant problem since it makes it difficult to set prices in existing digital and cryptocurrencies (Carstens, 2021).

Despite these limitations however, digital currencies are the ideal financial instrument to unlock the fourth industrial revolution and bridge the gap in financial inclusion for marginalized and underserved populations around the world. Thankfully, the limitations presented here are not absolute.

Note

1 Also referred to as the Blockchain Trilemma (Gemini, 2022).

Bibliography

Atlantic Council, 2022. *Central Bank Digital Currency Tracker*. [Online] Available at: https://www.atlanticcouncil.org/cbdctracker/ [Accessed 22 June 2022].

Carstens, A., 2021. *Digital Currencies and the Future of the Monetary System*. [Online] Available at: https://www.bis.org/speeches/sp210127.pdf [Accessed 5 August 2021].

Kenny, L., 2019. *The Blockchain Scalability Problem & the Race for Visa-Like Transaction Speed*. [Online] Available at: https://towardsdatascience.com/the-blockchain-scalability-problem-the-race-for-visa-like-transaction-speed-5cce48f9d44 [Accessed 5 August 2021].

Ledger Insights, 2020. *IMF Outlines Legal Issues for Central Bank Digital Currencies*. [Online] Available at: https://www.ledgerinsights.com/imf-legal-law-central-bank-digital-currencies-cbdc/ [Accessed 5 August 2021].

Lee, C., 2020. *How ITU is Building Trust in Digital Currency*. [Online] Available at: https://www.itu.int/en/myitu/News/2020/07/24/07/56/How-ITU-is-building-trust-in-digital-currency [Accessed 5 August 2021].

Makarenko, V., 2018. *Why Scalability is a Big Problem for Cryptocurrency*. [Online] Available at: https://medium.com/@makvitaly/why-scalability-is-a-big-problem-for-cryptocurrency-34f0909a757a [Accessed 5 August 2021].

Perkinscoie, 2021. *Virtual Currencies: International Actions and Regulations.* [Online] Available at: https://www.perkinscoie.com/images/content/2/4/v3/240289/Digital-Currencies-International-Actions-and-Regulations-01.pdf [Accessed 1 July 2021].

PWC, n.d. *Central Bank Digital Currencies: Towards Global Adoption.* [Online] Available at: https://www.pwc.com/it/it/publications/central-bank-digital-currencies-towards-global-adoption.html [Accessed 5 August 2021].

Seba Bank, 2020. *The Blockchain Trilemma.* [Online] Available at: https://www.seba.swiss/research/the-blockchain-trilemma [Accessed 4 July 2021].

UKTN, 2021. *Bitcoin and the Challenges for Financial Regulation.* [Online] Available at: https://www.uktech.news/bitcoin-and-the-challenges-for-financial-regulation [Accessed 5 August 2021].

26 What Happens Next?

This theory set out to highlight how the concept of value has evolved through history and to make suggestions its future evolution, or at least highlight how the tools we that we use as a species could evolve. The theory also set out to describe a logical framework for time as a store of value. To achieve its core purpose, the research identified a set of key objectives which included first defining the key concepts of the state, value, time, and digital economy. Other objectives of the research included understanding value in the context of informal economies/ underserved communities and developing an initial theoretical approach for time as a store of value.

These conclusions are presented here:

a) **Resource management (value creation) is at the heart of the social contract** – this important finding answers the question on what factors result in the formation of the political state. This conclusion was found after a critical review of the literature on the origin of the state. Across various political theories, resource management, which included managing/ protecting resources, was one of the central factors in why individuals left the state of nature and agreed to bind themselves by a social contract. While resource management is used here as a catch-all term, it does not assume the irrelevance of other important factors such as the fear of harm in the Hobbesian account on the state of nature. Furthermore, this conclusion is important in the context of contemporary society where resource management is no longer split solely between the state and the citizen, but now also includes the private sector.

b) **Utility is a core concept in value theory and utility has evolved in line with expanding production methods and consumer appetites** – this conclusion answers the question on the interpretations and evolution of "value" in economics. Utility, the good that a consumer receives from consumption, is at the heart of value theory because the good or happiness that consumers receive is directly related to how products and services are valued. Consumer utility is also influenced by a range of factors that have increased since the concept was first introduced in economics. This reinforces the claim that utility should be calculated as the additional good or happiness that the

DOI: 10.4324/9781003330417-34

consumer receives from consuming an additional unit of a product or services, as opposed to a total good or total happiness received.

c) **Competition and the private sector are key drivers of innovation (value creation)** – this conclusion answers the question on what factors drive innovation.

d) **The evolution of value through the industrial revolutions was influenced first by consumer methods and subsequently by consumer utility up until the beginning of the fourth industrial revolution** – this conclusion answers the question on the perception of value through the stages of industrialization in history. With the first industrial revolution and the drastic shifts created by new production methods and machines, economic value began to be defined from an objective perspective. As production methods increased and consumer choice improved, value theory became subjective. In the context of the fourth industrial revolution, value must evolve again to reflect the immensely diverse production methods available, as well as the extensively diverse consumer preferences and demands that influence every market.

e) **Individuals in the informal economy are willing to receive non-cash remuneration/payments** – this conclusion answers the question on appetite for non-cash transactions and alternative forms of payments in the informal economy. This conclusion was reached through the survey as well as through the observational study. The survey which was collected as part of the research behind this book highlighted how consumers in the informal economy are willing to receive alternative forms of payment other than cash. The observational study, although conducted with a closed group and on a small scale, also showed that families, individuals, and their subsistence businesses are willing to receive non-cash remuneration as long as the non-cash remuneration is calculated fairly and their needs are met.

f) **Digital currencies, an element of the digital economy, are ideally positioned to support capturing value in a way that facilitates financial inclusion for marginalized communities** – this conclusion answers the question on digital currencies as an effective tool to capture social and economic value. Digital currencies, however, need to move beyond existing cryptocurrencies which are limited (and inaccessible to low-income consumers in low-resource settings), to more robust and large-scale deployable solutions that leverage a range of technologies to rethink how value is measured and captured.

The state structure has evolved to include more stakeholders than just the government and citizens. In contemporary society, the private sector can play a significant role in upholding a new digital social contract around resource management. Given the evolution of value theory through history, and the use of money as a store of value, digital currencies, in particular a time-based digital currency, is a possible logical next step in the resource management process. This digital currency which forms the basis of a new digital social contract would ideally be managed by the private sector and would be used to drive financial inclusion of marginalized and underserved communities, effectively bringing them out of the new state of nature.

The concept of value will continue to evolve as technology unlocks even more opportunities for interaction among the stakeholders in society (and as the categories of stakeholders continues to increase). These evolutions will need to be recognized effectively to ensure that humanity can suitably adopt its methods and processes. Redefining how humanity measures and captures value is critical because it increases the chances of efficiently improving the lives of millions of people around the world who live in astute poverty. This book was developed against the backdrop of failing global financial and economic systems which have struggled to make significant strides in global poverty eradication. National policies in low- and lower-middle income economies are struggling with current models to reach marginalized communities, and a major factor in this is the currently limited approach to the application of value theory in society. Redefining value therefore allows humanity to develop innovative solutions that leverage technologies for transformative change. The philosophy of digital currencies should guide all future research and efforts in the digital currency space. It is important that digital currencies as a store of value consider designs with accessibility, deployability, and scalability. This approach ensures that digital currencies as a means of exchange can serve as a tool for financial inclusion for the millions of people without access to conventional financial services. Scalability is an important factor, as it ensures confident adoption by consumers. Introducing digital currencies as a means of exchange and making these available to large percentages of any population will require a rethink of monetary systems to ensure that these can effectively introduce digital currencies into the economy. As a species, we must continue to re-evaluate the social contract to reflect the true nature of interaction between individual and external stakeholders. Humanity will continue to evolve, as well as models of interaction and governance. Future researchers must continue to re-evaluate these social and economic relationships to ensure that any further changes to the social contract are discussed and potentially reflected. As in the case of the social contract, it is also important that humanity continue to re-evaluate how value is measured and captured, to ensure that the most effective instruments are available to capture social and economic value, and to facilitate trade for even the poorest members of society. Governments are recommended to pursue regulations that improve the innovation ecosystem and allow fintech solutions to thrive. This regulatory environment is important if the private sector is to effectively play its roles in driving financial inclusion for greater resource management (value creation) as part of a new social contract.

***

Humans interact as social beings with needs that must be met to survive. This interaction happens in the context of scarce resources, which leads to exchange. Exchange allows individuals or groups to trade what they have for what they need and allows for the management of scarce resources. The invention of money facilitated exchange on a much larger scale and broader scope. Technological inventions took this a step further and allowed money to evolve, as well as allowing financial systems to be built around money, exchange, and value. Despite these advancements, not all of humanity has been carried along and large populations are not able to interact because they are marginalized. Through each stage of industrial revolution, a critical technology or combination of technologies was complemented by radical shifts in how humanity approached value. The current stage of industrial revolution is no different. The radical shift in how humanity approaches value must be targeted at enhancing *vivos experientia* as exponentially as are the technologies available. Money must evolve again, and so must the institutions around it, so that all of humanity can interact and exchange to manage scarce resources in a new digital social contract where spending time creating value makes you a part of a community.

Index

Page numbers in **bold** indicate tables, page numbers in *italic* indicate figures and page numbers followed by n indicate notes.

Taylor & Francis Group
an informa business